THE CATECHISM IN EXAMPLES

REV. D. CHISHOLM

SENSUS FIDELIUM PRESS

The Catechism in Examples was originally published by R. & T. Washbourne, Ltd. in 1919, and is in the public domain.

Sensus Fidelium Press edition © 2023.

In this edition, editorial changes have been made to correct grammatical and punctuation errors, reword sentences for improved clarity, and make minor corrections to typographical errors. Additionally, certain names have been updated to reflect modern usage. Every effort has been made to preserve the original meaning and intent of the author, these changes were made to enhance the readability and accessibility of the text.

All rights reserved. The typography and editing of this edition are copyright of Sensus Fidelium Press. No part of this work may be reproduced in print or ebook formats without the express permission of the publisher, except for quotations for review in journals, blogs, or classroom use.

Print ISBN: 978-1-962639-24-8

SensusFideliumPress.com

CONTENTS

Preface   xix

PART I
WHY WE WERE MADE

1. GOD MADE YOU   3
    ST. DOMNINA AND HER FATHER IN HEAVEN.   3

2. GOD MADE YOU TO KNOW HIM   5
    THE LITTLE BOY IN THE SNOW.   5
    THE LITTLE BOY AT THE EXHIBITION.   6
    THE TWO LITTLE BOYS IN AMERICA.   6

3. GOD MADE YOU TO LOVE HIM   8
    HOW MUCH A LITTLE CHILD LOVED GOD.   8
    MARINA DE ESCOBAR   9
    "O JESUS, MY LOVE!"   10
    "OH! HOW UNGRATEFUL!"   10
    WHY A LITTLE GIRL LOVED HER MOTHER.   11
    ST. MARY MAGDALEN AND THE FLOWERS.   12
    A HOLY MAN ASHAMED OF HIS LITTLE LOVE FOR GOD.   13
    THE LITTLE BOY AND THE RICH LADY.   13
    JESUS ASKS US TO LOVE HIM.   14

4. GOD MADE YOU TO SERVE HIM   15
    ST. GERTRUDE'S RECOMPENSE.   15
    "O MY GOD, THOU HAST DECEIVED ME!"   16
    ST. ANTHONY'S GREAT BOOK.   17
    GOD SAYS I MUSTN'T   18
    THE MOTHER AND HER FOUR CHILDREN.   19
    "AUVERGNE, AUVERGNE, THE FOE!"   19

5. GOD MADE YOU TO BE HAPPY IN HEAVEN   22
    "I WAS BORN FOR GREATER THINGS."   22
    ST. TERESA SIGHS FOR HEAVEN.   23
    THE MONK AND THE BIRD.   24

6. GOD HAS GIVEN YOU A SOUL AND A BODY	26
SCIPIO'S MEDAL.	26
7. YOU MUST TAKE CARE OF YOUR BODY	28
ST. LEONIDAS AND HIS SON.	28
THE OLD MAN AND THE YOUNG SOLITARY.	29
8. YOU MUST TAKE MOST CARE OF YOUR SOUL	31
"SAVE YOUR SOUL."	31
ST. MACEDONIUS AND THE HUNTER.	32
A GREAT MISTAKE.	33
ST. AGNES.	34
ST. BERNARD'S LITTLE BROTHER NIVARD.	35
9. WHAT WE MUST DO TO SAVE OUR SOULS	37
THE SAINT WHO WAS AFRAID TO DIE.	37
THE THREE GREAT WORDS.	38

PART II
GOD'S GREAT GIFT OF FAITH

1. FAITH: A SUPERNATURAL GIFT OF GOD TO US	43
THE CHILDREN-SLAVES OF ALGERIA.	43
2. BY FAITH WE BELIEVE WHAT GOD HAS REVEALED	46
THE DREAM OF THE PRINCESS.	46
3. HOW GOD BESTOWS ON US THE GIFT OF FAITH	48
THE LITTLE INDIAN BOY.	48
THE BATTLE OF TOLBIAC.	49
4. VALUE OF THE GIFT OF FAITH: HOW WE SHOULD ESTEEM IT	53
OSKALOE, THE SAVAGE PRINCE.	53
5. THE GIFT OF FAITH MUST NEVER BE REFUSED	55
SS. BARLAAM AND JOSAPHAT.	55
RADBOD, KING OF FRIESLAND.	57

6. WE MUST NEVER BE ASHAMED OF OUR FAITH,
   MUCH LESS DENY IT   60
   THE COLONEL DISGRACED.   60
   FREDERICK OF PRUSSIA AND GENERAL
   ZEITHEN.   62
   A GIRL WHO LOST HER FAITH.   63

7. THE MARTYRS DIE RATHER THAN RENOUNCE
   THEIR FAITH   65
   ST. VITUS DIES FOR JESUS CHRIST.   65

8. FAITH NOT SUFFICIENT WITHOUT GOOD WORKS 67
   SERMON OF ST. JAMES THE APOSTLE.   67
   THE ARAB AND THE CATHOLIC.   68

9. THE GREAT SIN OF UNBELIEF   69
   ST. JANE FRANCES AND THE HERETIC.   69

10. HERESY   71
    THE HERMIT ACCUSED OF HERESY.   71

11. APOSTASY   73
    TRIED, AND FOUND FAITHFUL.   73

12. THE APOSTLES' CREED   76
    THE APOSTLES COMPOSE THE CREED.   76
    ST. PETER OF VERONA.   77

PART III
ONE GOD IN THREE PERSONS

1. THE EXISTENCE OF GOD   83
   THE GOD WHOM ST. PATRICK ADORED.   83
   THE ATHEIST IN DANGER OF DEATH.   84
   "I ADORE ONE ONLY GOD," SAID THE MARTYR.   85

2. WHO IS GOD?   87
   "COME BACK IN EIGHT DAYS."   87
   THE COUNTRYMAN GOING TO CHURCH.   88

3. GOD IS THE CREATOR OF ALL THINGS   89
   HOW A SAVAGE CAME TO KNOW GOD.   89
   GOD IN THE FIELDS.   90

4. GOD IS ALMIGHTY ... 92
   CANUTE'S ANSWER TO HIS COURTIERS. ... 92
   ST. PRISCA AMONG THE LIONS. ... 93
   THE THREE YOUNG MEN IN THE FIERY FURNACE. ... 94
   THE GREAT CONQUEROR, AND THE INDIAN CHIEF. ... 97

5. GOD IS EVERYWHERE ... 99
   ST. ATHANASIA'S VISION OF JESUS. ... 99
   THE EMPRESS AND THE BISHOP. ... 100
   "SILENCE! HERE IS BERNARDINE." ... 100
   AUGUSTINE AND HIS SISTER SOPHIA. ... 101
   BOLESLAUS AND HIS FATHER'S LIKENESS. ... 101
   ST. FRANCIS DE SALES AND THE CHILD AT CATECHISM. ... 102
   ST. ANTHONY IN TEMPTATION. ... 103
   "GOD SEES ME." ... 103
   BLESSED CRISPIN OF VITERBO. ... 104

6. GOD KNOWS AND SEES ALL THINGS ... 106
   ST. PHILIP NERI'S GREAT GIFT. ... 106
   ST. LIDVINA'S CONSOLATION. ... 107
   A LITTLE UNKNOWN SOUL. ... 107

7. GOD IS ETERNAL ... 109
   THE BIRD AND THE GRAINS OF SAND. ... 109
   ST. TERESA'S EXCLAMATION. ... 110

8. GOD IS INFINITELY BEAUTIFUL ... 111
   WHAT HE WOULD GIVE TO SEE GOD. ... 111

9. GOD IS INFINITELY MERCIFUL AND GOOD TO US ... 113
   ST. FRANCIS DE SALES AND THE PRISONER. ... 113
   CONTENT IN POVERTY. ... 114
   THE FATHER AND THE SICK CHILD. ... 115

10. GOD IS INFINITELY JUST AND HOLY ... 116
   THE HOLY MAN KILLED BY A WILD BEAST. ... 116

11. THE BLESSED TRINITY ... 118
   THE CHILD ON THE SEASHORE. ... 118
   ST. PATRICK AND THE SHAMROCK. ... 119

PART IV
JESUS CHRIST OUR SAVIOR

1. JESUS CHRIST THE ETERNAL SON OF GOD — 123
   ST. PAUL PROCLAIMS THE DIVINITY OF JESUS CHRIST. — 123

2. JESUS CHRIST IS TRUE GOD AND TRUE MAN — 125
   KING CHARLES IN DISGUISE. — 125
   JESUS CHRIST IS GOD. — 126

3. JESUS CHRIST COMES INTO THIS WORLD TO SAVE US — 127
   THE ANNUNCIATION. — 127
   THE BIRTH OF JESUS. — 127
   THE ANGELS APPEAR TO THE SHEPHERDS. — 128
   THE SHEPHERDS AT THE MANGER. — 128
   THE STAR IN THE EAST. — 129
   THE WISE MEN IN JERUSALEM. — 129
   THE WISE MEN AT THE CRIB. — 129
   THE MASSACRE OF THE INNOCENTS. — 130

4. THE DIVINE CHILDHOOD OF JESUS CHRIST — 131
   THE CIRCUMCISION. — 131
   BLESSED SUSO AND THE NAME OF JESUS. — 131
   THE COUNT ARMOGASTUS — 132
   ST. ANDREW THE TRIBUNE. — 132
   JESUS PRESENTED IN THE TEMPLE. — 133
   THE OLD MAN SIMEON. — 133
   ANNA THE PROPHETESS. — 134
   JESUS LOST IN JERUSALEM. — 134
   JESUS FOUND IN THE TEMPLE. — 135
   JESUS AT NAZARETH. — 135

5. ON THE LOVE OF JESUS CHRIST FOR US — 137
   THE CHILD IN THE WOODS. — 137
   ST. OZANNA AND THE HOLY CHILD JESUS. — 138
   THE NUN WHO WAS TEMPTED TO DESPAIR. — 139
   A STORY OF ALFRED THE GREAT. — 140
   THE LITTLE BOY'S DEATH. — 141
   ST. VINCENT OF PAUL IN CHAINS. — 142
   THE LION AND THE LAMB. — 142

6. JESUS CHRIST IN HIS SACRED PASSION	144
"I AM THY SAVIOR AND THY BROTHER."	144
GOD'S COMPLAINT.	145
THE VALUE OF A TEAR.	145
THE PRINCIPAL SUFFERINGS OF JESUS.	146
JESUS CONDEMNED TO DIE.	146
THE LITTLE GIRL'S CRUCIFIX.	147
VISION OF ST. MARGARET MARY.	148
7. JESUS DYING ON MOUNT CALVARY	150
JESUS NAILED TO THE CROSS.	150
JESUS HANGING ON THE CROSS.	150
THE SEVEN WORDS OF JESUS ON THE CROSS.	151
JESUS DIES ON THE CROSS.	152
JESUS LAID IN THE TOMB.	152
THE SOUL OF JESUS IN LIMBO.	153
8. THE RISEN LIFE OF JESUS CHRIST	154
JESUS RISES FROM THE TOMB.	154
JESUS APPEARS TO THE APOSTLES.	155
JESUS APPEARS TO ST. THOMAS.	155
HISTORY OF OUR LORD'S ASCENSION.	156
ST. PAUL'S ADVICE.	156
ST. JOHN FISHER AT DEATH.	156
"ARISE AND COME."	157
HEAVEN OUR TRUE COUNTRY.	157

PART V
JESUS CHRIST OUR TEACHER

1. "LEARN OF ME."	161
THE VISION OF PETER OF FECELANO.	161
WALKING IN HIS FOOTSTEPS.	162
THE DOCTRINE THAT JESUS TAUGHT.	164
THE MIRACLES OF JESUS CHRIST.	164
2. JESUS IN HIS INFANCY TEACHES US HUMILITY	166
THE GREATEST SINNER.	166
"WHAT MUST I DO TO BE GOOD?"	167
ADVICE OF FATHER LEFEVRE.	167
IN THE CEMETERY.	168
THE SOLITARY WHO BECAME PROUD.	168

BLESSED AMADEUS, DUKE OF SAVOY.	169
HUMILITY OF ST. ALOYSIUS.	170
ST. ANTHONY'S SURPRISE.	170
SATAN HATES HUMILITY.	170
3. JESUS IN HIS CHILDHOOD TEACHES US TO LIVE WITH GOD	172
ALWAYS GOD'S CHILD.	172
"I AM JESUS OF NAZARETH."	173
4. JESUS IN HIS PRIVATE LIFE TEACHES US OBEDIENCE	175
"YES, FATHER, I WILL GO."	175
THE FOUR SOLITARIES AND THE ABBOT.	176
ST. MARY MAGDALEN OF PAZZI'S OBEDIENCE.	177
ST. FRANCES OF ROME.	177
ST. BENEDICT AND THE LITTLE BOY MAURUS.	178
5. JESUS IN HIS PUBLIC LIFE TEACHES US TO BE MEEK	179
THE WAY TO PURCHASE HEAVEN.	179
WHAT I LEARNED AT SCHOOL.	180
ST. FRANCIS REGIS IN THE INN.	180
TWO LITTLE CHINESE CHILDREN.	181
"JESUS SUFFERED MORE THAN I DO."	182
6. JESUS IN HIS SUFFERING LIFE TEACHES US HOW TO BEAR OUR CROSS	183
A GREAT SCHOLAR WHO COULD NOT LEARN ANYTHING.	183
"I AM NOT AFRAID."	184
THE LADY'S CROSS.	185
"I AM INNOCENT."	186
THE COUNT ELEAZAR.	187
BROTHER JUNIPER'S PRECIOUS JEWELS.	188
BROTHER BERNARD'S GREAT JOY.	188
THE PATIENCE OF ST. NORBERT.	189
ST. ROSE OF LIMA'S PATIENCE.	189
THOSE WHOM JESUS LOVES BEST.	190
BLESSED ANGELA ON JOY IN SUFFERINGS.	190
ST. FRANCIS' PRAYER.	190
SAYINGS OF SOME OF THE SAINTS ABOUT SUFFERINGS.	191

ST. VINCENT OF PAUL IN HIS SUFFERINGS.	192
THE KNIGHT HILDEBRAND.	192

7. JESUS IN HIS GLORIOUS LIFE TEACHES US TO
    DESIRE HEAVEN — 195
    THE DEATH OF ST. JEROME. — 195

PART VI
JESUS CHRIST OUR JUDGE

1. THE GENERAL JUDGMENT — 199
    THE END OF JERUSALEM, AND THE LAST
    JUDGMENT. — 199
    THE "COMING OF THE SON OF MAN." — 201
    THE REMORSE OF THE WICKED. — 202
    ST. EPHREM'S SERMON ON THE GENERAL
    JUDGMENT. — 203

2. EXAMPLES OF THE TERROR OF EVEN THE
    THOUGHT OF THE LAST DAY — 205
    ST. CEDDA IN A THUNDERSTORM. — 205
    KING PHILIP AND HIS TWO NOBLES. — 206
    THE PICTURE OF THE LAST JUDGMENT. — 207
    "IF MEN BUT ONLY KNEW..." — 207
    THE PARTICULAR JUDGMENT. — 208
    THE HOUSE NOT BUILT. — 209
    THE EMPEROR AND HIS FAVORITE. — 211

3. THE SAINTS AND GOD'S JUDGMENTS — 212
    "NO ONE CAN IMAGINE." — 212
    THE HOLY MONK AGATHO. — 213
    THE DYING MONK. — 213
    BROTHER MORICO'S FEARS DISPELLED. — 214

4. HOW STRICT ARE THE JUDGMENTS OF GOD — 216
    GOD'S JUDGMENTS NOT LIKE THOSE OF MEN. — 216
    ST. STEPHEN OF CITEAUX. — 218
    A YOUNG MAN CONVERTED. — 219
    THE HOLY MAN NILUS. — 219

5. SIN THE ONLY CAUSE OF FEAR AT THE DAY OF
    JUDGMENT — 222
    WHAT ST. JOHN CHRYSOSTOM WAS AFRAID OF. — 222
    "MY JESUS, MERCY!" — 223

6. HOW BEST TO SECURE THE SENTENCE OF THE
   ELECT   226
   "I AM PREPARING FOR JUDGMENT."   226
   WHY GOD HAS GIVEN US TIME.   227

7. THE TERRIBLE JUDGMENT OF THE REPROBATE   228
   THE THREE TERRIBLE WORDS.   228
   A MAN WHO DID NOT SERVE GOD JUDGED.   230

PART VII
THE HOLY GHOST

1. WHO IS THE HOLY GHOST?   235
   JESUS PROMISES TO SEND THE HOLY GHOST.   235
   KING LEOVIGILD AND ST. GREGORY OF TOURS.   236

2. THE WORKING OF THE HOLY GHOST IN THE
   BEGINNING OF THE CHURCH   237
   THE DAY OF PENTECOST.   237
   SAUL AND BARNABAS SENT FORTH BY THE
   HOLY GHOST.   238
   CORNELIUS THE CENTURION IS RECEIVED
   INTO THE CHURCH.   239
   THE COUNCIL OF JERUSALEM.   242

3. FIRST GIFT OF THE HOLY GHOST—WISDOM   244
   THE YOUNG HERMIT AND THE ABBOT.   244

4. SECOND GIFT OF THE HOLY GHOST—
   UNDERSTANDING   246
   THE PIOUS MOTHER OF THE MACHABEES.   246

5. THIRD GIFT OF THE HOLY GHOST—COUNSEL   249
   THE BETTER PART CHOSEN.   249
   TANCREDS CHOICE.   251
   FLORA AND HER PIOUS FATHER.   252
   BLESSED NICHOLAS OF FLUE.   252
   ST. MARGARET OF SCOTLAND.   253

6. FOURTH GIFT OF THE HOLY GHOST—
   FORTITUDE   254
   THE LITTLE BOYS OF OZACA.   254
   ST. CONCORDIUS, MARTYR.   256
   THE LITTLE MARTYR BOY.   258

7. FIFTH GIFT OF THE HOLY GHOST—KNOWLEDGE	261
"HOW MUCH I PITY YOU!"	261
8. SIXTH GIFT OF THE HOLY GHOST—PIETY	264
ST. WENDELIN THE PIOUS.	264
9. SEVENTH GIFT OF THE HOLY GHOST—THE FEAR OF THE LORD	266
QUEEN BLANCHE AND HER SON ST. LOUIS.	266

PART VIII
THE CHURCH MILITANT

1. THE CATHOLIC CHURCH FOUNDED	271
JESUS ESTABLISHES HIS CHURCH.	271
"THOU ART PETER."	272
"FEED MY SHEEP."	272
THE APOSTLES SENT FORTH TO GUIDE AND INSTRUCT US.	273
2. THE POPE IS INFALLIBLE	275
DECREE OF THE VATICAN COUNCIL.	275
3. THE FOUR MARKS OF THE CHURCH	277
GONDEBRAND, KING OF BURGUNDY.	277
FÉNELON'S PIETY.	278
THE MAP OF THE WORLD.	279
THE CURE OF ARS' SERMON.	279
4. THE INFALLIBILITY OF THE CHURCH	281
A POOR MAN'S ANSWER.	281
THE POET WERNER.	282
5. THE NECESSITY OF BEING A MEMBER OF THE ONE TRUE CHURCH	283
THE BLESSED CURE OF ARS AND THE PROTESTANT.	283
"ONE FOLD AND ONE SHEPHERD."	284
VICTORINUS OF ROME.	285
6. HOW GOD LEADS HIS ELECT INTO THE ONE FOLD	286
"I MUST BECOME A CATHOLIC."	286

7. ZEAL FOR THE CONVERSION OF SOULS	288
ST. GREGORY, APOSTLE OF ENGLAND.	288
"THE VOICE OF THE IRISH."	290
"O MY GOD, GIVE ME THAT SOUL."	291
FATHER GASPAR AND THE INDIAN CHIEF.	292
8. IN THIS WORLD WE MUST SUFFER FOR THE FAITH	294
ST. JULITTA AND HER LITTLE BOY CYRUS.	294
9. WE MUST NEVER DENY OUR FAITH, NOR BE ASHAMED OF IT	297
WHY HE DID NOT OBTAIN THE SITUATION.	297
THE BRAVE SOLDIER'S ANSWER.	298
10. THE COMMUNION OF THE SAINTS IN HEAVEN	300
OUR HEAVENLY MOTHER MARY.	300
OUR LADY'S REPROACH.	301
ST. FELIX, OUR LADY'S DEAR CHILD.	301
BLESSED JANE OF ORVIETO.	302
ST. JEROME'S PRAYER.	302
ST. GREGORY AND ST. BASIL.	303
11. THE COMMUNION OF THE FAITHFUL ON EARTH	304
A BEAUTIFUL COMPARISON.	304
ST. PETER IN PRISON.	305
A SISTER'S PRAYERS.	306
ST. GENEVIEVE SAVES PARIS.	307

PART IX
THE CHURCH SUFFERING

1. PURGATORY, AND WHO GO THERE	311
A VOICE FROM BEYOND THE GRAVE.	311
WHAT ST. CATHERINE SAW IN PURGATORY.	313
A VOICE FROM THE TOMB.	313
THE SOUL OF ST. MARY MAGDALEN PAZZI SAW.	314
SISTER CATHERINE'S VISION.	315
A VOICE IN THE GARDEN.	316
2. THE INTENSITY OF THE SUFFERINGS OF PURGATORY	317
HIS CHOICE.	317
BROTHER ANTHONY CORSO.	319

THIRTY YEARS.	319
HOW TIME IS MEASURED IN PURGATORY.	319
3. HAPPINESS OF THE SOULS IN PURGATORY	321
THE ANSWER OF A SOUL FROM PURGATORY.	321
THE NUN'S DEATH.	322
4. WE CAN HELP THE SOULS IN PURGATORY	324
THE CHILDREN'S CRY.	324
BLESSED CONRAD'S PRAYERS.	325
AN ACT OF THANKSGIVING.	327
5. HOLY MASS OFFERED UP FOR THE SOULS IN PURGATORY	328
ST. MALACHY OF IRELAND AND HIS SISTER.	328
THE VISION OF ST. THOMAS OF AQUINAS.	329
THE PRIEST'S REQUEST.	330
"MAY THEY REST IN PEACE."	330
"HASTEN! COME QUICKLY! FOR MASS WILL SOON BE ENDED."	331
A GREAT CONVERSION.	332
THE MONK'S VISION.	332
ST. PETER DAMIAN.	333
6. HOLY COMMUNION HELPS THE SOULS IN PURGATORY	334
EFFECTS OF ONE GOOD COMMUNION.	334
ST. GERTRUDE'S GREAT CONSOLATION.	335
7. PRAYERS AND GOOD WORKS HELP THE SOULS IN PURGATORY	336
HELP IN THE HOUR OF NEED.	336
"BLESSED ARE THE MERCIFUL."	337
8. TO HELP THE HOLY SOULS IS BENEFICIAL TO OURSELVES	339
ST. GERTRUDE CONSOLED.	339
"O MY JESUS, HAVE MERCY ON THEM."	341
THE VOICES ST. BRIDGET HEARD.	342
9. TO NEGLECT THE HOLY SOULS IS INJURIOUS TO OURSELVES	343
THE VISION OF ST. ANTONINUS.	343
A MOTHER'S USELESS TEARS.	344
"O MY FATHER, HAVE PITY ON ME!"	345

PART X
THE CHURCH TRIUMPHANT

1. WHAT IS HEAVEN LIKE? 349
   ST. JOHN IN THE ISLAND OF PATMOS. 349
   THE GLORY OF JESUS CHRIST IN THE
   CHURCHTRIUMPHANT. 351
   THE GLORY OF THE SAINTS AND ANGELS. 352

2. A GLIMPSE OF THE GLORY OF HEAVEN 356
   EMMANUEL, THE PIOUS DOCTOR. 356
   "HEAVEN AT LAST." 357

3. OF THOSE TO WHOM GOD HAS PROMISED
   HEAVEN 360
   ST. CYRIL, THE BOY-MARTYR. 360
   "ONE DAY I SHALL REIGN!" 363
   THE VISION OF THEODOSIUS. 364

4. HAPPY THOSE WHO DIE IN BAPTISMAL
   INNOCENCE 366
   "I WANT THAT CHILD." 366
   EVANGELIST AND AGNES. 368

5. HAPPY THOSE WHO DO PENANCE HERE 370
   THE REWARD OF PENANCE. 370

6. JOY OF THE SAINTS ENTERING HEAVEN 372
   THE GOOD AND FAITHFUL SERVANT. 372
   THE HUNDREDFOLD REWARD. 373
   ST. TERESA'S EXCLAMATION. 374
   THE SHIPWRECKED FAMILY. 374

7. ALWAYS THINK OF HEAVEN'S JOYS 378
   "THAT CITY MUST BE MINE." 378
   ST. ADRIAN, MARTYR. 379
   THE PROPHET DANIEL IN BABYLON. 380

PART XI
SIN AND ITS FORGIVENESS

1. OUR OBLIGATION TO OBSERVE THE
   COMMANDMENTS OF GOD — 383
      GOD GAVE THE COMMANDMENTS IN THE
   OLD LAW. — 383
      CHRIST CONFIRMED THE COMMANDMENTS IN
   THE NEW LAW. — 385

2. WHAT SIN IS — 386
      WHAT SIN DOES. — 386
      THE SAINT WHO WAS FOUND WEEPING. — 387
      THE IMITATORS OF HEROD. — 387
      ST. PHILIP AND THE NOISY BOYS. — 388

3. GOD'S LOVE FOR THOSE WHO ARE INNOCENT — 389
      WHY JESUS LOVED ST. NICHOLAS SO MUCH. — 389

4. THE TERRIBLE STATE OF A SOUL IN SIN — 391
      THE ANGEL AND THE MONK. — 391

5. THE INGRATITUDE OF ONE WHO COMMITS SIN — 393
      ST. POLYCARP BEFORE THE JUDGE. — 393
      "NEVER! NEVER!" — 394
      THE PICTURE OF JESUS CRUCIFIED. — 394
      ST. CATHERINE'S WORDS TO JESUS. — 395
      ST. ALPHONSUS AT TWELVE YEARS OF AGE. — 395
      WHY ST. VINCENT DE PAUL HATED SIN SO
   MUCH. — 396

6. ORIGINAL SIN — 397
      CHRISTINA'S PRESENT. — 397
      THE LOST INHERITANCE. — 400
      THE PEARL IN THE MIRE. — 400

7. MORTAL SIN — 402
      ST. LOUIS HATRED OF SIN. — 402
      DON PEDRO'S CONVERSION. — 403
      THE BOY AND THE ROSE-BUSH. — 405
      THE SUSPENDED SWORD. — 406
      EMELIA AND THE PIECE OF COAL — 407

8. MORTAL SIN DESTROYS THE MERIT OF ALL OUR GOOD WORKS	409
THE WORK OF ART DESTROYED.	409
9. VENIAL SIN	411
"ONLY A VENIAL SIN."	411
ST. MACARIUS AND THE STOLEN FIG.	412
A HOLY CHILD'S GRIEF.	412
VENIAL SIN IN THE EYES OF GOD.	413
ST. MARGARET MARY'S LITTLE FAULTS.	413
DRAWN BY A HAIR.	414
10. HOW SIN IS PARDONED	415
THE LITTLE CHILD IN THE FIRE.	415
ST. FRANCIS DE SALES AND THE GREAT SINNER.	416
A SPARK THAT FELL INTO THE SEA.	417
HOPE OF PARDON.	418

PART XII
THE RESURRECTION OF THE BODY AND LIFE EVERLASTING

1. THE RESURRECTION OF THE BODY	421
ST. EULALIA'S LAST WORDS.	421
THE MACHABEES.	422
BLESSED WILLIAM OF CLAIRVAUX.	422
A LITTLE CHILD'S QUESTIONS.	423
2. WHAT LIFE EVERLASTING MEANS	425
APPARITION OF THE CHILD JESUS.	425
ST. THOMAS MORE'S FIDELITY.	427
ST. IGNATIUS ALWAYS THINKS OF HEAVEN.	428
3. THE JOY OF THE GOOD CHRISTIAN AT DEATH	430
THE DYING MAN'S SMILE.	430
VANITY, OR THE DYING GIRL.	431
JOY AT DEATH.	433
THE GOOD NEWS.	434
QUEEN ESTHER.	435
THE WORDS A SAINT HEARD IN HEAVEN.	436
THE BRIGHT CROWN.	437

- 4. THE ETERNAL REWARD FOR BEARING PATIENTLY OUR CROSS IN THIS WORLD — 438
  - COUNT OTHO'S DAUGHTER. — 438
  - THE BEAUTIFUL CROWN. — 439
  - ST. PLATO COMFORTED. — 440
  - "CONSIDER THY LAST END." — 441

- 5. OUR ETERNAL REWARD WILL BE MEASURED BY THE GOOD WE HAVE DONE ON EARTH — 442
  - THE DUKE OF CARINTHIA'S FEAST. — 442
  - "O PARADISE! O PARADISE!" — 444

- 6. THE SOULS OF THE JUST SHALL FIND ETERNAL REST IN GOD — 446
  - AN OFFICER CONVERTED. — 446
  - WHY HE WISHED TO DIE. — 447
  - "MY FRIENDS, TO PARADISE! TO PARADISE!" — 448
  - A SAINT WHO WAS ALWAYS TREMBLING. — 449
  - "WE DESIRE GOD ALONE AND HEAVEN." — 449

- 7. AN ETERNITY OF PUNISHMENT FOR THE WICKED — 451
  - "MAXIMUS, MY SON!" — 451
  - VICTORINE'S RESOLUTION. — 452
  - TWO SOLDIERS AT A SERMON. — 453
  - SATAN COMPELLED TO GIVE AN ANSWER. — 454
  - "I CANNOT BEAR THIS MUCH LONGER!" — 454

- 8. AMEN — 456
  - THE AMEN OF THE STONES — 456

PREFACE

St. Gregory the Great tells us that more men are drawn towards Heaven by the force of example than by the effects of argument. If this be true in reference to mankind in general, it is especially so with regard to the child. The child is formed on example. The truths of faith learned in the Catechism are for the most part unintelligible to him. He requires to have them sketched out as in a picture before he can take in their meaning. Children delight in stories, and they are not slow to catch the moral these are intended to convey. If these stories are lifelike, and within reach of their own practice, they try to imitate what is told in them. Long experience and the example of great and holy men, who have in this, as in other things, followed the example of Our Blessed Lord Himself, have convinced the author of this book of the necessity of bringing out in bold relief, by means of examples, the truths contained in the Catechism.

It was this that induced him to undertake this work. Each example has been carefully chosen to bring home to the mind of the child some one of the great truths of our holy Faith, and to fix it there. Each line of his book has been penned with scrupulous care, and in the simplest language, that religion might be made attractive, and that the child might see that it was in its power to do much for God in a humble way. He is conscious of many defects in his unpretending work; but he hopes that the result of his leisure moments, snatched from the continual turmoil of a laborious missionary life, may not be without its fruits. He had but one end in view—the greater glory of God and the sanctification of souls. If the perusal of this little work will make even one child more holy, or love our dear Lord more fervently, he will consider that he has not labored in vain.

PART I
WHY WE WERE MADE

1

GOD MADE YOU

My child, when you were very young, you were sent to school so that you might learn to read, write, and count. There, you also learned geography and many other useful things. When you grow up and are old enough to work, you will be sent to learn some trade or business, so that you may earn your livelihood.

Now, all these things are very useful, and even necessary. But there is one thing more useful and more necessary still, and that is to know God. You must learn what God has done for you, and what He wants you to do for Him.

The Catechism begins by telling you that God made you. Therefore, God is your Father, and you are His child.

ST. DOMNINA AND HER FATHER IN HEAVEN.

This great Saint, even when she was quite a child, was often found weeping. People who did not know her thought she must be very unhappy because she wept so much. But these tears were not shed because she was sad; it was the thought of how much her good Father in Heaven had done for her that made her weep.

"O my God, how good it was of Thee to think of me at all!" This is what she often said in her prayers. "Thou didst make me, not because Thou wert obliged to make me, but because Thou didst love me so much more than others; and not only didst Thou make me, but Thou gavest me many blessings besides. O my God, how good Thou hast been to me!"

One day a priest came to her house. She was reading a pious book when he came in. As usual, the tears that flowed from her eyes had fallen upon the book, and the pages of the book were wet, especially at those places where the holy name of God was written.

The priest asked her why she wept so much when she read good books, and why the places in her book where the name of God was written were more wet than other places.

Domnina answered him: "Why can you ask me such a question, reverend Father? Is there anything in this world so beautiful, so sweet, so lovely as the name of my dear Father in Heaven? I can never hear His name pronounced, or read it in a book, without feeling my whole heart filled with love for Him. He made me, therefore I am His child, and I know He loves me, poor and little though I am, just because I *am* His child, and I always try to keep this in mind; and I feel so happy when I think of this, that tears of joy flow from my eyes."

You also are God's child, for He made you. Like St. Domnina, you should try to keep this always before your mind, and thank Him for His goodness in making the choice of you to be His own child.

Cat. de Perseverance.

2

GOD MADE YOU TO KNOW HIM

THE LITTLE BOY IN THE SNOW.

In the kingdom of Poland, the cold is sometimes very great in the winter-time, and when people go out of their houses they cover themselves with fur clothing to keep themselves warm.

One very cold Sunday, three children were going along the road towards the chapel. It was the hour for Catechism. They were trembling with cold, because, being very poor, they were not able to buy fur clothes; moreover, their shoes were very bad and thin, and their feet were as cold as the frozen snow on which they were walking.

One of them, a little boy about seven years old, was weeping. His oldest sister, who was with him, knew that he wept because he was cold; so she said kindly to him: "Go home, my darling, and mother will make you warm; it is too cold today for you to come with us. God will not be angry with you for staying away from Sunday-school on such a cold day as this."

But the child said: "No, no; let me go with you. My feet are very cold, it is true, but even if they were frozen I would still go to Sunday-school to learn something more about God and the way to Heaven." And so he went along with them.

THE LITTLE BOY AT THE EXHIBITION.

During the great Exhibition in London, a gentleman went to visit it; his little boy Alfred was with him.

The child was astonished at the multitude of the things he saw, and was very anxious to know for what purpose they were made; so he kept continually asking his father to tell him. His father answered him as far as he could, and described to him the use of the various things as they passed along; and the boy saw that everything there had its own special use, and was made for some special purpose.

"You see, my dear boy," said the father to him, "that everything here has been made for a certain end. You also were made by God for a certain purpose—to know, love, and serve Him."

"Yes, father; these are the words of the Catechism: 'God made me to know Him, love Him, and serve Him in this world, and to be happy with Him in the next.'"

"My dear Alfred," replied the father, "keep these words always in your mind, and try every day to learn something about your Father in Heaven."

THE TWO LITTLE BOYS IN AMERICA.

Father Gaume wrote a letter from the wilds of America, to which he had been sent to preach the Gospel. In it he says: "There are two little native boys in my mission who have given me great consolation. The hut where they dwell with their parents is seven miles distant from our chapel, yet every day for six months these two boys came to hear me explain the Catechism. I have sometimes seen them at the door of the chapel early in the morning, waiting till I came to open it.

"One very cold and wet morning I went out as usual to the chapel. The boys were already there, and were trembling with cold. I said to them: 'My dear children, you might have remained at home today, since it is so cold.' But they answered that they would suffer even more cold rather than be absent from one instruction that they might learn more about God."

And you, my child, are perhaps within a short distance of the church, and so often neglect to go to hear the Word of God, or are inattentive to the instructions that are given you. This example, then, should inspire you with the resolution never to miss a sermon or an instruction, and to listen with great attention to the words you hear.

3

GOD MADE YOU TO LOVE HIM

My child, God made you to love Him. You must begin to love God as soon as you know Him, and must continue to do so all your lifetime; for if you do not love Him in this world you will never see Him nor be able to love Him in Heaven.

HOW MUCH A LITTLE CHILD LOVED GOD.

One Christmas Eve, a long time ago, a little maiden was kneeling in the chapel, and praying very earnestly to Him Who once came into the world, and was born in a stable at Bethlehem. She thought of the sufferings the Divine Child Jesus endured for love of her on that cold Christmas night, and her heart was all on fire with love of Him.

And as she prayed, a bright light filled the chapel, and Mary, Our Lady, appeared before her with the Divine Child in her arms. Our Lord said to her "My child, how much do you love Me?"

She answered in the words of St. Peter: "O Lord, Thou knowest that I love Thee."

"But how much?" asked the Infant Saviour.

"More than myself," murmured the maiden.

"And do you really love Me?" said the gentle voice again.

"Yes, yes, Lord," cried His little spouse; "I love Thee, and Thou knowest it, more than my heart and my life."

"How much more than your heart and your life?" inquired Jesus.

Then the maiden drooped her head. "I know not how to answer Thee, my dearest Lord," she said, and she could say no more. Her little heart was so full of love that it could contain itself no longer, and it broke. She lay on the floor of the chapel a few moments conscious, long enough to tell those who came to help her what had happened then she went to join the angels in loving Him in Heaven, Whom she had loved so much on earth.

MARINA DE ESCOBAR

A pious man named James de Escobar, who was by profession a lawyer, had a little daughter called Mary. This child was, from her infancy, so gentle and so meek that everyone spoke of her as a little saint. She had an aunt who stayed with her, for whom she had a special affection. The aunt, too, loved the child greatly, and spent most of her time teaching her little niece all about God and His holy law.

One day, when the child was only three years old, her aunt was telling her that God commands us to love Him "with our whole heart, and above all things." "My dear aunt," she said, "what does that mean? What is it to love God above all things?"

"To love God above all things is to love Him more than your father and your mother and me, and every other thing."

The child repeated these words to herself over and over again, until she knew them by heart; and very often people would hear her, when she thought no one was listening, saying, "O my God, I love Thee more than my father, and my mother, and my aunt, and every other thing. Yes, yes; I love nothing but Thee, O my God, and I wish to search for Thee until I find Thee."

Perfect. Chrét

"O JESUS, MY LOVE!"

St. Ignatius, the martyr, gave his life to show God how much he loved Him. "O Jesus, my Love!" were the words that were always upon his lips. It was by saying them so often that he got the strength and the consolation he needed in his many labors for God.

One day he was taken by the pagans before the judge because he was a Christian, and the judge told him if he wanted to save his life he must renounce Jesus Christ altogether.

But the only answer St. Ignatius made was his usual prayer: "O Jesus, my Love!"

The judge said: "Unless you cease to say these words, I shall order you to be put to the most awful tortures."

But the Saint, raising his hands to Heaven, answered: "Never will my lips cease to utter these words."

Then the pagans who were standing near him said to him in a tone of mockery: "When your head is cut off, your lips will not be able to speak these words, or any other words, and then you will be obliged to be silent."

"You have the power to do to me what you threaten; but when you have forced my lips to be silent, and when my tongue can no longer utter the name of my Jesus, my heart will say it as long as it beats."

When they led him to the place of death, the last words he was ever heard to say in this world were: "O Jesus, my Love!"

Rep. du Catéchiste.

"OH! HOW UNGRATEFUL!"

When the natives of Japan were told for the first time of the greatness and power and perfection of God, a feeling of awe came over them; and this was increased when they heard that this great God was always near them, and even in their very souls.

When the missionaries told them of the fall of our first parents, and of the infinite goodness of God in sending His own Divine Son to redeem them, their astonishment knew no bounds.

And when at length they began to tell them how that Jesus was born in a stable, and that He suffered and died on the cross for us, they all cried out "Oh, how loving! Oh, how good must the God of the Christians be!"

"More than that, my brethren," continued the Fathers, "God gives us a commandment that we must love Him with our whole hearts, and threatens us with terrible punishments if we refuse."

"Oh, surely that was not necessary," cried out one of the people— "surely, since He was so good to them, they could not but love Him, and think it the greatest honor to be allowed to do so. Surely the Christians must always be at the foot of the altar of their God, all penetrated with thanksgiving, all inflamed with love!"

"Ah, would to God that this were true!" said the missionary; "but it is far from being the case. There are Christians who not only will not love God, but who even spend their lives in offending Him."

Then these poor savages were filled with an indignation which they could not control. "Oh, who ever heard of such ingratitude! Oh, hard-hearted barbarians!" they exclaimed. "In what part of the world do these wretched men live, for they ought to be all destroyed from the face of the earth, and not allowed to live!"

Catechisme Pratique.

My child, you perhaps were at one time amongst the number of those who deserved these reproaches. Be very careful never to deserve them again, lest at the last day these poor people rise up in judgment against you and condemn you, because you did not love your God and Savior Who has loved you so much.

WHY A LITTLE GIRL LOVED HER MOTHER.

A little girl was one day playing with some toys in the room where her mother was sewing. All at once the child ran over to the place where her mother sat, and, climbing on her knee, threw her arms around her neck and kissed her. Then, laying her little head lovingly on her mother's shoulder, she whispered into her ear these words: "My own dear, sweet mother, I love you."

Her mother stopped her work, and, looking on her little one, smiled sweetly, and said: "Well, darling, why do you love me?"

"Oh, mother, can you not guess?" And her bright blue eyes were filled with tears as she continued: "It is because you loved me when I was too little to love you back—that's why I love you so much."

But God loved you, my child, as He Himself says, "with an everlasting love," and loves you more than any mother can love her child. Would it not, then, be most ungrateful on your part if you did not love Him in return?

If you saw God as the angels and the Saints see Him in Heaven, it would be impossible for you not to love Him, because He is so good and beautiful. But as long as you are in this world, you cannot see Him. That is to be your reward hereafter for loving Him here on earth.

But you can easily know that God must be very good and beautiful, since there are so many good and beautiful things in this world; and if your heart is filled with delight when you behold them, how much greater will be the joy and happiness you will feel in Heaven when you see, face to face, the great God Who made all these things.

ST. MARY MAGDALEN AND THE FLOWERS.

Every time St. Mary Magdalen of Pazzi saw a flower, or any other beautiful thing that God made, she would feel her soul all on fire with love of God. "O my God," she would say, "it was for love of me that Thou didst make that little flower, just to give me pleasure. Oh, how loving must Thou be, my dear Heavenly Father!"

A HOLY MAN ASHAMED OF HIS LITTLE LOVE FOR GOD.

There was a certain holy man who was so ashamed of his little love for God, that whenever he saw the beauty of the things God had made, he used to say: "Be silent, ye flowers and beautiful works of God. Whenever I look on you, you always seem to say to me: 'What an ungrateful wretch you are! God made us for love of you, and yet you will not love Him.' Yes, I hear you, and I know you say the truth; but oh, be silent, and do not always reproach me!"

My child, you must also love God because He made you. If He had not made you, you would never have been in this world at all. Yet He was not obliged to make you. He could have made others instead of you. But He made you because He had for you a special affection. Surely, then, you will not refuse to love Him.

THE LITTLE BOY AND THE RICH LADY.

A little boy was once sitting at the doorstep of a splendid mansion in one of our great cities; he was cold and hungry, and his clothes were only rags. He was an orphan, for both his parents were dead, and he was wandering over the country without friends to love him or a home to shelter him. He was glad when anyone offered him a crust of bread, or allowed him to sleep under the shelter of a stable or on a little straw.

As he was sitting there tired and weary, and tears running down his cheeks, the door opened and the lady of the house appeared. At first she was on the point of saying angry words to him, and of telling him to go away; but when she saw his sad face, and heard his sorrowful tale, she had compassion on him, took him into her house, and gave him some food.

While she stood watching him, a thought suddenly came into her mind. "Would you like to stay with me?" she said. "I think you would be happier here than wandering about without a home."

The little boy looked up to the face of the good lady; he could not imagine that he had heard rightly what she had said. So, when she asked him a second time, he threw himself on the ground at her feet, and for some moments could not speak, so great was his joy.

The lady was pleased with the boy, and in a short time adopted him as her child, and made him the heir of her great wealth; and the boy, in gratitude to his benefactress, loved her with the tenderest affection as long as she lived.

But God has done more for you than that. He created you and made you His child in this world, and has made you also the heir of eternal treasures in Heaven. Is He, then, not worthy of all your love?

JESUS ASKS US TO LOVE HIM.

One day, when the blessed Jane Mary Bonomi was preparing for Holy Communion, our Lord Himself appeared to her in all His glory, and, kneeling down beside her, showed her marks of great tenderness and affection.

Then He said to her: "My own beloved child, I ask you to love Me."

How great must have been the joy of that holy child when she heard these words from the lips of Jesus Himself. Yet, my child, He is always saying the same words to you in your heart: "My own beloved child, I ask you to love Me."

4

GOD MADE YOU TO SERVE HIM

My child, when we love God as we ought, it will be very easy to serve Him. When one person loves another, how careful he is never to displease such a one, and how anxious he is to do all that he knows will give him pleasure. It is in this way we must love God. We must keep away from everything which will displease Him; observe His commandments faithfully, and offer up to Him all our thoughts, words, and actions, and thus consecrate our entire being to His service.

There is a little prayer which you were taught to say every morning: "My dear Jesus, may I do all for the love of Thee this day." By that prayer, my child, you offer up to God all the thoughts, words, and actions of the day. If you do this fervently every day of your life, you will serve God well.

ST. GERTRUDE'S RECOMPENSE.

In the convent where St. Gertrude lived there were many pious young ladies who were always busy at work, and did much more than St. Gertrude, who was not strong in body. But the Saint gained more merit before God for the little she did than all the others, although they did so much.

The reason for this was because she did everything for the love of God, and they did many of their actions from some other motive. So they lost their reward for them; for God does not give any recompense for anything that is not done for Him. So, my child, be sure to do everything for the love of God.

If you desire to serve God and save your soul, you will have your cross to carry in this land of exile. But be not frightened, for Jesus has promised to help you when that time comes.

"O MY GOD, THOU HAST DECEIVED ME!"

A long time ago, there lived a great servant of God who was very anxious to lead a life of great perfection that he might gain Heaven.

As he was thinking one day how he could do this, he chanced to read that part of the Holy Scriptures where our Lord says: "He that will come after Me must deny himself, and take up his cross."

Now, these words made the humble man afraid. "How can I have the courage to suffer all my lifetime the afflictions Jesus Christ says all His disciples must suffer, and to take up the cross they must all carry? But I will try. I must gain Heaven, cost what it may; and I will now most willingly embrace a life of sufferings here that I may be with God in Heaven hereafter."

So he began to practice those virtues which make people Saints. He renounced his own will, he read pious books, and often meditated on heavenly things. He also went frequently to Holy Communion, and bore with great patience the afflictions he met with in the course of his life.

But instead of feeling this kind of life wearisome and hard to bear, his whole soul was filled with the greatest happiness and consolation.

One day he felt so happy that he cried out to God: "O my God, Thou hast deceived me! Thou didst say that those who want to be Thy disciples, and to get to Heaven, must bear their cross and suffer many things. I thought I would have many trials and afflictions, and much sorrow. But ever since I began to serve Thee I have always felt the greatest joy, happiness, and consolation, and I have found none of that bitterness Thou saidst I was to find in Thy service. O my God, Thou hast indeed deceived me!".

Catéchisme Pratique.

All the Saints tell us the same thing, my child, and if you try to be like them you also will be full of joy and happiness; you also will find consolation in bearing your cross, for the cross is heavy only to those who are afraid of it.

ST. ANTHONY'S GREAT BOOK.

In the deserts of the East there lived in the fourth century a holy hermit called Anthony. He had passed the greater part of his life in solitude, and knew but little of worldly learning, but he knew what was of infinitely more importance—how to serve and love God.

The fame of his sanctity, which had spread far and wide, reached the ears of some philosophers, who imagined that they knew all things, but they did not understand how a person could live so long in the desert all alone.

Eager to witness the kind of life he led, and to converse with one whom everyone admired and spoke of, they went to his cell in the wilderness. The gentle and noble appearance of St. Anthony filled them with a reverential awe; but when they began to converse with him they saw that all their boasted wisdom fell to the ground before his simple and admirable doctrine. They had come thinking to find a poor ignorant man, and they found one whose knowledge was greater than their own.

"Tell us, holy Father," they said to him, "in what book did you learn those sublime truths?"

The Saint raised up his hand towards Heaven. "That is my book," he said; "I have no other. Every person ought to study it, for it is full of marks of the wisdom and the power and the goodness of God.

By contemplating it you will soon be compelled to raise your thoughts to your Creator, and to burst forth in hymns of praise, of gratitude, and of love."

In Vit. Patrum.

GOD SAYS I MUSTN'T

One evening a mother sat at the fireside reading a story to her children. The story was about a little boy who was guilty of stealing.

When she had finished the story, she said to her children: "Why ought you never to steal as that boy did?"

William, the oldest child, immediately answered: "We ought not to steal because we ought never to do to another what we would not wish another to do to us."

"And what do you say, Robert?"

"I say I would not steal because, if I were caught, I know that you would punish me for it."

"And now, Mary, it is your turn to give a reason. Say, dear, why we ought not to steal."

"Because," said little Mary, looking meekly up into her mother's face — "because God says I mustn't."

"Right, my darling," said her mother, "that is the true reason, and the best reason that can be given. What God commands us to do, we must do; and what He forbids, we must be sure not to do. That is the real way to serve God." Then she said to the others: "If ever you are asked by anyone why you should not do what is wrong, let your answer be the one Mary has given, 'Because God says we mustn't."

III. Cath. American.

We often read and hear about the Saints, and we think that *we* cannot be saints. This is quite a mistake. If you serve God faithfully you will be a saint here on earth, and you will most certainly one day be a saint in Heaven.

THE MOTHER AND HER FOUR CHILDREN.

There was a mother who had four little children. She taught them in their very infancy to love God with their whole hearts, and to hate sin.

Every day she used to take them to her side, and teach them the truths which God has revealed to us, and make them say their prayers.

One evening, when she had finished this pious work, she looked upon them with eyes full of motherly tenderness, and as she looked she said to them: "Oh, my own dear children, what a happy mother I would be if I could only hope that one of you might be numbered amongst God's holy Saints."

Peter, the youngest of them all, climbed on his mother's knee, and, putting his little arms round her neck, said to her: "Mommy, I will be the saint." And he kept his promise. He never forgot the look his good mother gave him when he said these words, and in after-years he became the great St. Peter Celestine.

Let each one of us also say to our good Father in Heaven: "I will be a saint." All that is needed to become a saint is to love and serve God.

"AUVERGNE, AUVERGNE, THE FOE!"

Many years ago, two armies were at war with each other in France. They had not yet met in battle, but lay encamped not very far apart, although thick woods prevented them from seeing each other.

Night came on, and the French army planted their guards all round the camp, and kindled their fires to prevent their being taken by surprise.

A young soldier of the army, with four or five more, was posted a good way from the camp, not far from the edge of the woods.

They loaded their muskets, and commenced their slow, watchful march backwards and forwards under the glimmering light of the moon. The regiment to which these soldiers belonged was called the "Regiment of Auvergne."

All was still for some hours, and they heard nothing but the beetle humming by, or a wolf howling through the wood.

Once our young soldier heard a rustling among the trees. He stopped and listened. It ceased; he could hear nothing, so he moved on his beat again. Not long afterwards he heard it once more. He told his companions to be on the watch, and with his gun ready to fire, entered the woods.

It was now very dark—the moon was hidden behind the clouds—so he went along very cautiously. When he had gone forward about a bow-shot he came to an opening in the wood. Suddenly four soldiers sprang on him, drove his gun out of his hand by a sudden stroke, and pointed their bayonets at his breast, while one of them whispered fiercely in the darkness: "If you give any alarm you are a dead man."

The brave soldier had fallen into the hands of the enemy.

For a moment he stood still. What was he to do? His comrades were asleep in the camp, trusting to him to give the alarm if the enemy came near. He thought now that if he did not give the alarm the enemy would fall upon them and put them to death, and he saw that if he did give the alarm they would immediately kill him.

The hesitation was only for a moment. Remembering his duty to his King and to his country, he drew himself up, took a long breath, and shouted with all his might: "Auvergne, Auvergne, the foe!"

In an instant the bayonets were buried in his breast, and he fell to the ground in the agonies of death.

But his cry was heard. His dying ear caught the sharp crack of his companions' muskets as they fired the alarm, and soon the tramp of horses told him that he had not died in vain. Right nobly had he served his King.

My children, you have a King to serve—a heavenly one. Your foes are Satan and sin; these you must fight against. Like this brave soldier, you must be willing to die rather than fail in your duty to God; you must be faithful to Him even unto death.

Granville Fourth Reader, p. 10.

5

GOD MADE YOU TO BE HAPPY IN HEAVEN

My child, this world is not your home; you were made for Heaven; you were made to be happy forever with God in His eternal kingdom. Oh, how good God has been to you!

Now, since you were not made for this world, but for Heaven, you ought often to think of your future home, where you will dwell with your Heavenly Father, and of the joys He has prepared for you there if you serve Him faithfully here on earth.

"I WAS BORN FOR GREATER THINGS."

St. Stanislaus Kostka was born of a noble family, and was brought up amidst the splendors and luxuries of his princely position.

But even in his infancy, he despised all these things, and when he grew up he took the resolution of renouncing them all to embrace the holy poverty of a religious life.

When his friends were informed of his design, they tried to draw him from it. They often spoke to him of the happiness he would one day enjoy in the possession of great wealth. They pointed out to him the beauties of the vast domains of his ancestors, and the magnificence of the princely palace which would one day be his home. In a word, they placed before the eyes of his body as well as of his mind everything they thought would fascinate them.

Stanislaus did indeed look at them, but he also looked higher still. "My friends," he one day said to them, "these things are very beautiful, but I was born for greater things. God, my Father in Heaven, made me to possess the eternal riches of Heaven, and to see Himself forever there in His kingdom therefore, I keep my eyes fixed on Heaven that I may not allow them to be captivated by earthly things, which are so vile and worthless, when compared with those of Paradise."

ST. TERESA SIGHS FOR HEAVEN.

For the space of forty years, St. Teresa was never free from sufferings. She had a painful malady which gave her no repose. Yet in the midst of her pains, she was always calm and happy.

One of the sisters said to her once, when she was suffering more pain than usual: "Dear mother, you are suffering much today, yet you seem more joyful and more happy than usual."

"Yes, dear sister, the more I suffer now the happier I am, because I know that the more I suffer in this world the greater will be my reward in Heaven. Each moment of pain suffered with resignation to God's holy will is of immense value because of the happiness it will procure for me in Heaven."

So St. Teresa's thoughts were always in Heaven. One day one of the sisters asked her why she always smiled when she heard the clock strike.

She answered: "When I hear the clock striking it puts me in mind that I am a whole hour nearer to the end of my life, when I shall see my dear Heavenly Father, and be taken into my happy home in Heaven."

What a consoling thought it is for us in our life here to think that in Heaven our happiness will be forever and ever!

God made us to be happy with Him *forever* in Heaven.

THE MONK AND THE BIRD.

There was once a good religious who thought he should find time long in Paradise. The good God showed him plainly that he was mistaken.

One day in the summertime, when the sun was shining brightly, he was walking under the shade of the trees which grew in the garden of the monastery. His thoughts were, as usual, far away, in Heaven, and he began again to wonder what the Saints would do there during the endless ages of eternity.

As these thoughts were passing through his mind, he suddenly heard the most delicious music in the trees above his head. Looking up, he saw a snow-white bird that sang among the branches, and seemed to grow more and more beautiful the longer he looked at it.

He listened to it with a look of rapture upon his face, and followed the little bird as it flew from tree to tree. He wanted to catch it, but it escaped him, and flew far, far away, over hill and dale; and as its notes died away in the distance, he heard the monastery bell ringing the noonday Angelus. "It is time for me to return to the monastery," he said to himself; "I did not think it was so near this hour of day."

When he returned he was very much surprised to find at the gate a brother whom he had never seen before, and the brother did not know him either. This surprise was still greater when he saw nothing in the house but strange faces and new people; and yet it was the same old monastery, the same cloister, and the same quiet chapel.

"Where are our fathers?" he asked. "And our brothers, where are they?"

The others looked at him with astonishment. The Prior came to see him. "Who art thou?" he said. "Thou dost indeed wear the habit of our Order, but during the forty years I have been Prior here I have never seen thy face."

"My reverend Father," replied the monk, "it was but this morning that, with permission, I left my cell to walk in the quiet of the woods. While I was there, thinking of God and of Heaven, I heard the most beautiful music that it is possible to imagine, and I saw hopping from tree to tree a little bird—oh, such a beautiful one! I listened to it in rapture until the monastery bell rang out the midday Angelus. I was surprised that it had come so soon, for it seemed to me that, instead of for many hours, I had heard these thrilling notes only for a few brief moments."

"Hours!" exclaimed a very old and venerable monk who sat upon an oaken seat against the wall, and was looking fixedly into the face of him who had thus spoken, and who thought he recognized him; "it is years since thou didst leave the monastery. Is thy name Felix?"

"Yes, my Father, that is my name."

Then they searched in an old brown book, wherein were written down the names of all who had ever been in that holy house, and in it was recorded that, upon a certain day nearly a hundred years before, a monk called Felix had gone forth from the monastery at the hour of prime, and had never returned, and that he had been registered among the dead.

Then they all began to understand how that, in listening to that celestial song, the years had appeared to him like moments; and Felix, falling down upon his knees, bent his head humbly before God and murmured: "Ah, my God, now I understand that in the beauty of Thy heavenly city, and in the joy of Thy holy presence, a thousand years are as but a moment." Saying this, the monk bowed his face to the earth and died.

Oh, how glorious must be the beauty of Heaven, where God shows Himself in all His majesty to the Saints! And it is for that Heaven you were made, my child. Love and serve God now, that when you die it may be given to you.

6

GOD HAS GIVEN YOU A SOUL AND A BODY

God has given you a soul and a body. The soul is much more precious than the body, because God made it to His own image and likeness. How careful you should be never to destroy God's holy likeness by committing sin.

SCIPIO'S MEDAL.

Long ago, there used to be a curious custom among certain people; it was this: The children of all noble families had to wear on their breasts above their clothes a large medal, formed like a heart. On this medal were stamped the portraits of their fathers and mothers.

The reason why they wore this medal was, that they might have continually before their eyes the remembrance of their parents, and that the sight of it might keep them from doing anything that would bring dishonor to their parents' name.

A certain nobleman had a son named Scipio. This son wore round his neck a medal according to the custom. But he did not imitate the virtues of his parents, and by his bad conduct was bringing dishonor upon them. So the magistrates of the city commanded the medal to be taken from him, and ordered him to be punished.

When you were made, God, your Heavenly Father, put on your soul His image. You must, therefore, be very careful never to do anything unworthy of Him, otherwise He will no longer call you His child, and will punish you forever in hellfire.

7
YOU MUST TAKE CARE OF YOUR BODY

Y ou must also honor the body which God has given you, for it is His Holy Temple, and made to be happy along with the soul in heaven for all eternity.

ST. LEONIDAS AND HIS SON.

St. Leonidas, the martyr, had a son whose name was Origen. He loved him dearly because he was his youngest child. He watched over him with the greatest care that no evil might befall him, and he taught him to love God from his very infancy.

Origen grew up a pious child. He had a great horror of sin, no matter how small, and he seemed to have one only desire—that of pleasing God.

Leonidas had a feeling of reverence for his little boy. Often at night, when the child was sleeping in his little bed, he would go quietly up to him and uncover his breast and kiss it.

Once someone happened to surprise him in this act of piety, and asked him why he did so.

"Do you not know," he said, "that this child is the Living Temple of the Holy Ghost? In him He resides, for he is His chosen dwelling-place, and I love to honour the place where God reposes."

You, too, are God's Temple, my child. How carefully you ought to shun every evil, that you may keep pure and holy that temple which God has chosen for Himself, and which He created to be eternally happy in Heaven.

THE OLD MAN AND THE YOUNG SOLITARY.

There was once a young Solitary, whose one thought was the salvation of his soul.

Having often heard of the necessity of keeping the body in subjection, he used to entertain a great hatred for it, and treat it in a most cruel manner. Sometimes, even, for weeks he would not eat nor drink, and in a very short time he was reduced to a skeleton.

On one occasion an old man, who also had spent his life in the desert, meeting him, and seeing him reduced to this sad condition, asked him the cause of it.

"Of what use is this miserable body?" he answered, in reply; "it is of no value; it came from the dust of the earth, and must soon return to dust again."

"No, my friend," replied the old man, "you are very wrong; your body is indeed of great value. It is the dwelling-place of your soul, and through love for your soul, you ought also to love your body in a reasonable manner, and to preserve its existence as long as the will of God permits you. Let me lay before you a comparison: the eagle takes the greatest care of the egg in her nest, and woe betide the one who would dare to touch it. She does not do this for the sake of the egg, but for the preservation of the young eagle which it contains. But when the time of hatching has come, and the young bird comes forth from the shell to gaze upwards upon the sun, then the eagle cares nothing for the shell, but casts it away. So also should you take care of your body as long as the soul dwells with it, but when it goes forth to gaze upon the Sun of Justice, you need no longer care for the mortal covering which had enveloped it."

Thus spoke the wise old man. The young Solitary took his lesson to heart, and from that time forward treated his body in a more reasonable and Christian manner.

Hauterieve, VIII. 94.

8

YOU MUST TAKE MOST CARE OF YOUR SOUL

Since your soul is so much more precious than your body, you must take most care of it. Jesus Christ says to us, "What will a man give in exchange for his soul?" and again, "What will it avail a man to gain the whole world and lose his own soul?"

"SAVE YOUR SOUL."

Otto the Great, Emperor of Germany, had gone to Rome to visit the tombs of the holy Apostles there. On his way home, he passed through the land of Albania. The people who were along with him told him that there lived at a little distance a hermit, whose name was Nile, who was renowned throughout the whole country for his holy life. Otto thought that he would like to see him, so he left the highway and went to the place where the hermit dwelt.

When he had spoken to him for some time, the Emperor rose up to go away; but before leaving he said to him, "My Father, ask of me whatever you like, just as if you were my own son, and I will give it to you with the greatest joy."

St. Nile put his hand on the Emperor's breast, and said, in a solemn voice, "I ask of you, O Emperor, only one thing, and that is, that you will take care of your soul. Oh yes, I ask you, in the Name of God, to take care of your soul; for, although you are an Emperor, you must one day die like other men, and will have to give an account to God of everything you have done; and what will it avail you then if you have lost your soul?"

When the Emperor heard these words he began to weep, and, kneeling down at the Saint's feet, he took the royal crown off his head and answered, "O Holy Father, I will do what you ask me; but pray you to God for me, and give me now your blessing."

When he received the blessing of the Saint he rose up, and, still weeping and sobbing, went away along with those who had accompanied him.

Otto was then only about twenty years old. He had come to that time of life which is full of the greatest dangers. But he always kept in mind the solemn words of the Saint, and as soon as any temptation came to trouble him, he remembered his promise, that he would all his lifetime take most care of his soul.

So he led a life of great piety. His prayers were long and fervent, and he gave great alms to the poor. People used to say he was more like an angel in Heaven than a man upon earth. Thus he passed his life, and when the end came he died the death of the Saints, and he is now in Heaven, happy with God, because he followed the advice of St. Nile, and took most care of his soul.

Life of St. Nile.

ST. MACEDONIUS AND THE HUNTER.

A very holy man, whose name was Macedonius, one day heard a sermon upon those words, of Our Blessed Lord, "What will it avail a man to gain the whole world and lose his own soul?" They made so great an impression on his mind that he resolved to leave his home, and go into a great forest far away to live all alone, where no one would ever see him, and that there he would prepare for eternity. So he secretly went away. For some time people did not know what had become of him, and very soon he was forgotten as if he had been dead.

Many years afterwards it happened that a King came to hunt in the forest where Macedonius had gone to live. He had along with him many of his courtiers and others, who had gone to enjoy the chase. Suddenly he came to the place where the hermit dwelt. When he saw him he was full of wonder, and asked him what he was doing there. Macedonius, turning towards the King, asked him the same question, "What has brought *you* here?"

"I am come," answered the King, "to hunt in this forest."

"It was that same reason that brought me here," said Macedonius; "but I came, not to hunt the poor animals that wander about here, but to hunt for those eternal goods of Heaven which are so much more precious. I am here to try and gain Heaven."

The King went away, but he often thought on these words of the holy hermit.

Now, you are in this world as in a great forest, and you are here to hunt. Most men occupy themselves in hunting after riches, honor and fame, which are of no use to them. But the Saints, who had the thought of eternity always before them, hunted for those things which they are now enjoying in the kingdom of Heaven. My child, imitate their example.

A GREAT MISTAKE.

A priest once seeing the great care a man was paying to his horse, thus spoke to him:

"My friend, how much time does it take you every day to keep your horse in such fine condition?"

"About two hours," he replied.

"Now tell me as candidly, how much time do you give every day to the care of your soul?"

"Well, to tell the truth, not much. Every morning I bless myself, and I say an 'Our Father,' sometimes I add a 'Hail Mary,' and I never miss Mass on Sundays."

The priest said, "Since this is the case, if I belonged to you, I would rather be your horse than your soul."

ST. AGNES.

St. Agnes was born about the year 292. Her parents were very rich, but they were also good and fervent Christians, and brought up their only child in the fear of God.

When she was about twelve years old, a pagan met her coming home from school, and asked her to do what was very wrong, promising her, if she consented, to give her a great many valuable jewels. But Agnes at once rejected the temptation, and told him to begone, for she would never consent to offend her God for anything that the world could give her.

The young man was very angry when he heard this, and, soon afterwards discovering that Agnes was a Christian, he determined to make her yield to his wishes, or to accuse her to the pagan judge as belonging to that faith, and so she would be put to death.

When he told her what he intended to do, Agnes boldly answered, "Never will I consent to offend my God by sin, and joyfully will I suffer the loss of all things rather than lose my soul."

The young man accused her to the judge, and very soon Agnes was summoned before him. He tried first by kind words, and then by threats, to make her yield to him and renounce her faith, but to no effect. The firmness of the child filled him not only with wonder, but also with great wrath, and he handed her over to Aspasius, one of his underlings, that he might put her to death.

Aspasius commanded a great fire to be kindled, to consume her alive. But Our Lord was pleased to work a wonder in favor of His little girl, for when she was thrown into the fire, the flames divided in the middle, spreading themselves all around her without touching her, and spending their fury upon the idolaters who were standing by.

Then Agnes prayed to God, that now since she had confessed His holy Name, and had kept her soul undefiled in the midst of evil, and since He had shown forth His great power in her, He would be pleased to take her to Himself in Heaven.

When she had finished her prayer the fire suddenly went out of itself. Then Aspasius, fearing that she might escape, gave orders that the executioner should at once pierce her neck with a sword.

The man was so overcome with emotion at the sight of one so beautiful and so young, that at first he could not do this; but receiving a stern command from the prefect, he gave her the fatal blow, and her happy soul went at once to her God in Heaven, whom she had so tenderly loved.

Our soul is that pearl which is beyond all price. Like Agnes we should be willing to suffer all rather than stain it by sin, and the only thought of our lives should be to preserve undefiled that priceless treasure. It is sin alone that can kill the soul.

From her Life.

ST. BERNARD'S LITTLE BROTHER NIVARD.

St. Bernard, when quite young, saw how difficult it would be for him to save his soul in the midst of the temptations of the world, so he took the resolution to leave his father's house, and to go to some place where no one could ever find him.

His parents, and especially his mother, who loved him with great affection, tried by every means in their power to keep him at home, but their words had no effect on him. He spoke to them so eloquently of the happiness of living for God alone, and the necessity of making the salvation of our souls our chief work in life, that they finally gave their consent. Four of his brothers also resolved to follow his example.

During the six months that followed they dwelt together in a solitary place, making the final preparation for their departure; and at the end of that time they left the home of their childhood to serve God forever afterwards in solitude and prayer.

As they were leaving the courts of their father's house, they saw their little brother Nivard playing with some companions of his own age. He was their youngest brother, and as yet was only a child.

"Good-bye, dear little Nivard," said Guy, the eldest brother, to him; "we are going away to leave you, and we have made you sole heir of all that belongs to us, and of all that we may inherit when our parents die."

"No, no," cried out the child, "that must not be; that is not a fair division. You are all taking Heaven for your portion, and leaving me this miserable world for mine. No, I must go along with you."

For some years Nivard was obliged to remain at home; but when he grew up, and when he was no longer required to assist his aged parents, he followed his brothers into the monastery, and there labored to secure for himself the treasures of Heaven which can never be taken from him.

Life of St. Bernard.

9

WHAT WE MUST DO TO SAVE OUR SOULS

To save your soul, my child, you must worship God by faith, hope, and charity. You must believe all that God tells you, you must have confidence in Him that He will keep the promises He has made, and you must love Him with your whole heart.

THE SAINT WHO WAS AFRAID TO DIE.

In the lives of the Fathers of the desert, we read of a very holy anchorite who, during his whole lifetime, had the good habit of offering up every one of his actions to God in faith, hope, and charity. He never went anywhere, and never did anything, without saying to God that his greatest joy was to believe in Him and to hope in Him, and that he loved Him above all things.

This holy practice merited a special reward.

When the hour of his death drew near, this holy man lay on the ground of his cell, awaiting the summons from this life into eternity. He was full of fear at the terrible judgments of God, as sometimes the Saints are, who have a right notion of what sin is, so different from what we think about it.

But in the midst of his distress, when the thought of his sins was nearly driving him into despair, his angel guardian appeared to him.

"My child," said the angel, "do not be afraid. I am come to tell you that you are now going to see that God in whom you have so firmly believed; that you are to possess God in whom you placed all your hopes; and that you are now going to be united to God forever, whom you loved during life above all things."

The anchorite, consoled by this heavenly vision, passed out of this weary world into the bright light of eternity.

Catech. de Persévérance.

THE THREE GREAT WORDS.

In the lives of the religious belonging to the Order of St. Dominic, we read of one who was famous for his eloquence, and for the zeal with which he preached the holy Word of God.

"God made me to serve Him," he used to say. "I am in this world, O my God, to serve Thee. Show me then, dearest Lord, how I am to do so most perfectly, for this is the greatest, the only desire of my heart."

God was pleased with the fervor of this holy man, and answered his prayer.

As he was one day before the altar, pouring out his whole soul in the presence of God, and saying with more than usual fervor this little prayer, "O my God, what must I do to save my soul?" he heard a voice near him which answered him in these words: "Believe, Accomplish, Employ."

For a few minutes he repeated them to himself, trying to find out what they meant. But the more he thought over them the more difficult they seemed to be.

"O my God, make known to me the meaning of these words, for how can I understand them unless Thou dost explain them to me?"

This time, also, God was pleased to answer him. He heard the same voice again; it said: "My son, *Believe* all that God has revealed to you, *Accomplish* all that He has appointed to be done, by keeping His holy commandments, *Employ* the means He has given you to enable you to become holy and to reach Heaven."

The pious religious now clearly saw what God required of him to do, that he might serve Him in the most perfect manner. From that day till the hour of his happy death, he kept these words always before his mind; his whole life was thus spent in serving God most perfectly, and after death he was numbered amongst the Saints of God in Heaven.

It is in the same school that you, my child, will learn how to serve God as you ought. Do as this holy man did, and God will bestow on you the same reward.

Perfect. Chrét.

PART II

GOD'S GREAT GIFT OF FAITH

1

FAITH: A SUPERNATURAL GIFT OF GOD TO US

Faith is a supernatural gift of God, which enables us to believe without doubting whatever God has revealed.

My child, if you had not received this gift from God, you could never know Him in this world, nor see Him hereafter in Heaven.

THE CHILDREN-SLAVES OF ALGERIA.

In the province of Algeria, there was a slave market. In it, men, women, and even children were bought and sold, just as you see cattle bought and sold in our markets at home. When anyone of them was bought, he was driven home to his master's house, where he had to work all his lifetime, and got no wages, but often blows and ill-treatment, if he did not do the work which was given him to do.

One day there were a great many children standing in the market-place for sale.

It was a sad sight. They had been stolen from their happy homes far away by pirates, and brought to this place to be sold. Merchants were going about buying them to make them slaves.

Amongst these merchants, there was one who appeared to be

different from all the others. He went about among the children, chose out a few of them, and when he had paid the price that was asked, he took them along with him to the house where he lived, and spoke to them in these words:

"My children, you belong to me now. I paid a great price for you. If I had not bought you, some of those other cruel masters might have purchased you, and would perhaps have ill-treated you. But now you shall have nothing to fear from me. I have chosen you, and for what purpose?—To be my slaves? No; I am to be a father to you, and you are to be my children, and I am going to give you everything you can desire, to make you happy, for I love you, my children.

"You will have to remain here in this place for a little time, then I will come again, and take you all home with me to my own country, where I have large estates, and there you will be perfectly happy. When you grow up, I will give to each one of you a house and lands and wealth, which you will enjoy as long as you live."

When he had finished speaking the fortunate children burst into tears of joy, and falling down on their knees before their generous benefactor, tried to thank him, but they could not find words. They wondered why he had chosen them for this great happiness, instead of so many others who were left to their sad fate.

"My children," he said, "you have done nothing to merit this: it was entirely out of my own goodness that I made the choice of you. I am sure, then, you will be grateful, and never do anything to displease me, since I have been so kind to you."

They all promised to love and serve him all their lifetime, and never to forget the great favor he had bestowed on them.

My child, God has done something like this to you. You were a slave, and Satan was the cruel pirate who stole you, and thousands of others along with you, from the home of your Father in Heaven. But our dear Jesus came down amongst these slaves. He looked about and He chose you out of the multitude of your fellow-slaves, and brought you into His own house—that is, His Church—and said to you: "I have chosen you just out of My own kindness to you, and now you are to be My child, and I am to be your Father; and in My Church you will get every good thing you need; and in a short time, I will come and take you to Heaven, My country, and you shall be happy there forever."

Oh, what a treasure God has bestowed on you, in giving you the one true Faith!

2

BY FAITH WE BELIEVE WHAT GOD HAS REVEALED

By this gift of Faith, you are able, my child, to believe all that God has revealed to us. You must believe all that God has revealed, not because you can see or understand it, but because God has said it, and with the same certainty as if you really understood it all.

THE DREAM OF THE PRINCESS.

There was once a Princess who had been taught in her childhood the truths of faith in her Catechism. But when she grew up she began to go with companions who lived only for this world, and forgot God. Like them, she also neglected her duties, and gradually lost her faith; and like other unbelievers, she used to say she would not believe anything she did not see or understand.

One night she had a dream. Everything in life, even dreams, may, in the order of God's providence, be the means of inspiring us with good thoughts. She dreamed that she was walking through a great forest. She was alone. In the forest she saw a cottage, and at the door of the cottage there was a blind man sitting.

She drew near to him and said, "My good man, I see you are

blind; tell me, were you always blind, or is your blindness the result of an accident?"

"My lady," he replied, "I was born blind."

"Oh, how sad must be your lot!" replied the Princess. "You have never seen the beautiful sun, and you do not know what light is."

"No," he answered, "I have never seen the sun, and I have not the slightest idea what it is like, but I firmly believe that it must be something very beautiful."

The blind man then changing the tone of his voice, and assuming a serious look, continued, "You say you will not believe things which you do not see, or do not understand. Learn, then, from my example that many things are beautiful and beyond comprehension which you cannot understand, but which are really true, as true as the things which you can understand and see."

The Princess awoke, but the remembrance of the dream did not go away. It gave her a profitable lesson, and will give you one also, to believe firmly all the truths that God has revealed, whether you can understand them or not.

Migne, Dict., f. 385.

3

HOW GOD BESTOWS ON US THE GIFT OF FAITH

In the Sacrament of Baptism, God infuses the gift of faith into our souls. But He also in many ways brings to the knowledge of His Divine Faith and to the Sacrament of Baptism many of His children who have grown up in ignorance of the truths He has revealed. Happy are those who give ear to the voice of His Holy Spirit speaking in their hearts!

THE LITTLE INDIAN BOY.

In the "Life of St. Francis Xavier" we read the following beautiful story:

"There was once an Indian boy who led a very innocent life. He did not know God as we know Him, because there was no one in that country to teach him, and he grew up in the errors of the people among whom he lived. But young as he was, he soon saw that what they taught him, and what they themselves professed to believe, could not be true; and that it was impossible that gods made of stone or wood by the hands of men could have created this beautiful world and all that is in it. So he prayed to the Great Being, Who must be the Creator of such marvelous works, to be pleased to make known to him where He dwelt, that he might go and worship Him.

"It happened that someone spoke to him about the Turks, who followed the religion invented by Mahomet. His first impulse was to inquire what they believed and taught, but he soon found that it was little better than the religion in which he had been born.

"He next heard of the Jewish religion. At first he thought that at length he had found that of which he was so earnestly in search; but in a short time he felt within his soul that there was something wanting even in it. So he continued to pray as before: 'O Great Spirit Who made me, tell me Who Thou art, and where I can find Thee.'

"It was about that time that St. Francis Xavier arrived in his country, to preach to these poor Indians the one true Faith. When the young Indian heard that a stranger had come from a distant country, and was teaching the people the mysteries of our holy Religion, and especially when he learned that he had come to make known to them who God is, Who made all things, he went without delay to the place where the Saint dwelt. As he drew near, he seemed to hear a voice in his heart saying: 'Go to this man; he will tell you all about the true God, and how to serve Him.'

"He listened to the words of St. Francis with great joy; at last he had discovered a religion that could satisfy his soul, and in due time he received from the Saint the Sacrament of Baptism.

"From that hour to the end of his life he persevered in the fervent practice of the one true Faith, and never ceased to bless and thank God for having brought him into His Church, and for having made him His child."

THE BATTLE OF TOLBIAC.

About the middle of the fifth century, there lived in France a great and powerful King whose name was Clovis. He was not a Christian, but he was married to a noble Princess, who was not only a good Christian, but a great Saint. Her name was Clotilda.

Now, Clotilda loved her husband with the most tender affection, and the only thing that made her unhappy was that he was a pagan, and did not know about the true God. But she knew that God hears the prayers of those who pray to Him with confidence. So every day of her life she prayed to Him to bring her husband to the knowledge of the one true Faith.

God heard her prayer, and in His own good time granted it in a way which showed that nothing is impossible or difficult to Him.

Clovis loved his wife as much as she loved him, and often when they were alone she would speak to him of the greatness and the power of the God whom she adored. Clovis listened to her with the greatest attention; but when she asked him to leave the worship of idols, and serve the only true God, he always answered her, "No, I cannot do that just now, because if I did so, the people would all rise up against me, and perhaps take my kingdom from me, or put me to death; but I will become a Christian afterwards."

So the good Queen could only weep in silence when she saw him delay so long; and she continued to pray still more earnestly for his conversion.

It happened in the year 496 that a war broke out between the Franks, of whom Clovis was the King, and the Germans, who came with a great army into France to take part of it by force, and add it to their own kingdom. Clovis went out at the head of a powerful army to meet them, and a great battle was fought on the plains of Tolbiac.

Before he left home to go to battle, he went to say good-bye to his beloved Clotilda. Tears were in his manly eyes as he looked upon his dear wife, and thought that perhaps he might never see her again.

Clotilda also wept, and her heart was full of grief, for she knew the danger he was so soon to be in, and she knew also that if he died on the field of battle, he would never see God in Heaven, because he was still a pagan.

"My own dear husband," said the pious Queen, "you are going to fight a great battle: if you want to gain the victory, call upon the God of the Christians; He alone is Master of the whole world, and is called the 'God of armies.' If you call upon Him with confidence, no power on earth will overcome you; you will certainly triumph over your enemies, even if their numbers were far greater than yours."

The King promised to remember these parting words, and mounting on his war-horse, set out for the battlefield. Clotilda shut herself up in her oratory, and prayed without ceasing to God for him.

In the meantime, the two armies met, and the conflict was terrible. For a long time, it was doubtful which would gain the victory, for both armies fought with the greatest bravery. At length, the Franks began to give way; the commander of the infantry was wounded, and the soldiers turned and fled.

When the King saw this, he rode at the head of his cavalry to meet the victorious enemy, and soon drove them back. For some time the victory seemed to be on his side, but in the end, he had the grief to see his brave horsemen also flying before the Germans. He called upon them to turn back; he promised them great rewards if they drove back the enemy; he threatened them with death if they refused; but to no purpose—they seemed not to hear him, and fled away in terror.

At this moment Aurelian, a Christian General in his army, rode up to him, and said: "O my King, call upon the God of Clotilda, and you will yet gain the victory"

Then the King, remembering the words of the Queen, remained for a moment in deep thought. After this he raised his hands and eyes to Heaven, and cried out: "O Jesus Christ, Whom Clotilda calls the Son of the Living God, Who comest to the help of those who call upon Thee, and givest the victory to those who hope in Thee, I ask Thee to help me, for now I believe in Thee. If Thou wilt grant me the victory today over my enemies, and if I obtain from Thee this proof of Thy power, I will at once become a Christian. I have called upon my gods, and they have not heard me; so I know they have no power to help me, because they will not come to the assistance of those that call upon them. Thee, O God of Clotilda, do I now call upon; in Thee I now believe; grant, then, that I may overcome my enemies."

No sooner had he said these words than the Germans began to retreat. Their General was slain, and there was no one to command them. For a long time did the victorious Franks pursue them, and great was the slaughter. At length, a herald ran to the King, saying: "O King, cease to slay our people, and we will all submit to you." The King gave orders for an end to be put to the carnage, and then returned home with his victorious army.

Clovis, mindful of his vow, embraced the Christian Faith, and was baptized by St. Remigius with great pomp, along with an immense multitude of his subjects.

4

VALUE OF THE GIFT OF FAITH: HOW WE SHOULD ESTEEM IT

My child, since your faith is your most precious treasure, your esteem for it should be greater than for anything else; and your desire to increase it in your soul should make you consider as nothing the difficulties you must meet with in preserving it.

The following example will show you how the great gift of faith was esteemed by the poor savages of Canada, and will be a lesson for you, who are so much more favored than they.

OSKALOE, THE SAVAGE PRINCE.

"When holy Mass was done," writes one of the missionaries in his letter, "Oskiloe, one of the chiefs, followed by a great many people belonging to his tribe, came to us, and asked to speak to us. Then, addressing himself to Father Marault, he said: 'O my Father, you have come to us at last! How glad we are to see you! And for such a long time have we been waiting for you! It is now five Sundays since we came here expecting to find you. Our provisions are nearly all done, and we cannot catch any fish because the rivers are in flood. What will become of us, Father? Nevertheless, we would rather die than go home without going to our confession this year. This, then, is what we have made up our minds to do. If the fishing still continues bad, we will fast for ten days, that we may remain with you and hear God's holy Word. No doubt this will cause us to suffer much; but that does not matter; we will suffer it all with joy, that we may attend to our souls' salvation. And if at the end of ten days the Great Spirit does not send us any fish, necessity will force us to go home; but it will cause us the greatest sorrow to go away.'"

What fervour! And yet, my child, you possess the same faith as they did.

Hautrieve, v. 50.

5

THE GIFT OF FAITH MUST NEVER BE REFUSED

The man who has not the happiness of possessing the true religion must do what lies in his power to come to the knowledge of it, and as soon as he has discovered it, he must at all hazards embrace it, for it is that precious pearl of which there is mention in the Gospel, to obtain which, everything he possesses on earth must be sacrificed. Yet how many, my child, are found who place no value on it.

SS. BARLAAM AND JOSAPHAT.

St. Josaphat, whom the Church honors on November 27, was the son of Abenner, King of the Indies. This pagan King, fearing that his son might become a Christian (for he had been warned by a certain astrologer that this would happen), took the most severe measures to keep him from the knowledge of the Christian religion. He shut him up, even in his earliest childhood, in a large castle with no one but his tutor to live with him, who was instructed to bring him up a pagan, like his father, and never, under pain of death, to speak to him of the Christian faith, and to see that nothing would be put in his way that would ever make him hear about it or inquire into it.

The tutor obeyed his orders to the letter, and for many years the young Prince never saw but the castle in which he dwelt, and the fields which surrounded it.

One day, however, when he had already reached the age of manhood, his father at length yielded to his oft-repeated request that he might be allowed to go forth into the great world to visit it. He had not gone far, when he met a poor man bent nearly to the ground through old age. Josaphat was astonished at this sight so new to him, and he asked his tutor what had brought the man to that sad condition. The tutor answered that it was the effect of old age.

"And shall we also, when we are old like this man have the same infirmities?" said the Prince.

"Yes, all men must follow in the same path which leads to old age, then to death."

"And shall I also have to die one day?" asked Josaphat. "And if so, what will become of me after my death? What will happen to my soul?"

"Ah! as to that," replied the tutor, "it is a problem which it is impossible for anyone to understand, and which we must not try to solve; it is a mystery which God Himself has covered with a veil."

This answer did not at all satisfy the young Prince, and only made him the more desirous of discovering that which his tutor wanted to conceal from him. All his thoughts from that moment were fixed on death, and the state after death. He felt that God, Who had created him, could not leave him without letting him know what was to happen to him after this life was over, "It cannot be possible," he thought, "that God could refuse to enlighten me upon that important subject if I humbly ask Him in prayer."

So he besought God in fervent prayer to make him know the truth. God heard his prayer, and in a wonderful way answered it by sending to him a humble anchorite named Barlaam.

That holy man came to him under the disguise of a pearl merchant, who, presenting himself at the castle, was admitted, that the Prince, who was exceedingly fond of such things, might admire them and perhaps purchase some of them.

As the Prince was admiring the luster of some of the pearls, Barlaam took the opportunity of a moment in which he was alone with him to tell him of another pearl which was more beautiful and precious than any of those he had just seen. Josaphat wanted to see it at once.

"It is a pearl that cannot be seen with the eyes," said the old man. "The pearl of which I speak is called Truth."

"Truth," exclaimed the young Prince, "that is just what I am looking for, and what I wish to possess at all price. I beseech you, O stranger, to tell me what is Truth."

Then Barlaam spoke to him of Jesus Christ, and of the eternal happiness which He purchased for us by His death. This was for the young man the light for which he had been seeking. He opened his eyes to it at once, and soon afterwards, having, by the grace of God, found means of secretly escaping the vigilance of his guard, he fled from the castle, left the kingdom of his father, and at length found the place in the desert where Barlaam dwelt. There, forgetting the crown of the earthly kingdom which was his inheritance, and all the worldly things that were to be his, he thought only of practicing the holy religion of Jesus Christ, and thus became a Saint. He is now reigning with Jesus Christ in Heaven, and the Church on earth venerates him as one of her powerful intercessors before the throne of God.

Lives of the Saints, Nov. 27.

When a person throws away this great gift of God, or does not accept it when God offers it to him, he may never get it again, and so will lose his soul.

RADBOD, KING OF FRIESLAND.

Radbod was King of Friesland. During his reign a holy Bishop went into that country to preach the true Faith. The name of the Bishop was Vulfran. When the King heard the truths of our holy Religion explained to him, he expressed his great desire to be admitted into the Church by baptism.

When the preparations were being made for his reception into the Church, a strange thought came into his mind. He began to wonder what had become of the souls of all his relations and his predecessors in the kingdom, since he was told that to obtain the Kingdom of Heaven it was necessary to be members of the Christian religion, so he asked the Bishop to come and speak to him.

"O holy Bishop," he said, "tell me what has become of the Kings who have ruled over this mighty nation before me, and all those nobles whose fame is so great, and who are now dead. Are they in that beautiful Heaven which you have told us is to be given to those who are good, or are they all lost in hell, where you tell me the wicked are sent to when they die?"

But the Bishop answered: "O Prince, do not think of these things, but leave them in the hands of God, and from the thought of how unfortunate they were in dying without the knowledge of the one true Faith, you will give God eternal thanks that you have been so favored as you are, and strive with your whole heart to profit by such a great grace."

But the King answered: "Then I will not become a Christian; I choose to go where my predecessors have gone, rather than to be along with the small number of the poor in Heaven; I cannot make up my mind to believe in these new doctrines. I prefer to follow the religion and the customs which my nation has followed till now."

The Bishop tried to show him how wrong it would be not to follow the light which God gave him, but all he could say to him was of no avail; the King remained obstinate. But many of the people accepted God's grace, and became fervent Christians.

Still, the King did not feel quite at ease in his mind at what he had done, so in a short time he sent a message to another Bishop called St. Willibrord, who lived at some distance, to tell him that he wanted to speak to him.

St. Willibrord, who knew what the King had said to the other Bishop, made answer to the messengers: "Since the King, your master, has despised the words of the holy Bishop Vulfran, do you think he will listen to mine? Besides, it is now too late, for this very night I have seen him in a vision bound in chains, as if he were already dead and lost eternally. Nevertheless, I will go with you."

On the way to the place where Radbod dwelt, they met some people who told them that the King was dead. He died without baptism by his own fault.

Eccles. History, A.D. 719.

6

WE MUST NEVER BE ASHAMED OF OUR FAITH, MUCH LESS DENY IT

You must never be ashamed of your Faith, my child, much less deny it, for Jesus Christ has said: "He that shall be ashamed of Me, and of My words, of him the Son of man shall be ashamed, when He shall come in His Majesty" (Luke IX. 26).

THE COLONEL DISGRACED.

There was once a young Colonel in the army who owed his promotion to the goodwill of his Sovereign.

A short time before he had been raised to that rank, there had been a war between his country and one of the other kingdoms of Europe; but it was now at an end, and there was peace between them.

During this time of peace, the Colonel asked from the King leave of absence, as he had a great desire to travel, and visit the great cities of Europe and other places of which he had often read. This permission was easily obtained, and he set out on his journey.

Now, it happened that while passing through the kingdom which had lately been at war with his own, he was invited to join a company of the chief officers and to dine with them.

During the course of the repast the conversation turned upon the late war. Some of the company spoke very freely, not only against the country to which the young Colonel belonged, but even against the King himself. They said many bitter things about the way he governed his people, as well as about his private character, and they laughed and found amusement at his expense.

These words hurt the Colonel very much. He loved his King, not only because he owed his present position to him, but because he knew him to be upright and good. But now he was at a loss how to act. He said to himself: "If I stand up here in defense of my King and country, or if I show how angry I feel, they will only laugh the more, and I will not be able to do any good, because I am only one, and there are so many against me. I will pretend, therefore, not to heed what they say, for their words cannot do my Sovereign any harm."

So he made no reply to all their severe remarks, and pretended not to be hurt by what they were saying. He sometimes smiled, when he saw the others laughing, and even added a little word by way of joke, that he might not seem to be offended at them.

When the visit was over, he returned to his lodgings, well pleased with the manner in which he had conducted himself during the day. "After all," he said to himself, "in the circumstances in which I was placed it was best to act as I did."

But the news of what had occurred reached the ears of the King at home. His indignation was very great, especially when he thought of how kind he had been to the young officer. So as soon as the latter came home, he sent for him.

"What is this I have heard about you?" said the King in an angry tone.

The Colonel hung down his head, and began to make excuses by explaining the difficult position in which he found himself, and said that he did what he thought was the best to be done.

But the King answered: "You did very wrong. It was your duty to have upheld your King and your country even at the risk of your life. Your cowardly conduct has made you unworthy to wear the uniform of a soldier any longer, so begone forever from my presence, degraded and disgraced."

My child, you are a soldier of Jesus Christ, and you must not be ashamed of Him or of your holy Faith. Whenever you hear anyone speak against it, be sure to defend it, not only by your words, but also by your whole conduct.

FREDERICK OF PRUSSIA AND GENERAL ZEITHEN.

When the Seven Years' War was ended, the great General Zeithen became one of Frederick of Prussia's greatest favorites. He was often invited to dine at the royal table, and always occupied the place of honor at the King's right hand, unless there happened to be some Prince of the royal blood present.

Now this General was a devout Catholic, and faithful in the practice of his religious duties.

One day the King sent him an invitation to dine with him, as he had invited a number of guests that day. But Zeithen sent an answer, asking the King to have the goodness to excuse him from attending on that occasion, as it was one of the days on which he had the custom of going to Holy Communion, and he wished to keep himself in a state of recollection and devotion all that day.

Not very long afterwards, when he went to the Court, the King began to taunt him. "Well, General," he said, "how did you get on the other day at that Communion of yours?"

At these words the King laughed, in which he was joined by all the courtiers around him, who thought it was an excellent joke.

But Zeithen raised his head with great dignity, and walked over to the place where the King was standing. Having bowed to him, he said in a voice firm and solemn: "Your Majesty knows well that I am a brave soldier, that I have fought courageously for you and for my country; and you know, too, that I am ready to do more still— yea, to die if needs be in defense of our rights and liberties. But there is over us a Being more powerful than you or I, or all men together—our God and Savior Who, to redeem the world, shed the last drop of His Blood. Now, I will not stand here and permit Him to be offended by words of irony and disrespect, even by you, O King, for in Him is centered my faith, my hope, all my consolation. Had it not been for the protection He granted to our arms, we never could have gained the victories we did gain, and if you do not honor Him, then you need not expect to see your country prosper. This, then, is what I have to say to you; I hope your Majesty will excuse me."

The King, instead of being angry at his boldness, was greatly moved, and could not refrain from shedding a tear. He laid his hand upon the General's shoulder, and said to him: "Happy Zeithen, I respect your religion and its practices. Follow them faithfully as you are doing now, and I promise you, you will never again hear from my lips words like what you heard today."

Hist of Prussia.

A GIRL WHO LOST HER FAITH.

A young girl called Agnes left her father's house a short time after she had made her first Communion to live with a relative who was not a Catholic.

Agnes had been well instructed in the truths of our holy Faith, and on the day of her first Communion there was not one of all the children who knelt at the altar who gave so much edification as she did. Before she left home her parents made her promise never to neglect her religious duties, and she promised faithfully that she would sooner die rather than offend God. "Oh, how could I ever grieve Jesus by committing sin," she said, "since He has been so good to me, and has loved me so much?"

But in a short time a great change came over the child. She at first kept her resolution, and went regularly to the holy Sacraments; but one day someone spoke to her in a tone of ridicule of her piety, and even called her a hypocrite. This was her first temptation, and she neglected to ask God for His grace. She from that moment became ashamed of her faith, and very soon entirely neglected her duties. At length, in about three years, she lost her faith altogether.

Some years afterwards she died suddenly; she died without having time to repent, and so went to receive from the just Judge the terrible sentence she had merited.

7

THE MARTYRS DIE RATHER THAN RENOUNCE THEIR FAITH

The holy martyrs considered it the greatest glory to die in defense of their religion, and even many children willingly laid down their lives rather than throw away God's holy gift of faith.

ST. VITUS DIES FOR JESUS CHRIST.

There lived in the early days of the Church a little boy whose name was Vitus. He loved God from the first moment that he was capable of doing so, and many times a day did his infant lips tell Him that he loved Him with his whole heart.

When the Emperor heard about him and of his great fervour, he was angry; but he thought he would easily make him renounce his faith, because he was so young, so one day he sent for him.

"My dear child," he said to him in his gentlest voice, "I am going to give you gold, and jewels, and splendid clothes, and everything else you would like to ask for, if only you will change your religion, renounce your faith, and blaspheme Jesus Christ."

But the foolish Emperor did not know that God had promised to speak by the mouths of His servants when called upon to give testimony for Him.

Vitus answered: "Jesus Christ is my Master and my Saviour; He died for me upon the cross. I will never say one word that may offend Him, and with my whole heart I will always love Him."

"Very well, then," said the Emperor, suddenly changing the tone of his voice; "if you will not obey my orders, I will cast you into a cauldron of boiling oil. Make your choice, then, at once, between the pleasures I offer you, and the torments I threaten."

But the child was not dismayed. With a courage which came from Heaven, he calmly answered: "I will cheerfully suffer not only that torment, but I am willing to die the most cruel death rather than deny the Faith of Jesus Christ."

The Emperor was filled with rage at the answer of the child, and gave orders that the cauldron should be immediately prepared.

When the oil began to boil, he said to the executioners: "Take off his clothes now and throw him in."

They did as they were told, and the holy martyr suffered this awful torture without a murmur. As he stood in the cauldron, he raised his hands and eyes to Heaven, and said: "Lord Jesus, receive my soul."

When he had said these words, angels were seen coming down from Heaven, and they placed a beautiful crown upon his head, and into his hands they put a green palm-branch—the sign of victory—and carried his soul to the judgment-seat of Jesus Christ.

The great Judge looked lovingly upon the boy, and with a sweet smile on His lips, thus spoke to him: "My own beloved child, you have suffered a most cruel death for the love of Me; come now, and I will give you eternal joy in Heaven."

You, my child, may not have to suffer death for your holy Faith as St. Vitus had, but you may have to suffer much persecution because you are a Catholic. Be faithful, then, and when God's time comes, angels will carry your soul also to God's judgment-seat, where you will be received by your Divine Master in the same loving manner as St. Vitus was, and obtain the same reward.

8

FAITH NOT SUFFICIENT WITHOUT GOOD WORKS

It is not enough for us, in order to reach Heaven, to believe all the truths that God has revealed to us. To reach Heaven it is necessary for us also to show forth our faith by our good works.

SERMON OF ST. JAMES THE APOSTLE.

"My brethren, what shall it profit if a man say he hath faith, but hath not works? Shall faith be able to save him?

"And if a brother or sister be naked and want daily food, and one of you say to them, 'Go in peace; be you warmed and filled,' yet give them not those things that are necessary for the body, what shall it profit? So faith also, if it have not works, is dead in itself.

"But some man will say: 'Thou hast faith, and I have works; show me thy faith without works, and I will show thee, by works, my faith. Thou believest that there is one God. Thou dost well: the devils also believe and tremble. But wilt thou know, O vain man, that faith without works is dead? Was not Abraham our father justified by works, offering up Isaac his son upon the altar? Seest thou that faith did co-operate with his works, and by works faith was made perfect. And the Scripture was fulfilled, saying: 'Abraham believed God, and it was reputed to him to justice, and he was called the friend of God.' Do you see that by works a man is justified, and not by faith only?

"And in like manner also Rahab the harlot, was not she justified by works, receiving the messengers, and sending them out another way? For even as the body without the spirit is dead, so also faith without works is dead."

St. James II. 14 *et seq.*

THE ARAB AND THE CATHOLIC.

It is said that an Arab one day asked a Catholic whom he met, and whose conduct was far from corresponding with the Faith he professed, if he believed in God. The Catholic was indignant at being asked such a question, and answered in a tone which showed how displeased he was: "Of course I believe that there is a God; did you ever hear of a Catholic who did not believe in God?"

The Arab answered: "You may, indeed, say with your lips that you believe in God, but certainly your actions tell me that you do not."

Could this also not be said by many of those around us who have not the true Faith: "Do you Catholics believe that there is a God? Certainly your actions go far to prove that you do not. And might God not address to many amongst us that bitter reproach which He addressed of old to the people of the Jews by the mouth of His prophet: 'I have created My children, and I have nourished them, and I have brought them up, and they have despised me. An animal without reason knows the house of its master, but man does not know Me.'"

9

THE GREAT SIN OF UNBELIEF

Those who refuse to believe what Jesus Christ teaches us in His holy Church are guilty of a great sin, and God will punish them for it.

ST. JANE FRANCES AND THE HERETIC.

A gentleman, who followed the heresy of Calvin, came to pay a visit to the parents of St. Jane Frances de Chantal. She was then only five years old.

One day, while she was playing in the room where the gentleman was conversing with another person, she heard him say that he did not believe in the real presence of Jesus Christ in the Blessed Sacrament.

The child looked up from her playthings, and, going over to him, said: "So you don't believe that Jesus Christ is present in the Blessed Sacrament?"

"No, child," he said, "I do not."

"Yet Jesus Christ has positively declared that He *is*," replied the child. "So by saying these words you mean to say that Jesus Christ is a liar! Well, if you had said as much about the King of this country in my father's presence, he would send you away from his house, and perhaps kill you! And do you think the great God will not punish you some day, because you have dared to call His dear Son a liar, by saying that you do not believe what He tells you?"

The gentleman was so confounded by these words of the little girl that he did not know what to say. He thought he would appease her by giving her some little presents, so he gave her some very beautiful ones.

But she was very angry at this, and when he put them into her hands she at once threw them into the fire, and said to him while they were burning: "Look, that is the way in which God will punish in the next world all those who refuse to believe the words of His Divine Son Jesus Christ."

From her Life.

10

HERESY

Heresy is an obstinate refusal to believe what God has revealed. The name of heretic is the most disgraceful name that can be given to anyone; and of all sins, this is the one that gave the Saints the greatest horror.

THE HERMIT ACCUSED OF HERESY.

Amongst the holy men who dwelt in the deserts of Egypt, there was one named Agatho, who was remarkable above all the rest for his great humility and patience.

Some of the brethren wanted to put his humility to a trial. So one day they went to his cell, and said to him: "Brother Agatho, we have come to speak to you of your great pride and self-conceit. Why do you despise us, whom you think to be less pious than yourself? No doubt it is because, being very wicked yourself, you think you can disguise it by trying to make us appear worse than you are."

The holy man heard all they said without showing the least sign of displeasure. "My brethren," he said, "I am indeed a most grievous sinner." Then, casting himself at their feet, he continued: "Oh, pray for me to God, that He may take away my sins; your prayers alone will find mercy for me from my offended judge."

"But," said the others, "we must tell you also that some people say you are a heretic."

The Saint at once lifted up his hand, and said: "Oh no, that is quite false! However wretched I am in other respects, or however guilty I may be of other sins, I am not so great a wretch as to forfeit my share in Jesus Christ by heresy: far be this from me!"

The brethren at these words, casting themselves at his feet, said to him: "Brother, tell us why you, who suffered so many other false accusations without saying the smallest word in your own defense at once showed so great a horror when you were accused of heresy?"

The man of God answered: "When you accused me of pride and self-conceit, I knew it was quite true, and therefore it was only right to bear patiently what I really deserved. Did not Jesus Christ, our Master and Model, although He was Innocence itself, keep silent when accused of sin? And ought not I to do so since I am really guilty? But as to heresy, it is quite different. To be guilty of that crime is openly to deny what God has said. Heresy destroys faith, without which no one can see God, and it gives the soul over to Satan. Therefore, as no one should wish to be an enemy of God, or be separated from Him in eternity, so no one ought to consent to be called a heretic."

Lives of Fathers of the Desert,

11

APOSTASY

When one who has received the gift of faith, and by his sinful life or neglect, has ceased to believe and profess the truths revealed by God, he is guilty of the crime of apostasy, which is one of the greatest sins that can be committed.

TRIED, AND FOUND FAITHFUL.

Anyone who neglects his duty to God for the sake of the world, or for the fear of losing the esteem of men, is not worthy to be called a child of God, and sometimes those who do this meet their punishment even in this world.

At the beginning of the fourth century the Roman Empire in Gaul was governed by an Emperor named Constantius Chloris. He was a pagan, but he did not persecute the Christians, as many of the other Roman governors did; he even gave to many of them high positions in his province, because he knew that if they were faithful to their God they would be faithful also to their temporal Prince.

One day, to the astonishment of all the people, he published a solemn edict, in which he decreed that every Christian who held any office in his household should, on a certain appointed day, go to the temple of Jupiter, one of the heathen gods, and offer sacrifice, and that if anyone refused to do this, he was immediately to be deprived of the office he held, and be banished from the country forever.

This decree was the cause of great consternation and alarm among the Christians. They had till then enjoyed peace; their religion was even respected by the pagans; and now, on a sudden, without any warning, an edict was issued against them.

The governor eagerly awaited the appointed day to see how the Christians would act.

When the day came, a great crowd of people were seen approaching the palace gates. They were a band of Christians, who came to resign the offices they held.

"We have come, O Prince," they said, "to give back into your hands the favors you granted to us. Willingly would we still continue to serve you, as we have always done, but we have a Master in Heaven Who is above all, and whose law must be obeyed before the orders of temporal Princes. And since His law forbids us to worship any other god but Himself, we cannot obey your decrees. Yea, we are willing to die rather than be wanting in our fidelity to Him."

Constantius said nothing, but let them depart. Then, going up to the temple of Jupiter, he saw there some other Christians offering sacrifice according to the command that had been given. They were ready to deny their God rather than lose their temporal position.

But they were soon punished for their apostasy. For the Emperor, assembling together his army and the rest of the people, publicly, before them all, reinstated those Christians who had been faithful to God, in all their former dignity, and restored to them all the honors they had resigned rather than offend God.

Then, turning to those miserable ones who had offered sacrifice, he said: "O impious wretches, you do not deserve to be called men—you, who denied your God and your religion for a little worldly honor and ease; listen to what I have to say to you: you can never more share my confidence; I take away from you all the offices you have enjoyed till now, and I give them to those faithful men who were willing to die rather than offend God, and I order you to depart from my household, that my eyes may never again behold you."

Thus were rewarded, even in this world, those who had proved themselves faithful, and thus also were punished those who denied their faith.

One of the courtiers asked the Emperor why he had done this.

Constantius answered: "I desired to know whom I could trust. Men who sacrifice their religion to their interests are likely to fail in their other duties. I could not expect that those who were not faithful to God would be faithful to me."

Not only did the Emperor thus publicly praise and reward those faithful men, but he chose them as his special counselors and committed to their care his person and his whole household.

When we are tempted for some temporal consideration to be unfaithful to God, we should remember that on the day of our baptism we promised solemnly to serve Him to the end of our lives, and that if we do not keep our promise, we shall most certainly be punished, if not in this life, at least in the next.

The History of the Church,

12

THE APOSTLES' CREED

My child, the Catechism tells us that the Creed is the sum of our belief made by the twelve Apostles; that is to say, that it contains the chief things God has revealed, and which we have to believe. Therefore, when you say the Creed in your prayers, how fervently you should say it! For it is a solemn declaration to God that you believe all the things He has revealed.

THE APOSTLES COMPOSE THE CREED.

Before the Apostles went forth to preach the Gospel throughout the world, they assembled together for the last time, and drew up that short formula of belief which, even at the present day, is known as the Apostles' Creed.

It is composed of twelve parts, or articles, and there is a tradition, which the great historian Baronius has recorded in his "Annals," that each of the Apostles made one of the articles it contains, inspired by the Holy Ghost.

St. Peter began in these words: "I believe in God the Father Almighty."

To which St. John added: "Creator of Heaven and earth."

St. James said: "And in Jesus Christ His only Son Our Lord."

Then St. Andrew said: "Who was conceived by the Holy Ghost, born of the Virgin Mary."

Then St. Philip said: "Suffered under Pontius Pilate, was crucified, dead, and buried."

St. Thomas then said: "He descended into hell; the third day He rose again from the dead."

St. Bartholomew next said: "He ascended into Heaven, sitteth at the right hand of God the Father Almighty."

Then St. Matthew spoke, saying: "From thence He shall come to judge the living and the dead."

Next St. James, the son of Alpheus, said: "I believe in the Holy Ghost, the Holy Catholic Church."

St. Simon Zelotes then added: "The Communion of Saints, the forgiveness of sins."

St. Jude came next; he said: "The resurrection of the body."

Finally, St. Matthias said: "And life everlasting."

It is the great St. Augustine himself who has told us in his writings that the above was the manner in which the Creed was composed. (*Sermo. 115, de Temp.*)

Baronius: *Anno* 44.

ST. PETER OF VERONA.

In the year 1205, a little boy was born in Verona. His parents gave him the name of Peter. They both belonged to a sect of heretics who taught that God did not make the world, but that it was made by a wicked spirit. So the child was in the greatest danger of being brought up in this false doctrine; but God preserved him from it.

Peter was sent to a Catholic school when he was old enough to go thither. His parents were obliged to send him there, because there was no school in Verona belonging to their sect, and they did not want him to be brought up without education. They thought that there would be no danger of so young a child learning much about the Catholic doctrine, and they persuaded themselves that if he did learn something about it, it would be an easy matter to take it out of his mind when he grew up. But in this they were mistaken.

The first thing that Peter learned at the Catholic school, after his prayers, was the Apostles' Creed. God inspired his young heart with a great desire to understand all the truths that it contained. So after learning with great diligence the words of the Creed, he tried to learn also the meaning of each of the twelve articles it contained. If he met with anything he could not understand, he went to his master, and asked him to explain it to him. Thus in a short time, young as he was, Peter understood all the Christian Doctrine as contained in the Creed.

One day when he came home from school he met his uncle, who had come to pay a visit to his parents. He was also a heretic.

He took the boy on his knee, and said to him: "Tell me, Peter, what did you learn at school today?"

The child answered with the utmost simplicity: "I learned the Apostles' Creed. Would you like to hear me say it? I can say it from beginning to end."

Peter then began in a solemn voice to say the Creed, and when he had finished, he looked up into his uncle's face, as if to say: "Don't I know it well?"

His uncle, with an angry look, said to the boy: "You are wrong; it was not God that created the world, but a wicked spirit."

"Yes, it was God," replied the boy. "He made not only the things we can see, but also the things that we cannot see, for at the very beginning of the Book of Genesis it is written: 'In the beginning, God created the heavens and the earth.' I believe, therefore, in God the Father Almighty, Creator of Heaven and earth, and I will live and die in that belief."

It was God Himself Who spoke by the mouth of the child.

His uncle was astonished at the words of the little boy, and went and told his parents. They became alarmed when they saw the firm root the Catholic Faith had already taken in the child, and they tried to destroy it by threats and promises; but to no effect. Peter remained firm, and they saw themselves obliged to cease importuning him.

When he grew up to manhood he entered the Dominican Order, in which, by his eloquent sermons, he converted many heretics to the true Faith. Some of them, whose hearts were hardened against the grace of God, became so angry when they saw the multitudes who were returning to the true Church that in their anger they resolved to put him to death. They waylaid him, and assassinated him between Como and Milan on April 6, 1252.

His last words when expiring were: "I believe in God the Father Almighty, Creator of Heaven and earth."

His assassins and a great multitude of heretics were converted by the sight of the many miracles God was pleased to work through his intercession, and the prayers offered up at his tomb.

PART III
ONE GOD IN THREE PERSONS

1

THE EXISTENCE OF GOD

My child, the first words of the Apostles' Creed are these: "I believe in God the Father Almighty, Creator of Heaven and earth." And when you are asked, when at catechism, "Are there more Gods than one?" your answer is: "There is only one God."

THE GOD WHOM ST. PATRICK ADORED.

When St. Patrick was a young boy, he was captured by a band of pirates, and brought by them as a slave into Ireland. There he fell into the hands of a brutal pagan, who sent him to tend his cattle, and pass the night in the place where they were sheltered.

One day he had a dream, in which he was admonished to go to the seashore, and that there he would obtain his freedom. He obeyed, and found there a ship which was about to set sail, on board of which he was received after many entreaties and supplications.

The vessel was driven out of its course by a storm, and the sailors were glad when they safely reached land, although it was on a lonely and barren place on the Scottish shore. In a very short time the provisions they had taken with them were consumed, and although they had penetrated inland in search of food, they could find none, nor did they meet any human being or see any habitation. Overcome with hunger, the companions of St. Patrick, who were pagans, asked him to have recourse to his God that He might help them in their distress, saying to him that if the God of the Christians was so great and so powerful as He had described Him to them, He surely would not permit them to die of hunger.

Animated with a lively faith and confidence in his God, Patrick answered that if they would only become Christians, and turn to the worship of the one true God with their whole heart, He would soon deliver them from the death by hunger that threatened them. He himself retired to a lonely place, and prayed for a short time in silence. Scarcely had an hour elapsed before they saw a herd of wild boars near them. They immediately laid hold of some of them, and thus procured for themselves abundant food.

They sailed for twenty-four days looking for an inhabited country, and during all this time food never failed them. At last they landed at a place where they found a number of huts, and where they were hospitably received by the people who dwelt on that coast. Faithful to the promises they had made, they one and all embraced Christianity.

GODESCARD: *Vie des Saints*, 17 Mar.

THE ATHEIST IN DANGER OF DEATH.

The atheist Volney was one day taking an excursion by sea on the coast of North America, along with some friends as impious as himself.

Suddenly a boisterous storm arose, which in a short time assumed a threatening aspect, and those on board began to fear for their safety. Their noisy conversation soon lapsed into silence, and the lips of those men, who were accustomed to speak of God as if He did not exist, or had no command over the world, began to move; in a word, they began to pray.

Volney himself, taking a rosary from the most hidden part of his clothing, began to recite with great fervor the "Hail Mary," which he continued to do as long as the ship was in danger.

When the wind had abated, and the peril seemed passed, someone who had observed what had occurred, went to him and said: "My dear sir, I thought I saw you saying your prayers a little time ago. Who were you praying to? I was of the opinion that you disbelieved in the very existence of a Supreme Being? Of what use was it, therefore, for you to pray?"

"Ah! My friend," replied the philosopher, full of shame at having been detected, "it is one thing to profess disbelief in one's own house, where there is no danger threatening, but quite a different thing to do so when one is standing in the presence of imminent death."

Noel Catéch de Rodez, I. 78.

"I ADORE ONE ONLY GOD," SAID THE MARTYR.

St. Fructuosus, Bishop of Tarragona, in Spain, suffered martyrdom because he would not offer sacrifice to the gods of the pagans. In the year 259, he was apprehended along with two other Christians, who were deacons, whose names were Augurus and Eulogius.

The Governor Emelian said to Fructuosus, "Have you heard what the Emperors have decreed?"

Fructuosus answered: "I do not know what they may have decreed, but it matters not to me, because I am a Christian."

Emelian answered: "They have commanded that everyone must offer sacrifice to the gods."

Fructuosus answered: "I adore the one only God, Who made Heaven and earth, the sea, and all things that are in them."

Emelian said: "Do you not know that there are many gods?"

"No; I never knew that there was more than one God."

"Then you shall soon be taught that there are many gods."

Fructuosus, well knowing that by these words the judge meant to put him to death if he would not renounce his belief in the one true God, raised up his hands to Heaven and began to pray.

Emelian, seeing this, said to the deacon Augurus: "Do not you, at least, listen to the words of Fructuosus, and do not imitate the bad example he has given."

Augurus replied: "I also adore the one Almighty God."

Then, turning to Eulogius, Emelian said: "And you, do you also adore Fructuosus?"

"No," replied Eulogius, "I do not adore Fructuosus, but I adore the God he adores."

Emelian said to Fructuosus: "Are you a Bishop?"

"Yes," he answered, "I am."

"Then you shall not be that much longer."

Saying these words, he gave orders that the three confessors should be burned alive. This was done, and they went to Heaven to receive a never-ending reward from Him Who said that He would confess before His Father in Heaven those who would confess Him before men on earth.

2

WHO IS GOD?

We are told in the Scriptures that there was once a holy mother who wanted to encourage her child to do his duty; so she took him to her side, and said to him: "I beseech thee, my son, look upon Heaven and earth, and all that is in them, and consider that God made them out of nothing, and also all mankind" (II Macc. VII. 28).

My child, your mother, the Catholic Church, says the same words to you: "God made Heaven and earth, and all things in them, by His only word."

God is a Spirit infinitely perfect, Creator and Sovereign Lord of all things.

"COME BACK IN EIGHT DAYS."

One day, some people went to the house of a certain philosopher, who was supposed to be one of the wisest men that was in the world at that time.

"We have been sent to you, sir," said one of them, "to ask you to tell us plainly what God is."

The philosopher answered: "I will think about it; come back in eight days, and I will give you my answer."

When the eight days had passed, the messengers returned as he had told them to do.

But the only answer he gave them was the same as he had given them before: "I will think about it; come back again in eight days."

At the end of that time they returned, but he gave them still the same answer.

This time they became angry, and said to him: "How long are you going to keep us waiting? How many more times are you going to tell us to return in eight days?"

He answered them: "I will give you the same answer as often as you put the same question to me. I know that there is a God, but Who, or what God is, no mortal man can tell."

No, my child, no man can understand God, because He is infinite. Yet this infinite God created *you* and loves *you* with an infinite love.

THE COUNTRYMAN GOING TO CHURCH.

A great and learned man, who did not believe in God, once met a simple countryman going to church to hear Mass. He said to him: "My good man, where are you going?"

"To church, sir," he answered.

"And what do you do in church?"

"I worship God," replied the countryman.

"Tell me," said the other, in a tone of mockery, "whether your God is a great or a little God."

"He is both, sir," said the man reverently.

"How can that be?"

"He is so great," answered the poor man, "that the Heaven of heavens cannot contain Him, and He is so little that He can live in my heart."

The learned man declared that this answer had more effect on his mind than all the books he had ever read.

3

GOD IS THE CREATOR OF ALL THINGS

HOW A SAVAGE CAME TO KNOW GOD.

In the year 1721, missionaries were sent from Denmark into Greenland to preach the Gospel. They were kindly received by the inhabitants of that far-away country, and many of these, touched by the grace of God, became fervent converts.

One day one of the missionaries was conversing with some of those who had embraced the Faith. He was thinking of the great grace God had given them in bringing them into His holy Church.

"God has indeed been good to you, my brethren," he said. "How unhappy must you have been until now, never to have known your Creator, and to have lived as if there was no God at all to watch over you or to love you!"

One of them answered: "It is quite true, Father, that we were indeed poor and ignorant pagans—that we knew nothing about the great God, nor about Jesus Christ, for how could we have known about them unless you had come and told us? But you must not think that we had no idea about a great Being Who ruled over us. I often used to say to myself: 'A kayak (boat) with all its equipment cannot make itself, but it requires great skill to make it well, and also much labor. A person who does not understand that much is not capable of understanding anything. Now, the formation of even the smallest bird requires much more skill than the making of the best kayak, and no one could ever make a bird. But man is greater in every way than all the other creatures that are in existence, and who made him? He comes from his parents, it is true, and they came from their parents; but where did our first parents come from? And the sun, and the moon, and the stars, who made them? Where did they come from? And the earth and the sea. They could not make themselves. Who was it, then, that made them? Someone must have done it, and whoever made them must be greater than the greatest man, both in wisdom and in power, and he must also be exceedingly good, because he has made all these things, and ourselves too, with so much perfection.' I used often then to think upon these things, and wonder about them, and when you came to preach God to us, then I saw at once Who it was that did all this, and I am full of happiness and joy when I think how good God was in sending you here to tell us."

Hist. of Greenland,

GOD IN THE FIELDS.

A little boy, who was most diligent in attending instructions, was one day at work in the fields with a man who did not know much about his religion. The man said to the boy: "How do you know there is God?"

The boy answered: "You must indeed be blind if you require a proof of the existence of God, for everything about us speaks to us of Him."

"How so?" asked the man.

"Look there at the corn; it is drying up, and the fruit is dropping off the trees because there has been no rain this season. The farmers, with all their complaining and fretting, cannot create one drop of rain. There are some things man cannot do. It is God alone Who can make the sun shine and the rain fall, for He is the maker and preserver of the whole world."

God is called the Creator of all things because He made all things out of nothing. A mason who builds a house cannot do so without stones and lime. A carpenter requires wood to make articles of furniture. But God made Heaven and earth, and the millions of created things that are in them, out of nothing. He said: "Let them be made," and immediately they were made.

4

GOD IS ALMIGHTY

My child, God can do all things, and nothing is impossible or difficult to Him. If you want a proof of the almighty power of God you have only to look at this great and beautiful world in which you dwell. It was God Who made it.

CANUTE'S ANSWER TO HIS COURTIERS.

Long ago, at the beginning of the eleventh century, when England was a Catholic kingdom, it was governed by a pious King whose name was Canute.

Some of his courtiers, who wanted to flatter him in order to obtain his favour, one day said to him: "O King, thou art indeed the greatest of all Kings; thou art master of the seas, which obey thy voice and are submissive to thy will."

Canute said nothing in answer to these words, but gave orders that his throne should be taken to the seashore, and placed upon the beach as the tide was coming in. When this was done, he went thither with his courtiers and sat down.

When the waves were coming near to the place where he sat, he with a loud voice cried out to them: "O waves, I command you to retire, and not dare to approach your royal master."

But in a few moments the water came up, heedless of his words, and, rushing onwards, wet his feet, and those of the courtiers who were with him.

Then, turning towards them, he said: "O foolish men, behold how little is the power of a King. Learn from what you see that God alone is great, that He alone has power to command the sea, and to say to it, 'Thus far shalt thou go and no farther.'"

ST. PRISCA AMONG THE LIONS.

In the year 275, a little girl of thirteen, named Prisca, was brought before the Emperor Claudius, and accused of being a Christian.

"Are you a Christian?" he asked.

"Yes, I am, by the grace of God," replied the holy virgin.

"Will you go to the temple of Apollo along with the other girls of your age, and offer sacrifice to him?"

"May the great God preserve me from such iniquity," was her heroic answer.

The Emperor was angry. "Take her to the amphitheater," he cried out, "that the lions may tear her to pieces."

They placed her in the middle of the arena, and let the lions loose to devour her. They sprang towards their innocent victim, and the multitude thought that in another instant she would be destroyed.

But God would not permit the lions to touch her. When they reached the place where she stood, they sat down tamely at her feet as if they were harmless lambs.

Prisca gave thanks to God for this manifestation of His almighty power, saying: "Blessed art Thou, O Lord Jesus Christ, for Thou givest eternal peace to those who believe in Thee."

And when she had said this she was surrounded with a bright light, and a voice from Heaven was heard saying: "Daughter, be of good courage and fear nothing, for I am the Lord Whom thou hast called upon in thy trial, and I will never abandon thee."

But the judge, enraged beyond measure, ordered her to be led outside the city to be beheaded. When she received the stroke of death, the voice came from Heaven the second time, saying: "Because thou hast fought valiantly for My Name's sake, O Prisca, enter now into the Kingdom of Heaven with all My Saints."

My child, in all your trials, remember that you also are the child of the same Almighty God Who did these wonderful things. If you serve Him faithfully in this life, He, at the last day, by His almighty power, will raise you up from the dead, and reward you also with the eternal joys of Paradise.

THE THREE YOUNG MEN IN THE FIERY FURNACE.

"King Nabuchodonosor made a statue of gold, sixty cubits high, and six cubits broad, and he set it up in the Plain of Dura in the province of Babylon. Then Nabuchodonosor the King sent to call together the nobles, the magistrates, and the judges, the captains, and rulers, and governors, and all the chief men of the provinces, to come to the dedication of the statue which King Nabuchodonosor had set up. And they were gathered together, and they stood before the statue which King Nabuchodonosor had set up.

"Then a herald cried with a strong voice: 'To you it is commanded, O nations, tribes, and languages: that in the hour you shall hear the sound of the trumpet, and of all kinds of music, ye fall down and adore the golden statue which King Nabuchodonosor hath set up. But if any man shall not fall down and adore, he shall the same hour be cast into a furnace of burning fire.'

"Upon this, therefore, at the time when all the people heard the sound of the trumpet, and all kinds of music: all the nations, tribes, and languages fell down and adored the golden statue which King Nabuchodonosor had set up.

"And presently at that very time some Chaldeans came and accused the Jews, and said to King Nabuchodonosor: 'O King, live for ever. Thou, O King, hast made a decree that every man that shall hear the sound of the trumpet and of all kinds of music, shall prostrate himself and adore the golden statue; and that if any man shall not fall down and adore, he should be cast into a furnace of burning fire.

"'Now there are certain Jews whom thou hast set over the works of the province of Babylon, Sidrach, Misach, and Abdenago; these men, O King, have slighted thy decree; they worship not thy gods, nor do they adore the golden statue which thou hast set up.'

"Then Nabuchodonosor, in fury and in wrath, commanded that Sidrach, Misach, and Abdenago should be brought: who immediately were brought before the King.

"And Nabuchodonosor the King spoke to them, and said: 'Is it true, O Sidrach, Misach, and Abdenago, that you do not worship my gods, nor adore the golden statue I have set up? Now, therefore, if you be ready, at what hour soever you shall hear the sound of the trumpet and of all kinds of music, prostrate yourselves, and adore the statue which I have made: but if you do not adore, you shall be cast the same hour into the furnace of burning fire: and who is the God that shall deliver you out of my hand?'

"Sidrach, Misach, and Abdenago answered, and said to King Nabuchodonosor: 'We have no occasion to answer thee concerning this matter. For behold our God, Whom we worship, is able to save us from the furnace of burning fire, and to deliver us out of thy hand, O King. But if He will not, be it known to thee, O King, that we will not worship thy gods, nor adore the golden statue which thou hast set up.'

"Then was Nabuchodonosor filled with fury: and the countenance of his face was changed against Sidrach, Misach, and Abdenago, and he commanded that the furnace should be heated seven times more than it had been accustomed to be heated. And he commanded the strongest men that were in his army to bind the feet of Sidrach, Misach, and Abdenago, and to cast them into the furnace of burning fire. And immediately these men were bound, and were cast into the furnace of burning fire, with their coats, and their caps, and their shoes, and their garments: for the King's commandment was urgent, and the furnace was heated exceedingly, and the flame of the fire slew those men that had cast in Sidrach, Misach, and Abdenago.

"But these men, that is, Sidrach, Misach, and Abdenago, fell down bound in the midst of the furnace of burning fire. And they walked in the midst of the flame, praising God and blessing the Lord.

"Now, the King's servants that had cast them in ceased not to heat the furnace with brimstone and tow, and pitch, and dry sticks, and the flame mounted up above the furnace nine-and-forty cubits: and it broke forth, and burnt such of the Chaldeans as it found near the furnace.

"But the Angel of the Lord went down with Azarias and his companions into the furnace, and he drove the flame of the fire out of the furnace, and made the midst of the furnace like the blowing of a wind bringing dew: and the fire touched them not at all, nor troubled them, nor did them any harm. Then these three as with one mouth praised and glorified and blessed God in the furnace.

"Then Nabuchodonosor the King was astonished, and rose up in haste, and said to his nobles: 'Did we not cast three men bound into the midst of the fire?'

"They answered the King and said: 'True, O King.'

"He answered, and said: 'Behold I see four men loose, and walking in the midst of the fire, and there is no hurt in them, and the form of the fourth is like the Son of God.'

"Then Nabuchodonosor came to the door of the burning fiery furnace, and said: 'Sidrach, Misach, and Abdenago, ye servants of the Most High God, go ye forth, and come.' And immediately Sidrach, Misach, and Abdenago went out from the midst of the fire.

"And the nobles, and the magistrates, and the judges, and the great men of the King gathered together, considered these men, that the fire had no power on their bodies, and that not a hair of their heads had been singed, nor their garments altered, nor the smell of the fire had passed on them.

"Then Nabuchodonosor, breaking forth, said: 'Blessed be the God of them, to wit, of Sidrach, Misach, and Abdenago, Who hath sent

His Angel, and delivered His servants that believed in Him. And they changed the King's word, and delivered up their bodies that they might not serve, nor adore any god, except their own God. By me, therefore, this decree is made, that every people, tribe, and tongue which shall speak blasphemy against the God of Sidrach, Misach, and Abdenago shall be destroyed, and their houses laid waste, for there is no other God that can save in this manner.'

"And the King promoted Sidrach, Misach, and Abdenago, in the province of Babylon."

Daniel, chap III.

THE GREAT CONQUEROR, AND THE INDIAN CHIEF.

Vasco Nunez was a great Spanish General who, by his bravery, conquered the West Indies, and brought them under the Spanish rule. In return for this he was made Viceroy of the conquered provinces.

One day a poor Indian chief, named Mumitama, was brought before him, accused of having formed a plot to take away his life.

The poor man tried in every way to prove his innocence, that he might escape death; but all in vain—the evidence seemed to be against him, and he was condemned to die.

When he saw that there was no longer any hope, he went forward to the foot of the tribunal, and, falling on his knees, reverently put his hand on the hilt of the Viceroy's sword.

"Most noble conqueror," he said, "how could you for an instant think that I could be guilty of such a great crime? Did I not see this sword always hanging at your side? How could I ever dare to attempt the crime of which I am accused, since I have only weapons of wood, knowing that with one blow you could strike me dead?"

These words were said in a tone which showed how much he thought the great conqueror superior to himself. He saw that life and death were in his hands, and therefore he humbled himself before him. They also served to convince Vasco of the poor man's innocence, and procured his release.

My child, this is but a feeble image of how little we are in the presence of God, Who is so great; and it should be a lesson to you, never to offend Him, since He could in one moment take you out of this world, and punish you forever for doing so.

5

GOD IS EVERYWHERE

My child, when you kneel down to say your prayers, you say: "Our Father, Who art in Heaven." Heaven is the home of the angels and the Saints, and it is in Heaven that God shows Himself to them in all His glory.

But God is not in Heaven only; He is everywhere. He is in the house and in the fields, and in the streets, and on the roads, and in the most secret and hidden places, and even to the uttermost parts of the earth.

ST. ATHANASIA'S VISION OF JESUS.

There was once a great Saint who tried to do all things to please God. Her name was Athanasia.

She used to keep in mind that God was always near her, and to think that she saw Jesus walking by her side. This thought made her every day more perfect, because she knew that He was really there, and saw all she did.

Our Lord was so pleased with her for this, that He sometimes appeared to her in a visible manner, surrounded with a bright light, and accompanied by many angels.

The angels said to her one day: "Athanasia, this is Jesus Himself, Who, when on earth, was so meek and humble of heart. Continue to be like Him, and always bear in mind that He is near you, and you shall one day rejoice with Him in His glorious kingdom."

The remembrance that God is everywhere is the greatest consolation for those who serve Him, because they know He sees them, and all that they do for Him, and that He will reward them for it in Heaven.

THE EMPRESS AND THE BISHOP.

Eudoxia, Empress of Constantinople, hated St. John Chrysostom, because he always spoke to her of her faults, which she did not try to correct.

One day, being very angry, she said to him: "I am going to banish you from this city, and send you into the most distant parts of my empire. In this way I will put an end to these reproaches."

St. John answered: "Do you imagine that by these words you will make me afraid? Oh no! The God Whom I serve is everywhere; His immensity fills Heaven and earth. Send me into any part of the world you please: I will find God there, as much as in this city; and I care not where I am, since God is always with me."

"SILENCE! HERE IS BERNARDINE."

When St. Bernardine was a little boy, he was so good and innocent that his companions looked on him with a kind of reverence. They never said an unbecoming word when he was with them, and if they saw him approaching when they were speaking in that way, they immediately ceased, saying one to the other: "Silence! Here is Bernardine."

If the presence of a holy child had so much influence on his companions, how much greater should be the influence on us of the thought of God's presence.

AUGUSTINE AND HIS SISTER SOPHIA.

Augustine was one day alone in the house with his sister Sophia; their parents had gone out.

"Sophia," he said, "come, we have a good opportunity of getting some nice things to eat, for we are alone in the house."

"Yes, I will go with you," she said, "but we must go where no one will see us."

"Let us go into the pantry, then, where there are some nice things; no one will see us there."

"But," she said, "you surely have forgotten about the man who is cutting the firewood just outside the window; he will certainly see us. So we cannot go there."

"Then we will go into the kitchen, for there are—"

But she interrupted him, saying, "No, we cannot go there either, for the woman who is washing in the courtyard will hear and see us, and will be sure to tell our parents."

"Well, I know a place where no one will see us—the cellars where the wine is kept. It is quite dark there, and we will enjoy ourselves to our hearts' content."

Sophia answered, "It is quite true no one can see us there; but God is there, and He can see us in the dark as well as in the light. His eye is upon us everywhere, and He will punish us if we do wrong."

Augustine answered, "You are right, dear sister; I forgot that, but I will try to keep it in mind for the time to come."

So, my child, God sees you wherever you are; and when anyone tempts you to do wrong, think of this.

BOLESLAUS AND HIS FATHER'S LIKENESS.

Boleslaus IV, King of Poland, had the greatest affection for his father. He got a portrait of his father, and put it into a beautiful frame, and hung it around his neck.

Every time he wanted to say anything or do anything important, he would take this portrait into his hand, look at it for a moment, and lovingly kiss it. "O my father," he would say from time to time, "God forbid that I should ever say anything or do anything that would not please you, if you were beside me."

God, your Heavenly Father, is always beside you, and if you, like King Boleslaus, always thought of that, you would never do anything wrong.

Cat. Hist., I. 89.

ST. FRANCIS DE SALES AND THE CHILD AT CATECHISM.

One day St. Francis de Sales was explaining the Catechism to some little children at Sunday-school. The lesson was upon the happiness of Adam and Eve in the garden of Paradise before they fell into sin.

"My children," he said, "one of the greatest pleasures our first parents enjoyed in Paradise, was the happiness of seeing God, and speaking to Him as familiarly as children speak to their parents."

A little boy was heard to say, "Oh, what a pity it is that we cannot speak to God now as they could do! How much I would like to be able to speak to Him, and hear Him speaking to me."

The holy Bishop heard these words, and, turning toward the child who had spoken them, he said: "My dear child, you can speak to God if you like; we have indeed lost Paradise on account of sin, but we have not lost God. He is everywhere, and is always near us, so that we can speak to Him whenever we like, and as often as we like, and we feel in our hearts that He hears us and answers us."

So, my child, although God is so great, and fills Heaven and earth, yet He loves you, little and sinful though you are, more than all the other things He has made. There is just one thing He wants you to give Him, and that is your heart—"*My child, give Me your heart*"; that means to say that He wants you to love Him. What a privilege this is to be able to love so great and so good a God! My child, you will surely grant Him this request.

ST. ANTHONY IN TEMPTATION.

When the great St. Anthony left the world to serve God in the desert, and to labor there to save his soul, the devil used to assault him with many temptations. Not only did he tempt him, but he used sometimes to appear to him in various ugly shapes to frighten him.

One day, after tempting him in various ways, and being repulsed every time, he became so enraged that he even assaulted him with blows, and tormented him in a way similar to what he had done to Job in former times.

Before he left him, Anthony was all covered with wounds and bruises.

Suddenly there appeared in his cell a great brightness, and immediately Satan with his wicked angels disappeared. Then St. Anthony knew that Our Lord Himself had come to visit him.

"O my good Jesus," said he lovingly, "where wert Thou? where wert Thou? Why didst Thou not come before now to drive Satan away, and to keep him from hurting me?"

To this loving complaint, Our Lord answered: "Anthony, I was here beside you, and I saw all your conflict. It was with my permission that you were wounded, that I might heal you; that you were afflicted, that I might comfort you. Like a good soldier, you have fought well. Never be afraid of your enemies, but fight them bravely, for I am always near you to help you."

With these words St. Anthony was greatly comforted. Our Lord also healed his wounds and filled his soul with a sweet peace.

RIBAD: *Lives of the Saints*, p. 100.

"GOD SEES ME."

One day, a young man, who was often tormented with bad thoughts, went to a holy priest and said to him: "Father, I am constantly tormented with bad thoughts, and I am most anxious to banish them from my mind; tell me the best means of putting them away."

"My child," said the priest, "if your head were made of glass, so that everyone could see these thoughts, how long would you keep them in your mind?"

"Oh! I would put them away instantly, for I would be filled with shame if anyone knew that I was thinking about them."

"God sees every one of your thoughts as clearly as if they were covered by thin transparent glass," said the priest; "therefore, when these wicked thoughts come to your mind, say to yourself, 'God sees me,' and immediately they will fly from you."

So, my child, when you are tempted to do evil, say to yourself, "God sees me, and God will judge me." If you only said these words often, how good and happy you would always be!

Also, be sure to keep in mind that Jesus, Who loves you dearly, is always near you. Whenever you are tempted, then, say at once, "O my Jesus, help me!" He will immediately give you the grace to put away the temptation, and thus you shall persevere in His grace.

BLESSED CRISPIN OF VITERBO.

St. Crispin of Viterbo became a great Saint, because he thought continually of God; and, although he had very many temptations during his long lifetime, he overcame them all, because he always remembered that God was near him.

He died in the year 1750. At the moment of his death, one of the brothers of his Order had a vision, in which he saw the holy man carrying a heavy sack on his shoulders, over a road which was very rough, and covered with deep mud.

He saw also that on the road were placed here and there pieces of wood and large stones, and that Crispin, as he walked along, was always careful to put his feet upon them, so that the mud did not even touch the end of his tunic.

When he had walked for a long distance in this manner, he came to a field covered with beautiful flowers, in the middle of which there stood a magnificent palace. A multitude of young men, clad in gorgeous attire, came out to meet the old man, and, going up to him, welcomed him with great joy, and led him into the palace. The vision then disappeared.

The good religious, coming to himself, cried out, "Brother Crispin is dead, and is in Heaven. God has just shown me the holy man walking through the temptations and dangers of the world, without being in the least stained by them, because he was always careful to walk in the presence of God, and at every step he took he always tried to please Him. I saw him entering the Kingdom of Heaven, where he is now enjoying the visible presence of God along with His happy Saints."

So, my child, like St. Crispin, think of God in everything you do, and, like him, you shall one day enjoy His visible presence in Heaven.

6

GOD KNOWS AND SEES ALL THINGS

God knows and sees all things, even our most secret thoughts. If you are always trying to please God, my child, this will be your greatest consolation, because then you will know that He sees all the good you do, and will reward it; but if you are living in a state of sin, this thought should make you afraid, since you cannot hide anything from His all-seeing eye, and since He punishes sin with such terrible chastisements.

ST. PHILIP NERI'S GREAT GIFT.

St. Philip Neri received from God the gift of knowing at a glance the state of the souls of his penitents. He knew when a soul was in the state of grace by the brightness in which it shone, and when it was in the state of sin by the darkness surrounding it.

One day a young man omitted, through shame, to confess some mortal sins he had committed. St. Philip said to him at the end of his confession: "My son, you have not come here in sincerity. You have omitted such and such sins," naming them one by one. The young man, seeing that the Saint knew the state of his soul, made an exact confession of his whole life, and became a fervent Christian.

There was another young man, who always kept in mind that God was near him, and in this way was always in the state of grace. St. Philip always saw a great splendor on his countenance, and declared that it seemed to him as if he were looking on the face of an angel.

My child, it is not a Saint that sees your soul, but God Himself; if you are free from sin, you appear beautiful in His eyes, like one of His heavenly angels, but if you are in mortal sin, how hideous you must be in His sight!

ST. LIDVINA'S CONSOLATION.

St. Lidvina was the daughter of very poor parents, and during her whole lifetime was afflicted with many sufferings. She was covered from head to foot with most painful ulcers. Her bed, also, was made of hard, rough boards, on which she lay for thirty-eight years. For want of sufficient clothing, she suffered much from the cold, and during the last year of her life, she had to endure the most painful sufferings that can afflict the human frame.

She had also much to suffer from the people around her, who not only heaped reproaches on her, and spoke to her in a most unkind way, but even increased her bodily pain by striking her.

Yet Lidvina never complained, but was always patient and resigned. God knew and saw everything she had to suffer, and that was enough for her; and when the end of her sorrows came, she died in peace, and God took her to her home above; the poor sickly despised sufferer became an object of veneration to the faithful, and her name has been enrolled in the catalog of the Saints.

A LITTLE UNKNOWN SOUL.

"I have read," writes the famous L. Veuillot, "that one day there came to Heaven a little soul unknown to the world. During its trial on earth it had not done anything extraordinary, for it had occupied a humble place in the world, and had only to do those things which fall to the lot of the poor.

"Yet the good God assigned to it a very glorious place in Heaven, and there was a murmur of astonishment among the great Saints, who, in their day of trial, had done and suffered so much for God.

"All looked towards the angel guardian who had brought in this beautiful soul. The angel bowed before God as if to obtain permission to speak to the heavenly court, and from his lips there fell these words, which all Heaven heard:

"'This soul, when on earth, always took what God sent it, sunshine or toil, sorrow or joy, and never complained. Whatever God sent was always welcome, and it never questioned why He did what He did, but always thought that God knew best. And God, Who knew and saw every act of its life, now rewards it with this great glory.'"

What a beautiful lesson there is in this story! O my child, remember that God sees and knows all you do, and that He, in His goodness, will reward you in Heaven for even the smallest act you perform for His sake.

7

GOD IS ETERNAL

My child, God had no beginning; He always was, is, and will be forever.

A few years ago, you were not in existence at all; no one spoke of you, no one even thought about you. A few years after this you must die. Your body will be put into the grave, and you will soon be forgotten; the world will go on without you after you leave it, as it did before you came into it.

But before the world was made, God was from all eternity, and when the world comes to an end, God will be for all eternity. But, O my child, who can understand the eternity of God?

THE BIRD AND THE GRAINS OF SAND.

Imagine that you saw a little bird coming every day to the seashore, and taking away one grain of sand in its beak. How many years, think you, must pass before it could carry away all the sand that lies upon the beach?

But if this little bird, instead of coming every day, came only once in a thousand years, and took each time it came only one grain of sand, count, if you can, the immense number of years that must pass before it could carry it all away.

Yet, my child, this little bird would be able in this way to carry off all the sand that is on the seashore, and also every grain of dust that is on the earth, and God would still be as far from the end of eternity as He was when the bird took away the first grain of sand. O Eternity of God!

ST. TERESA'S EXCLAMATION.

When St. Teresa was quite a child her greatest desire was to be alone, that she might think of God and speak to Him. The thought of eternity was always before her mind, and the words "Forever, forever, forever," always on her lips.

This world had no attractions for her, because she knew that it would end so soon; hence her constant prayer was that God would be pleased to let her die soon, in order that she might at once get to Heaven to see Him there, and to live forever with Him.

8

GOD IS INFINITELY BEAUTIFUL

God is infinitely beautiful. The greatest joy of the blessed in Heaven is to see God face to face, and look upon Him in His glory.

WHAT HE WOULD GIVE TO SEE GOD.

Father Jourdain, a religious of the Order of St. Dominic, was casting out an evil spirit from the body of a young man, as we read that Our Blessed Lord sometimes did.

When he had been cast out, the good Father asked him to tell him in what place he would desire to be forever.

"In Heaven," answered the evil one.

"And why would you wish to be there?"

"That I might be able to look upon the face of my Creator."

"Would you, who are lost, wish again to see God?" he asked.

"Ah, yes," he replied; "it was granted to me once, and that only for an instant, to look upon Him. To see Him again, even for one short instant, I would be willing to suffer till the Day of Judgment all the pains of Hell."

These last words, spoken in a tone of despair, so overcame the priest that he fainted. When he recovered, he again spoke to the wicked spirit:

"Since you have already seen God, I conjure you to give me some idea of His beauty and greatness."

The evil one answered: "That is quite impossible! No mind can conceive it, much less can any tongue express it."

"But give me some comparison," urged the Father.

"Imagine, then, if you can, that all the beauty of Heaven and earth, all the richest and most beautiful of all created things, were put together; then think that you saw all the stars of the firmament shining as so many suns, that the sun itself shone with the brightness of all these stars and that all this made but one—that magnificent object would be greater than any human mind could ever comprehend. But all this, in comparison with the infinite beauty of God, is less than nothing; it is as if you compared the thickest darkness of the most obscure night with the glowing light of the brightest noonday sun."

Oh, my child, how beautiful must our good Father in Heaven be! How carefully you should live that you may one day see Him in all His glory. That wicked spirit can never see God, but you can; it is for this you were made. You are in this world for one thing only—to prepare yourself to see Him, and be happy with Him forever in heaven.

9

GOD IS INFINITELY MERCIFUL AND GOOD TO US

My child, since God loves us so much, and desires so much to see us eternally happy, He watches over us with the greatest care, and bestows on us the gifts He knows will be most useful to us. But as the Scripture says: "His mercy is above all His works."

God is infinitely merciful to sinners who have rebelled against Him. It was for them He came down from Heaven. He says, "I came not to call the just, but sinners to penance" (Luke V. 32).

ST. FRANCIS DE SALES AND THE PRISONER.

One day St. Francis de Sales was informed that there was in the prison of the city in which he dwelt, a man condemned to death, and who was crying out in despair that he was lost. The Saint, full of compassion, went to the prison to try to prepare him for a happy death.

"It is quite useless," said the unhappy man, when he discovered why the Saint had come; "it is quite useless to speak to me of God's mercy, for there is no hope for me."

"But, my child," said the Saint, "would you not rather be with God in Heaven forever than with Satan?"

"Certainly," he answered; "but what can God do for such a wretch as I am?"

"Ah, my son, it was for sinners such as you that Jesus Christ came from Heaven."

"But would it not be an insult, for a criminal like me to have recourse to the mercy of God?"

"An insult!" exclaimed the Saint. "On the contrary, it would be an insult to Him if you thought that He would refuse to pardon sinners for whom He died."

"But is not God just? If so, then He must condemn me, because I have been so wicked."

"Yes, God is just, but He is also merciful, and He will pardon you, if only you with a humble and contrite heart ask His forgiveness."

Touched by these words, the poor man burst into tears, and cried out: "Then, O my Jesus, I throw myself into the arms of Thy mercy; I give myself entirely to Thee." And he died a most edifying death.

God shows His mercy and goodness to us in the care He takes of us; and those who confide in Him with a childlike confidence are always happy and content, no matter how much they may have to suffer.

CONTENT IN POVERTY.

A pious Christian was once asked by one of his friends the secret of his being always content, although living in great poverty.

"Oh, it is not difficult," he answered, "to be always content. When I am in sorrow or distress, I go into my house, and, kneeling down in the presence of God, I say to Him: 'O my good God, Thou art my Father, and Thou surely wilt not forsake me and mine in this hour of need. Oh no! Hast thou not said that, even if a mother could find it in her heart to forget her child, Thou at least wouldst never forget us? If in this world a father knows how to bestow on his children the best of what he possesses, how much more wilt Thou bestow Thy blessings on those who put their trust in Thee!'

"In this way, when I think of the goodness of God, and His power and love, all thoughts of sadness leave my mind, for I know God is so good that He will never forsake me."

THE FATHER AND THE SICK CHILD.

A father had a child whom he loved with all the tenderness of a father's heart. The child became very ill, and the physician ordered some very bitter medicine to be given him. The child refused to take it because it was so bitter, but his father commanded him to take it, and even used force to compel him to swallow it.

A neighbor, who heard the cries of the child, came into the house, and saw the father administering the medicine. "Oh, cruel man!" he cried out, "take pity on the child. Do not make him suffer in that way."

But the father turned towards him and said with anger: "Be silent! Do you think that I would cause my darling child to suffer in this way if it were not for his good, and necessary for his recovery? No; it is because I love him so dearly that I am forcing him to do what is so disagreeable."

It is in this way that our Heavenly Father treats us when He sends us trials, for it is one of the surest signs that He loves us. Oh, my child, throw yourself into the arms of your Heavenly Father with the greatest confidence, and He will take care of you.

10

GOD IS INFINITELY JUST AND HOLY

God is infinitely just and holy, and will give to everyone according to his works.

THE HOLY MAN KILLED BY A WILD BEAST.

In one of the deserts of Egypt, not far from the River Nile, there lived a very holy man, who served God most faithfully. No one knew that he lived there, except one poor man, who from time to time brought him some food.

Not very far away from this place, in a large town, there was a very rich man, who seemed to have but one thought in his mind—namely, how much enjoyment and pleasure he could obtain for himself. He never thought of God, nor of the life to come, but lived as if he had been made for nothing else but eating and drinking.

One day he died. Death came upon him suddenly without any warning, and he died as he had lived.

On the day of his funeral he was carried to the grave with great pomp and ceremony; all the people of the town seemed to follow his remains.

It happened on the same day, after the funeral was over, that the poor man set out to the desert where the solitary lived, with his usual supply of food.

When he came to the place where he used to find him, he was horror-stricken to see the ground covered with shreds of cloth and wet with blood. There were also unmistakable signs that the holy man had been devoured by a wild beast.

He threw himself upon the ground, and began to weep for the loss of him whom he had known so long and served so patiently. But what gave him the greatest sorrow was the awful way in which he had met his death. He began to wonder how God, Who is infinitely just, could permit one who had served Him so well all his days, to die such a terrible death; whereas the rich man, who had never loved Him at all, had received such an honorable funeral.

"O my God," he said, "I will not rise from this spot till Thou hast made known to me the reason of this."

God heard his humble prayer, and sent an angel to speak to him.

"Wait till the Day of Judgment, and then you will know the reason of many things that now appear strange to you. But be assured that God is infinitely just, and that nothing happens without His permission.

"The rich man," he continued, "once did a little good action, and God has given him a temporal reward for it in the splendid funeral that was given him; but because of his evil life he is now suffering in eternity. As to the poor solitary whom you knew to be so good, his soul is now in Heaven with God, and in eternal happiness; but because of some small sins he had fallen into, God permitted this cruel death to happen to him that they might be blotted out."

The good man went home consoled, and never afterwards doubted the justice of God in any events that happened.

11

THE BLESSED TRINITY

My child, there is only one God, but in this one God there are three Persons—the Father, the Son, and the Holy Ghost. Each of these three Persons is God, yet there are not three Gods, but only one. This is what is meant by the Mystery of the Most Holy Trinity.

THE CHILD ON THE SEASHORE.

One day the great St. Augustine was walking on the seashore. He was thinking of the mystery of the Most Holy Trinity, and trying to find out how he could explain it to the people in his sermons and in the books of instruction which he wrote.

Suddenly he saw before him on the shore a child playing. He had made a little hole in the sand, and was taking water out of the sea with a small shell, and pouring it into the hole.

The Saint stood for a few moments watching the child. At length, going up to him, he said, "My child, what are you doing here?"

"I am going to empty the sea into that hole which I have made in the sand."

"That is quite impossible," said the Saint. "Do you not see that the ocean is so great, and the hole you have made is so small?"

"So you think I cannot do it? But it would be easier for me to do this than for you to understand the mystery of the Holy Trinity."

Saying these words, the child disappeared. It was an angel whom God sent to his servant to teach him how impossible it is for anyone in this world to understand the greatness of God.

Life of St. Augustine.

ST. PATRICK AND THE SHAMROCK.

When St. Patrick was teaching the Irish people the truths of our holy Faith, he saw that they were unwilling to believe the mystery of the Holy Trinity, because they could not understand how there could be three Persons in one God, that each Person is God, and that there are not three Gods, but only one God.

Bowing down towards the ground, he plucked a leaf of shamrock which grew at his feet, and holding it in his hand that they might all be able to see it, said: "Behold this little plant which bears on one stalk three small leaves; they are distinct from each other, but are exactly alike, and form but one leaf, and rest on one stalk. So it is, my brethren, with the great God I preach to you. He is one in nature, and three in Person."

The people immediately believed, and on that day many thousands received the Faith.

My child, thank God from your inmost soul that He has brought you to know Him here, and ask Him for the grace of being His faithful child on earth, that you may see Him face to face in Heaven.

PART IV
JESUS CHRIST OUR SAVIOR

1

JESUS CHRIST THE ETERNAL SON OF GOD

When God created man, He did not immediately bestow on him the eternal happiness of Heaven; it was His Divine will that he should be placed on trial for a time, that by his obedience to his Creator he might merit that everlasting glory for which he was made.

Our first parents, Adam and Eve, in the garden of Paradise, disobeyed God by eating of the forbidden fruit, and brought upon themselves, and upon us and all their posterity, eternal ruin. Heaven was forever closed against us, and we would never possess God, but be cast away from Him forever.

But God, in His mercy, promised to send us a Redeemer who would restore to us the heavenly inheritance we had lost. This Redeemer Whom God sent was His only Son Jesus. Jesus Christ is the Second Person of the Blessed Trinity, the Eternal Son of God.

ST. PAUL PROCLAIMS THE DIVINITY OF JESUS CHRIST.

St. Paul, writing to the Hebrews, begins by promulgating the Divinity of Jesus Christ in these words:

"God, Who at sundry times and in divers manners spoke, in times past to the fathers by the prophets, last of all, in these days hath spoken to us by His Son, Whom He hath appointed heir of all things, by Whom also He made the world:

"Who, being the brightness of His glory, and the figure of His substance, and upholding all things by the word of His power, making purgation of sins, sitteth on the right hand of the Majesty on high; being made so much better than the angels, as he hath inherited a more excellent name than they. For to which of the angels hath he said at any time: 'Thou art My Son, today have I begotten Thee'? and again: 'I will be to Him a Father, and He shall be to Me a Son'?

"And again, when He bringeth in the first-begotten into the world, he saith: 'And let all the angels of God adore Him.' And to the angels indeed He saith: 'He that hath made His angels spirits, and His ministers a flame of fire.' But to the Son: 'Thy throne, O God, is for ever and ever; a scepter of justice is the scepter of Thy kingdom. Thou hast loved justice, and hated iniquity; therefore God, Thy God, hath anointed Thee with the oil of gladness above Thy fellows. And, 'Thou in the beginning, O Lord, didst found the earth: and the work of Thy hands are the heavens. They shall perish, but Thou shalt continue: and they shall all grow old as a garment, and as a vesture shalt Thou change them, and they shall be changed: but Thou art the selfsame, and thy years shall not fail.' "

Hebrews, chap. I.

2

JESUS CHRIST IS TRUE GOD AND TRUE MAN

My child, the Son of God, in becoming man for us, did not cease to be God; Jesus Christ is both God and man. He is God because He has the nature of God, and He is man because He has the nature of man. When He was in this world He appeared to be like the rest of men, but under that outward appearance He concealed His Divinity, so that He was, as the Catechism tells us, "true God and true man."

KING CHARLES IN DISGUISE.

After the Battle of Worcester, Charles II was obliged to conceal himself in the woods lest he might fall into the hands of his enemies. He was even obliged to disguise himself. His hands and face were covered with paint; his royal robes were laid aside, and he put on the clothes of a common laborer; he carried in his hand a heavy ax as if he were a woodsman. Those who met him thought he was only a laborer in the woods; no one ever imagined that he was a King; only those who were with him knew that he was their Sovereign.

So, my child, although Jesus Christ has clothed Himself with our lowly nature, He is still our God, and the great Creator of Heaven and earth; and although many refuse to believe in Him, you at least, who are in the number of His friends, should know and love Him.

JESUS CHRIST IS GOD.

About the end of the fifth century, the Vandals, a people who dwelt in Africa, raised a persecution against the Christians who dwelt there, because they professed that Jesus Christ was true God as well as true man.

Huneric, their King, seized three hundred of them in one day, and brought them before his tribunal at Typasium. "You must declare that Jesus Christ is not God," he said to them; "if you refuse, I will command that your tongues be pulled out, and your right hands be cut off in the public square of the city."

Not one of the three hundred yielded to his order; they all declared that to the last moment of their lives they would profess their faith in the Divinity of Jesus Christ, and would be willing to lose not only their tongues and their hands, but even their very lives in defense of their belief.

They were then led to the place appointed, and the barbarous order of the King was executed. But God, by a miracle, rewarded His servants for their fidelity to His Divine Son. For, although their tongues were cut out by the root, they continued to cry out as before: "Jesus Christ is God! Jesus Christ is truly God!"

Many of them lived for a long time after this event, and the historians of the time, who saw them and heard them, have recorded that they went about from place to place saying these words, and that many heretics were converted and returned to the true Faith.

3

JESUS CHRIST COMES INTO THIS WORLD TO SAVE US

The Holy Gospels record as follows the Divine Infancy of Jesus Christ:

THE ANNUNCIATION.

When the time came for Our Savior to appear in this world amongst us, the archangel Gabriel was sent to Mary in her home at Nazareth, to announce to her that she had been chosen to be His Mother. Mary was afraid when she heard the angel's message; but when she knew that it was the most holy will of God, and that she should forever remain a spotless virgin, she gave her consent, and God the Son, the Second Person of the Blessed Trinity, came down from Heaven and was made man for us.

THE BIRTH OF JESUS.

When the time of Mary's delivery was near, the Emperor Augustus issued a decree that the whole world should be enrolled, and that everyone should go to his own city for this purpose. Mary and Joseph, her husband, belonged to the tribe of David, the chief city of which was Bethlehem. It was therefore to that city they were obliged to go to inscribe their names.

When they reached the city of Bethlehem they could find no place in which to dwell, and were obliged to take shelter in a stable by the wayside.

It was in that lowly stable that Jesus was born at midnight. His mother Mary wrapped Him lovingly in swaddling clothes, and laid Him in a manger.

THE ANGELS APPEAR TO THE SHEPHERDS.

Now, it happened that there were some poor shepherds in the neighborhood watching their sheep. At the moment Jesus was born, they suddenly beheld a bright light shining in the heavens above them, and they became afraid. And as they gazed on the light, behold an angel stood by them, who told them not to be afraid, because there was born to them that day a Savior in the city of Bethlehem. And the angel told them how they would be able to find Him.

At the same instant there appeared a multitude of the heavenly army singing these words: "Glory be to God in the highest, and on earth, peace to men of good will."

THE SHEPHERDS AT THE MANGER.

When the angel returned to Heaven, and the vision was ended, the shepherds said one to another: "Let us go over to Bethlehem, and see this word that is come to pass, that the Lord hath showed to us."

So, going over in haste to the place pointed out by the angel, they found the Holy Child in the manger, with Mary and Joseph at His side; and when they had adored their newborn Savior they returned, glorifying and praising God for all that they had heard and seen.

THE STAR IN THE EAST.

At the same time there appeared in the east a star of wonderful brightness. Three wise men, who were Kings in those far distant lands, saw the star, and, remembering an ancient prophecy that the appearance of a certain star would point out the time of the Redeemer's birth, they said to each other: "This is the sign of the great King. Let us go and look for Him, and offer Him our gifts."

So these wise men set out on their long journey towards Jerusalem. The star they saw in the heavens guided them on their way till they came to that city.

THE WISE MEN IN JERUSALEM.

When they reached Jerusalem, the star suddenly disappeared, and they thought they had come to the end of their journey.

"Where is He that is born King of the Jews?" they cried out on entering the city. "We have seen His star in the east, and we are come to adore Him."

When Herod heard these words he was troubled, and all the people with him. Sending for the chief priests and scribes, he inquired of them the time and place of Our Divine Lord's birth. They answered him that the prophet had foretold that Bethlehem was to be the city in which the Savior should be born.

Then Herod sent the wise men to Bethlehem, saying to them: "Go and diligently inquire after the child, and when you have found Him, bring me word again, that I also may come and adore Him."

THE WISE MEN AT THE CRIB.

When they left the King, the star again appeared, and went before them till it came and stood over where the Child was. And entering into the house, they found the Child with Mary His Mother, and, falling down, they adored Him. And opening their treasures, they offered Him gifts, gold, frankincense, and myrrh. When they were about to return home, an angel of the Lord appeared to them, and told them that they should not return to Herod, so they went back another way to their own country.

THE MASSACRE OF THE INNOCENTS.

When Herod saw that the wise men did not return, he became very angry, for he wanted to find out where Jesus was, that he might kill Him. And he sent an order secretly that all the male children about Bethlehem, from two years old and under, should be slain.

But an angel of the Lord appeared to Joseph in his sleep, saying: "Arise, and take the Child and His Mother, and fly into Egypt, and be there until I shall tell thee."

Joseph immediately obeyed the angel, and fled into Egypt with Our Lady and her Divine Child, and thus He escaped the hands of Herod.

Next morning the soldiers reached Bethlehem, and slew all the children without mercy, so that there was great lamentation in the city. These little martyred children are called the holy innocents.

4

THE DIVINE CHILDHOOD OF JESUS CHRIST

THE CIRCUMCISION.

My child, when Jesus was eight days old He was circumcised, and on that day began to suffer pain for the love of us. He also at the same time received the holy Name of Jesus, which signifies Savior because in His infinite love He came to save us, His people, from our sins. Oh, how grateful you should be to Him! How much you should love Him in return, and with what love you should reverence His holy Name!

BLESSED SUSO AND THE NAME OF JESUS.

The blessed Suso had so great a devotion for the holy Name of Jesus that he one day took a sharp instrument, and with it cut the letters of that holy Name on his breast.

When he had done this he knelt down before his crucifix, and said to his beloved Master: "Thou seest, O Lord, how much I love Thee, and the great desire I have of being united to Thee. Oh, dwell now and forever in my heart, and may Thy holy Name be ever written there."

My child, if God does not want you to write His holy Name on your breast, as the blessed Suso did, He desires you to write it in your heart by loving Him above all things.

THE COUNT ARMOGASTUS

The Count Armogastus was one of the most remarkable men who lived during the reign of the Emperor Theodoric, not only for his courage, but still more for his strict religious life.

The Emperor, who was a heretic, and who did not believe in the Divinity of Jesus Christ, endeavored to persuade his favorite statesman to renounce his belief in that mystery, and become an Arian like himself. But the nobleman refused, and declared that Jesus Christ was true God, and that he would die rather than deny that truth.

"Then," said the Emperor, "you shall get your choice: you must either do what I have asked of you or die."

"Then I at once choose to die," said the heroic man.

The Emperor did not immediately order him to be executed, for he hoped by putting him to the torture to make him yield. So he commanded the soldiers to bind him tightly with strong cords. When this was done, Armogastus raised his eyes to Heaven, and said but one word—the Name of Jesus.

As soon as he had uttered that holy Name, the cords that bound him were broken to pieces, as if they had been thin threads.

The Emperor was filled with anger when he saw this, and ordered him to be bound with ropes; but all in vain. The holy man again uttered the Name of Jesus, and they were instantly broken.

ST. ANDREW THE TRIBUNE.

St. Andrew was a tribune or officer in the Roman army. On account of his courage, he was stationed on the banks of the River Euphrates to protect that part of the empire.

In the year 297, an immense army of Persians went to attack him unawares, and he and his whole army would certainly have perished had he trusted to human resources. But, seeing all earthly power of no avail, he raised up his eyes to Heaven, and invoked the holy Name of Jesus. Then he charged the enemy, and, by the power of that holy Name, put them to flight.

JESUS PRESENTED IN THE TEMPLE.

When Jesus was forty days old, His parents carried Him to Jerusalem to present Him to the Lord. When they arrived at the Temple, the high priest took the Child from the arms of His Mother, and offered Him to His Eternal Father. Then, as they were very poor, they made the offering appointed for the poor—namely, two turtle-doves.

THE OLD MAN SIMEON.

There dwelt at that time in Jerusalem an old man named Simeon, who, as the Scriptures tell us, "was just and devout, waiting for the consolation of Israel. And he had received an answer from the Holy Ghost that he should not see death before he had seen the Christ of the Lord.

"And he came by the spirit into the Temple. And when His parents brought in the Child Jesus, he took Him into his arms and blessed God, and said: 'Now Thou dost dismiss Thy servant, O Lord, according to Thy word, in peace, because my eyes have seen Thy salvation, which Thou hast prepared before all the people; a light to the revelation of the Gentiles, and the glory of Thy people Israel.'

"And His Father and Mother were wondering at those things which were spoken concerning Him.

"And Simeon blessed them, and said to Mary His Mother: 'Behold, this Child is set for the fall and for the resurrection of many in Israel, and for a sign which shall be contradicted; and thy own soul a sword shall pierce, that out of many hearts thoughts may be revealed.'"

ANNA THE PROPHETESS.

And there was one Anna, a prophetess, who was a widow and far advanced in years, being fourscore and four, who departed not from the Temple by fastings and prayers, serving day and night. Now she at the same hour coming in, confessed to the Lord, and spoke of Him to all who looked for the redemption of Israel.

You see, my child, how God rewarded these holy people for a long life spent in serving Him. If you serve God as faithfully as they did, you also shall receive the same reward. You shall see the same Divine Jesus, if not during this short life, at least forever in eternity.

JESUS LOST IN JERUSALEM.

Jesus came from Heaven to show us by His example how to please God. In His very childhood we see how careful He was to fulfill in everything the holy law of God.

Mary and Joseph went every year to Jerusalem at the solemn day of the Pasch. When Jesus was twelve years old they brought Him along with them, and when the solemnity was ended they returned home; "but the Child Jesus remained in Jerusalem, and His parents knew it not. And thinking that He was in the company, they came a day's journey and sought Him among their kinsfolk and acquaintances, and not finding Him, they returned into Jerusalem seeking Him."

My child, think of the sorrow that must have filled the soul of Our Blessed Lady when she lost her Son. Think of her grief during the three days she wandered about Jerusalem seeking Him, and how diligently she sought for her Jesus whom she had lost. Oh! If you ever have the misfortune to lose Jesus by sin, seek Him with the utmost diligence, and rest not, like Mary, till you have found Him again.

JESUS FOUND IN THE TEMPLE.

At the end of the third day, "going into the Temple, they found Him there, sitting in the midst of the doctors, hearing them and asking them questions; and all that heard Him were astonished at His wisdom and His answers.

"And seeing Him they wondered; and His Mother said to Him: 'Son, why hast Thou done so to us? Behold, Thy father and I have sought Thee sorrowing.'

"And He said to them: 'How is it that you sought Me? Did you not know that I must be about My Father's business?'"

You, my child, can learn from the example of Jesus to be most diligent in listening to the instructions you receive from the priest. Jesus was infinitely wise, and did not need any instruction; yet for your sake, and to show you what you should do, He, for three days, listened to those who were appointed to explain the law of God.

JESUS AT NAZARETH.

After this, we read that Jesus went down to Nazareth, and was obedient to Our Blessed Lady and St. Joseph. You can imagine the Divine Child in that lowly home, helping His Blessed Mother and St. Joseph in their humble occupations, and obeying them. Like Him, therefore, endeavor to be obedient to your parents in all things, since that virtue is the one God loves to see in all His children; help them in all their labors as Jesus did His most holy Mother and St. Joseph, and you will be the joy of your parents, you yourself will be happy, and God will give you the reward He has promised to dutiful children —a long and happy life and a good death.

Jesus lived at Nazareth until he was about thirty years of age, when the time came for Him to go forth publicly into the world to preach the Gospel of the Kingdom of God.

It would be impossible to write down in this little book all that Jesus did during His public life. St. John the Evangelist, at the end of his Gospel, wrote these words: "There are also many other things which Jesus did, which if they were written every one, the world itself, I think, would not be able to contain the books that should be written" (St. John XXI. 25). But in the next chapter—"Jesus Christ our Teacher"—you will learn how He has taught us to live in this world, that we may hereafter obtain the happiness for which we were made. "Jesus Christ came down from Heaven to teach us the way to Heaven."

5

ON THE LOVE OF JESUS CHRIST FOR US

My child, if I were to ask you where Our Savior was born, you would answer me at once, "In a stable at Bethlehem"; and if I asked you why he was born in a stable, you would tell me, "He was born in a stable because He loved us." Yes, everyone knows this.

Why is it, then, that people who know this will not love God? It is because they have no gratitude, because their hearts are hard like stones. No wonder that our good God should complain so often of men's ingratitude. He Who is our only joy and consolation never complained of all the sufferings He endured for us, but He did complain very much of the hard-heartedness of those whom He loved and who would not love Him in return.

THE CHILD IN THE WOODS.

A certain holy monk of Brabant was going through a forest one Christmas night. He was thinking about the love of the good God, in sending His beloved Son Jesus to be born on that night for us. As he was passing along, he thought he heard the cries of a newly born child not far from him. He turned towards the place from whence the sound came, and behold, he saw lying on the snow a beautiful child, crying and trembling in the cold.

Filled with compassion for the poor infant, he said, as if speaking to the child, "My little child, how is it that you are thus left alone, lying on the cold snow? Who has had the cruelty to leave you there?"

Then the little child—for it was a vision of Jesus Himself that the monk saw—answered him: "Alas! how can I help crying, when I see Myself abandoned by everyone, when I see that nobody receives Me or has pity for Me." Having said this, he disappeared.

The monk then understood that this vision was given him to show him that men whom Jesus came from Heaven to save, instead of loving Him and receiving Him with joy, do not make room in their hearts for Him, but cast Him out, as the Jews did, to a poor stable, and leave Him there to cry, without giving Him even one word of pity.

St. Liguori.

ST. OZANNA AND THE HOLY CHILD JESUS.

One of the greatest blessings God can bestow upon us is to give us a father and mother who love Him.

The parents of St. Ozanna loved God with their whole hearts, and they taught their little daughter to do the same. When she was about six years old, her love for her dear Father in Heaven was so great that nothing could please her that did not speak to her of God and of Heaven.

One day, in her childish simplicity, she asked God to tell her what she could do for Him that would give Him the greatest pleasure, and a voice said distinctly to her: "My daughter, love Me with your whole heart."

Her Angel Guardian, on another occasion, led her into Paradise, and showed her the glory God gives to His Saints. When she returned to her senses after this vision, she said, "My own dear Lord, I give myself from this moment to Thee; just do with me whatever is most pleasing to Thee, for I want to live for nothing else."

Immediately Jesus appeared to her in the form of a lovely little child with a beautiful countenance. On His head was a crown of sharp thorns, and on His little shoulders a very heavy cross. He stretched out His arms towards the little girl, and smiled upon her. Then, opening His Divine lips, He said: "Dearest Ozanna, I am Jesus, the Son of the Blessed Virgin Mary; if you wish to please Me, you will have to suffer much while you are in this world; but be not afraid, dearest, for I will never forsake you."

When He had said these words He disappeared, leaving the holy Child filled with Divine love. From that day she made the sufferings of Our Lord the special object of her meditation. The crosses she had to carry were sometimes very heavy, but Jesus had promised never to forsake her, and she is now happy with Him in Heaven.

Life of St. Ozanna.

My child, if you ask Jesus to tell you what you could do that would give Him the greatest pleasure, He would answer you as He did St. Ozanna: "Love Me with your whole heart." Make Him, then, the same promise that she made, and say: "My dearest Jesus, I give myself to Thee; I want to live for Thee alone."

THE NUN WHO WAS TEMPTED TO DESPAIR.

In the Life of St. Philip Neri, it is related that there was once a nun whom the Devil tempted to despair. He tried to make her think that it would be quite impossible for her to get to Heaven, because she had so often offended God during the course of her life.

The temptation made her very miserable, and all the words of encouragement that kind friends said to her did not bring back peace to her soul.

St. Philip, hearing of this, went one day to see her. Everyone looked upon him as a great Saint, and followed his advice as if they had heard it from the lips of Jesus Christ Himself. So the nun was very glad when she was told that he wanted to speak to her.

"My child," he said, in a voice full of sweetness, "can you tell me the reason why the Son of God came down from Heaven and died upon the cross?"

"Yes, Father, it was for poor sinners—to save them from Hell, and to open Heaven for them."

"Now tell me," said the Saint, "what are you? Are you not a sinner?"

"Oh yes, Father, I am a great sinner; I have offended God so much."

"Well, since that is the case, you should feel very happy, because it was specially for you that Jesus came—to purchase the Kingdom of Heaven for you."

These words had the desired effect. The good religious now saw how Satan had been trying to deceive her. From that time till the day of her happy death the thoughts of despair never gave her any more trouble.

Life of St. Philip Neri.

A STORY OF ALFRED THE GREAT.

Alfred the Great was one day hunting along with a large company of his nobles. Suddenly there fell upon their ears a sound like the crying of a little child, which seemed to come from the top of a high rock not far distant.

The King ordered one of his attendants to go and see what was the cause of so strange a noise.

On mounting to the top of the rock he found an eagle's nest, and lying in the nest a little child, which seemed to be only a few days old. To all appearance it had been left there by its cruel parents that the eagle might destroy it.

Alfred wept when he saw the sad condition of the poor child, and ordered it to be put at once under the care of a nurse.

"Since its own parents have forsaken it and left it to die," he said,

"I will adopt it, and love it as if it were my own child, and I will bring it up in my own palace."

The courtiers applauded this kind act of the King; it added one more to those many deeds of generosity which had already made him an object of love to his people.

My child, our first parents left us to die, by their great sin. Terrible would have been our fate for all eternity had not Jesus Christ, the great King of Heaven, come on earth to rescue us from so great an evil.

THE LITTLE BOY'S DEATH.

There lived a long time ago at Messina a little boy whose name was Dominic Ansalom. In a church in that town there was a picture representing Our Blessed Lady with the Divine Infant in her arms. Dominic loved this picture, and was very often seen saying his prayers before it, and gazing on it with a look of great affection.

It happened that he became very ill, and could not any longer go to pray before it. He asked the priest as a great favor to bring the picture to his house, that he might see it again before he died. His request was granted.

As soon as the picture was brought into the room he saluted it with these words: "O my Jesus, have mercy on me." Then, turning to his parents, he said: "Oh, look! Oh, how beautiful is the little Jesus!"

The last night of his life, when his friends were weeping around his bed, he alone was full of joy. Before he expired he raised his eyes and hands to Heaven, as if he saw something very beautiful, and, with a countenance beaming with joy, he exclaimed: "Oh, how lovely! Oh, how beautiful is my dearest Jesus!" These were his last words.

O my child, what a beautiful death! Dominic died in this manner because he loved Our Lord and kept away from sin. Jesus also loved him and took him to Heaven in his innocence. Like that little boy, love Jesus, and when the hour of your death comes Jesus will take you also to Himself in Heaven.

ST. VINCENT OF PAUL IN CHAINS.

One day when St. Vincent of Paul was at Marseilles, he went to visit the poor galley-slaves who were sent to that city to fill up the time of their punishment.

There was amongst them one man who seemed sadder than the others. "Tell me, my good man," said the Saint, "what is it that makes you so sad?"

The man replied: "I have a wife and little family who live far; far away from this place; it is many years since I have seen them, and my heart yearns to speak to them again, and to embrace my darling little ones, but whilst I am here I can never enjoy that happiness. That is what makes me so sad."

St. Vincent went to the overseer, who did not know who the Saint was, and asked permission to take the poor man's place that he might have the happiness of seeing his friends again. This strange request was granted; the chains were taken off the poor man and put on St. Vincent, and he was made to work in the place of the criminal, till, in a short time, it being discovered who he was, he was instantly set free.

St. Vincent was not obliged to take the place of the galley-slave; it was his love for him that made him do so. Jesus Christ did more for you, my child. He saw you never could have seen your Heavenly Father, nor the home for which you were made; and He, out of love for you, came down from Heaven, and put on our human nature, that He might in His own Divine Person make reparation to His Father for your sins. Oh, how good has Jesus been to you, and how worthy He is of your love and gratitude!

THE LION AND THE LAMB.

In ancient history, we read that a merchant went to the palace of a certain King, and sold him false stones as real jewels. After some time the deception was discovered, and in punishment of it, the merchant was condemned to be devoured by lions.

On the day fixed for his death, a great multitude had assembled to witness it. The King himself was there, surrounded by his Court. A deep silence reigned in the crowd as they saw the condemned man led into the arena.

At length, the hour fixed for the execution came, and the King gave the signal. The gate of the arena was thrown open, and behold, instead of an angry lion, a little lamb came frisking in and ran towards the man, who thought his last hour had come.

A sudden enthusiasm seized upon the multitude when they saw this, for they knew that the King had shown the poor man mercy, and they cried out with one voice: "Long live the King!"

My child, your Heavenly Father has treated you in the same way. You offended Him by sin, and His justice required that you should forever suffer for your offense against Him. But in His mercy, He had pity on you, and sent His own beloved Son—"the Lamb of God, Who taketh away the sins of the world"—to redeem you. Oh, surely you will never offend Him again.

6

JESUS CHRIST IN HIS SACRED PASSION

My child, from your infancy you have been taught all that Jesus did and suffered for the love of you, and every year, when Holy Week comes round, the Church puts you in mind of it, that you may ever love Jesus more and more, and never wilfully yield to sin, which caused Him all His sufferings; and also that you may be willing to suffer for love of Him all the trials and sufferings of this short life.

"I AM THY SAVIOR AND THY BROTHER."

When St. Thomas of Canterbury was preparing for martyrdom by prayer and great works of penance, Our Lord appeared to him one day as he was making his thanksgiving after Mass. Jesus said to him: "Thomas, thou shalt honor My Church by thy holy martyrdom."

The Saint in surprise said: "O my Lord, Who art Thou?"

"I am Jesus Christ, thy Savior and thy Brother." Our Lord spoke to him in this way to give him courage to suffer and die for His sake. He says the same to each one of us: "My child, I am thy Saviour and thy Brother. Take up thy cross and follow Me, and thou shalt have a great treasure in Heaven."

GOD'S COMPLAINT.

It was the sin of ingratitude that made God complain long ago, in the old law, by the lips of His prophet Isaias: "Hear, O ye heavens, and give ear, O earth, for the Lord hath spoken. I have brought up children, and have exalted them, but they have despised Me. The ox knoweth its owner, and the ass his master's crib, but Israel hath not known Me" (Isa. I. 2). So Jesus has to complain that we His people, whom He loves so much, love Him so little.

THE VALUE OF A TEAR.

A little child by the name of Catharine used to go to a school taught by the nuns.

One day the Sister who was in charge of the school was giving the children an instruction on the sufferings of Our Blessed Redeemer, to which the little girl listened with the greatest attention.

"My children," she said, "one tear shed through compassion for the sufferings of Jesus is of far greater value before God than almost anything else we can do."

Catharine heard these words, and the next day, when she went to Holy Mass, she kept her eyes fixed on the cross, and thought of the cruel sufferings which Jesus endured for the love of us.

Very soon the tears began to run down her cheeks. "O my dear Jesus," she said, "I wish I could suffer something instead of you."

The Sister heard these words, and saw her weeping. "My child," she said, "what is the matter with you?"

"I am weeping because I am sorry to see Jesus suffering so much."

The Sister remembered the instruction she had given to the children the day before, and she too wept with joy to see a tear shed through love for Jesus crucified.

THE PRINCIPAL SUFFERINGS OF JESUS.

The night before His death, Jesus went into the Garden of Gethsemane with His disciples. The thought of all the sufferings He was about to endure came before His mind, and filled Him with anguish. He prayed to His Heavenly Father that, if it were possible, He would take from Him the bitter chalice of these sufferings; but seeing that it was His Father's will that He should endure them, He willingly submitted, saying, "Not My will, but Thine be done."

Then Judas, one of His disciples, who, for thirty pieces of silver had sold Him into the hands of the chief priests, came into the garden at the head of a band of soldiers. Going up to Our Divine Lord, he, with a kiss, betrayed Him into their hands. Jesus was then led away like a malefactor to the tribunals of the high priests, who insulted Him, and heaped upon Him every outrage their wicked minds could conceive.

He was then brought before Herod, who mocked Him and treated Him as a fool; and before Pilate, who commanded Him to be scourged. He was delivered over to the cruel soldiers, who struck Him on the face, spat upon Him, and mocked Him. They crowned Him with a crown of thorns, and, putting a reed into His hand, they bowed the knee before Him, and treated Him as a mock King.

These and many other sufferings had Jesus to endure at their hands; but He bore all patiently. During all that time He thought of you, my child, and offered them up to His Heavenly Father that the sins you had committed might be blotted out.

JESUS CONDEMNED TO DIE.

But what grieved Our Divine Lord more than all His sufferings was the ingratitude of the Jews. He had spent His whole life amongst them doing them good; and now in return they went in a body to Pilate, and cried out that He should be put to death.

Pilate was a cowardly man, and, fearing to displease the people, who were continually crying out, "Take Him away, take Him away! Crucify Him, crucify Him!" he pronounced upon Him the sentence of death.

Immediately a heavy cross was prepared and brought to Jesus, Who, with great affection, embraced it, because He loved us so much, and, putting it on His shoulders, set out for Mount Calvary. On the journey He met His most blessed Mother, whose sacred heart was pierced with a sword of grief as she beheld Him, her own dear Jesus, bearing the heavy cross. Many times also did He fall on the way, and much had He to suffer from the soldiers but for your sake, my child, He meekly bore all.

My child, when you look at the cross, think of all these things. The sight of a crucifix has often changed the greatest sinner into a saint; and how can we be surprised at this when we remember that it was our sins that caused Jesus to suffer and to die?

THE LITTLE GIRL'S CRUCIFIX.

There was a little girl of eleven years of age who was very troublesome and idle. She always liked to have her own way, and would become very angry at the least contradiction.

This went on for a long time. Promises and threats made no impression on her, and her superiors began to despair of ever being able to correct her.

But suddenly an unexpected change came over her, which no one could account for. Her evil habits had entirely disappeared, and she became one of the most obedient and gentle children in the school.

One of her teachers observed that, from time to time, she put her hand upon her breast, and seemed to press it against something she carried there; so one day she asked her why she did so.

The child blushed when she heard the question, and did not answer it. But when her superior urged her to tell her, she whispered into her ear these words: "It is to help me to be good."

"How can that help you to be good, my child?" she asked.

The child, with some confusion, drew forth from under the band of her dress a large crucifix, which was suspended from her neck by a ribbon. "When I am tempted to be naughty," she said, "I press this image to my heart, and then I find it easy to be good. But be sure, Sister, not to tell this to anyone."

O my child, think frequently of the sufferings of Jesus, and make acts of contrition for your sins which caused them. This will give some consolation to His Sacred Heart.

Since Jesus has done so much to make us happy in this world and in the next, the least we can do in return is to love Him with our whole hearts.

Yet Our Lord Himself complained to St. Margaret Mary that His people do not do this, but, on the contrary, show Him contempt and ingratitude.

VISION OF ST. MARGARET MARY.

One day, as St. Margaret Mary was kneeling before the altar, Jesus appeared to her in a visible manner in all the splendor of His glory, His five wounds shining like five bright suns. He showed her His adorable Heart all surrounded with flames, and told her the great extent to which the excess of His love for man had carried Him.

"Behold," He said, "behold this Heart which has loved men so much, and made every effort to testify that love. In return I receive from the greater number only contempt and ingratitude.

"It is this," He continued, "which I feel more deeply than all that I suffered in My Passion; for if they would only return My love, I would consider all that I have done for them as nothing, and, if possible, I would even wish to do more; instead of which I meet with coldness and repulses from men in My anxiety to do them good.

"At least, then," added He, "do thou give Me satisfaction by atoning for their ingratitude as far as thou art able."

Life of B. Margaret Mary.

My child, you also will try to make up for the ingratitude of men, and for your own past ingratitude, by loving Jesus with your whole heart. In return, He will write down your name in His Sacred Heart, never to be blotted out.

7

JESUS DYING ON MOUNT CALVARY

My child, oh, how great was the love of Jesus for us! He loved us so much that He even died for us on the cross, that by His death our sins might be blotted out, and that we might forever be happy with Him in Heaven. Let us read, then, with great devotion the account of His death.

JESUS NAILED TO THE CROSS.

When Jesus reached the top of Mount Calvary, the soldiers stripped Him of His garments, and rudely threw Him down upon the cross. Then, taking a hammer and nails, they, with the utmost cruelty, fastened His hands and His feet to the cross. When this was done, they dragged the cross to the hole in the rock they had prepared for it, and, raising it up, they made it fall into the hole, which caused Him to suffer unutterable agony.

JESUS HANGING ON THE CROSS.

Jesus hung for three hours on the cross, thinking of you, my child, suffering for you and praying for you. His most holy Mother Mary stood there, her heart pierced with sorrow, while at her side stood St. John, the beloved disciple.

To add a still greater insult to the many they had already heaped upon Him, they crucified Him between two thieves. Then the crowd who had assembled began to insult Him and blaspheme Him, wagging their heads and saying: "Vah! Thou that destroyest the temple of God and in three days dost rebuild it, save Thy own self! If Thou be the Son of God, come down from the cross."

In like manner also the chief priests, with the scribes and ancients, mocking, said: "He saved others; Himself He cannot save! If He be the King of Israel, let Him now come down from the cross, and we will believe Him."

THE SEVEN WORDS OF JESUS ON THE CROSS.

During the three hours of His terrible agony on the cross, Jesus opened His Divine lips seven times to show us that even then He was thinking of us and praying for us.

His first word was a prayer to His Heavenly Father for those who were putting Him to death: "Father, forgive them, for they know not what they do." O my child, how could anyone refuse to forgive his neighbor who may have injured him, since Jesus forgave and prayed for those even who were taking away His life?

The second word was to His most holy Mother and His beloved disciple St. John. "Woman," He said to her, "Behold thy Son"; and to St. John He said: "Behold thy Mother." At that moment he gave us, in the person of St. John, His own most blessed Mother to be our Mother, and from that moment she has ever looked on us as her dear children.

The third word that Jesus spoke was to the good thief, who had asked His forgiveness, saying: "Lord, remember me when Thou shalt come into Thy kingdom." Jesus said to him: "Amen, I say to thee this day shalt thou be with Me in Paradise."

The fourth time that Jesus opened His lips was to cry to His Heavenly Father: "Eli, Eli, lamma sabacthani?"—that is, "My God, My

God, why hast Thou forsaken Me?" As if He had said: "My God, You have so much loved the world that in giving Me to death for its redemption, You seem to have forsaken Me."

The next word He said was: "I thirst." His enemies hearing it took the opportunity of tormenting Him still more, for they took vinegar mingled with gall and put it to His mouth that He might drink.

The sixth word was: "It is finished." As if He said: "O Father, I have obediently fulfilled all the commands Thou gavest Me; wherefore now, if it please Thee, receive Me again to Thyself."

The seventh word was the prayer which every dying Christian who has served God loves to utter as he leaves this world for ever: "Father, into Thy hands I commend My spirit."

My child, you must often meditate on these last words of your dying Lord, for by doing this you will keep from sin, and obtain consolation in your trials.

JESUS DIES ON THE CROSS.

When Jesus had with a loud voice said these last words, bowing His head, He gave up the ghost.

"And behold the veil of the temple was rent in two, from the top even to the bottom; and the earth quaked and the rocks were rent, and the graves were opened, and many bodies of the Saints that had slept arose, and coming out of the tombs after His resurrection, came into the holy city and appeared to many.

"Now, the centurion and they that were with him watching Jesus, having seen the earthquake and the things that were done, were sore afraid, saying: 'Indeed, this was the Son of God. And all the multitude that were come together to that sight and saw the things that were done, returned striking their breasts."

JESUS LAID IN THE TOMB.

"And when it was evening there came a certain rich man of Arimathea, named Joseph, who also himself was a disciple of Jesus.

He went to Pilate and asked for the body of Jesus. But Pilate wondered that He should be already dead, and sending for the centurion, he asked him if He were really dead. And when he had understood it by the centurion, he commanded that the body should be delivered up.

"And Joseph, buying fine linen, and taking Him down, wrapped Him in the fine linen, and laid Him in his own new monument which he had hewed out in a rock, and he rolled a great stone to the door of the sepulcher and went his way."

Such, my child, is the history of Our dear Lord's death, given us in the sacred Scriptures. Often, and especially during Passiontide, read it with very great devotion and love, for it was for you He suffered all these torments and died that cruel death.

THE SOUL OF JESUS IN LIMBO.

My child, as soon as Our Divine Lord had expired on the cross, His soul descended into that part of Hell called Limbo, to free the just who were there. What joy must have filled that prison when these holy souls saw that they were now to be delivered and taken up to Heaven, which Jesus had opened for them by His death.

8

THE RISEN LIFE OF JESUS CHRIST

The Apostles' Creed describes the glorious life of Our Divine Lord Jesus Christ in these words: "The third day He rose again from the dead; He ascended into Heaven, sits at the right hand of God the Father Almighty."

JESUS RISES FROM THE TOMB.

Early on Sunday morning, the first day of the week, the soul of Jesus returned to the grave, and re-entering His sacred Body, by His own power, He rose gloriously from the dead.

"And when it began to dawn," says the Scripture, "Mary Magdalene and the other Mary came to see the sepulcher. And behold there was a great earthquake, for an angel of the Lord descended from Heaven, and coming, rolled back the stone and sat upon it: and his countenance was as lightning, and his raiment as snow: and for fear of him the guards were struck with terror, and became as dead men.

"And the angel answering said to the women: 'Fear not you; for I know that you seek Jesus Who was crucified. He is not here, for He is risen as He said. Come and see the place where the Lord was laid;

and, going quickly, tell ye His disciples that He is risen, and behold He will go before you into Galilee; there you shall see Him.'"

JESUS APPEARS TO THE APOSTLES.

"Now when it was late that same day, the first day of the week, and the doors were shut where the disciples were gathered together for fear of the Jews, Jesus came and stood in the midst and said to them, 'Peace be with you.' And when He had said this, He showed them His hands and His side. The disciples therefore were glad when they saw the Lord.

"He said therefore to them again: 'Peace be to you; as the Father hath sent me, I also send you.' When He had said this, He breathed on them; and He said to them: 'Receive ye the Holy Ghost; whose sins you shall forgive they are forgiven them, and whose sins you shall retain they are retained.'"

JESUS APPEARS TO ST. THOMAS.

"Now Thomas, one of the twelve, who is called Didymus, was not with them when Jesus came. The other disciples therefore said to him: 'We have seen the Lord.'

"But he said to them: 'Except I see in His hands the print of the nails, and put my finger into the place of the nails, and put my hand into His side, I will not believe.'

"And after eight days again, His disciples were within, and Thomas with them. Jesus cometh, the door being shut, and stood in the midst and said: 'Peace be to you.'

"Then He saith to Thomas: 'Put in thy finger hither, and see my hands; and bring hither thy hand, and put it into My side, and be not faithless, but believing.'

Thomas answered and said to Him: 'My Lord and my God.'

Jesus saith to Him: 'Because thou hast seen Me, Thomas, thou hast believed. Blessed are they that have not seen and have believed.'"

Forty days after Jesus rose from the dead He ascended into

Heaven, to take possession of His kingdom and to prepare a place in it for us."

HISTORY OF OUR LORD'S ASCENSION.

On the fortieth day after His resurrection from the dead, Jesus led out His Apostles and disciples as far as Bethania, to the Mount of Olives. There raising up His hands He blessed them; and "while they looked on He was raised up and carried up to Heaven, and a cloud received Him out of their sight.

"And while they were beholding Him going up to Heaven, behold two men stood by them in white garments, who also said: 'Ye men of Galilee, why stand you looking up to Heaven? This Jesus Who is taken up from you into Heaven shall so come as you have seen Him going into Heaven.'

"And they adoring went back to Jerusalem with great joy" (St. Luke XXIV.; Acts I.).

ST. PAUL'S ADVICE.

My child, St. Paul tells us that if we really love Jesus Christ we should have our hearts in Heaven, not in this world. "Seek the things that are above," he says, "where Christ is sitting at the right hand of God. Mind the things that are above, not the things that are upon the earth." This is what the Saints did, and by doing this they reached that happiness they now possess.

ST. JOHN FISHER AT DEATH.

St. John Fisher was condemned to die because he would not deny his Faith, and would not yield to the iniquitous desires of an ambitious King.

As he was advanced in age and weak from the sufferings he had endured, he leant upon his staff as he was led to the place of his death. But when he reached the scaffold he threw away the staff, saying: "Take courage, my feet, you have not much more to do; a few steps more, and you will bring me into the house of my God, where my sufferings shall be changed into joy."

My child, the Saints were frail and weak like you. What was it, then, that gave them so much courage and joy in their trials? It was the thought that Jesus had gone before them into Heaven to prepare a place for them.

"ARISE AND COME."

St. Pardulphus, Abbot of Gueret, spent his whole life in works of penance. He thought continually of the place which Jesus went up to Heaven to prepare for him, and from this thought he drew that courage which made him persevere to the end.

When the day of his death drew near, he saw in a vision a ladder reaching from earth to Heaven. St. Michael, the archangel, stood beside him, and said: "O Pardulphus, man of God, arise, come quickly and ascend this ladder. At the top of it you will meet Jesus Christ, and you shall receive from Him the crown of glory He has prepared for you as a reward for your sufferings on earth."

My child, Jesus has prepared a place for you also in Heaven. Take courage, then; bear your cross patiently, and you shall one day occupy it.

HEAVEN OUR TRUE COUNTRY.

In the life of the holy martyr Pamphilius, we read that many pagans who saw the great joy that filled the Christians when they were condemned to die for Jesus Christ, wondered how they could be so happy. And when they were told that it was because they were so soon to see God in Heaven, and to enjoy the happiness God had prepared for them, they also wished to become Christians, that they might share in that happiness. It was in this way that God brought them into His holy Church.

They had not long to wait for the martyr's crown. For the Prefect of Cesarea, hearing of what had taken place, sent soldiers to bring them before him.

One of the first questions he put to them was: "What country do you belong to?"

"Our country is Heaven," was the answer; "it is there where our God and our Savior dwells. When He had suffered and died for us, and rose again from the dead, He went up to Heaven to prepare a place for us. So Heaven is our home."

The Prefect was very angry at the tone of confidence in which they said these words, and commanded them to suffer the most inhuman tortures.

But the holy martyrs were not frightened. They kept their eyes constantly fixed on Heaven, and encouraged each other with these words: "In Heaven is our God and our Saviour: Heaven is our country, Heaven is our home; let us take courage, we will soon be there." And thus they persevered to the end.

Life of St. Pamphilius.

PART V

JESUS CHRIST OUR TEACHER

1

"LEARN OF ME."

"Learn of Me."

These are the words of Jesus Christ Himself, and He says them to all His children, that they may try to be like Him. You must, therefore, my child, try to imitate Jesus Christ, and learn from His example how to become perfect.

He has also taught you by His words how you can save your soul. You must, therefore, not only listen to these words, but also put them into practice; for He again says: 'Blessed are those who hear the words of God and keep them.'

THE VISION OF PETER OF FECELANO.

A very holy young man called Peter of Fecelano, who lived in Sienna, had one night a beautiful vision.

He thought he was standing in a great church, the floor of which was covered with dust and little rough stones. Suddenly the heavy door at the front of the church was thrown open, and someone entered.

Peter looked to see who had come in, and he saw that it was Our Blessed Savior Himself, under the appearance of a poor man, suffering great pain from wounds in His hands and in His feet. He walked slowly and with difficulty over the rough stones, onward through the church, till He came to the altar, leaving the prints of His feet upon the ground. The floor of the church was also covered with blood, which had run down from His wounds.

When He reached the altar, He sat down on a beautiful throne that was there, all bright and shining like the sun.

Very soon after He had taken His seat upon the throne, another person came into the church; it was His most holy Mother Mary, and she walked exactly on the footprints of her Divine Son. When she came up to the altar, He received her with the greatest joy, and placed her on a throne at His right hand.

Then others came in: they were the holy Apostles and the martyrs. After these came many others of every nation, and of every state of life—Kings and Princes and poor men and women—all of whom took great care to walk in the footsteps of their Divine Master.

When they reached the altar where He was, they also were received with great love by Jesus, Who, after embracing them one by one, made them all sit down beside Him on thrones of light.

In a very short time, as Peter was gazing at this beautiful vision in the sanctuary, it disappeared, and he awoke.

"It is not difficult," he said to himself, "to know the meaning of what I have seen. If I wish to reach Heaven, I also must take care to walk in the footsteps of Jesus Christ, as Our Blessed Lady, and the Apostles, and the Saints have done. It may be through sufferings and trials, and over rough ways; but that matters not, if I can only reach the sanctuary of Heaven and obtain a place there, in the happy company of Jesus and His Saints forever."

Catechisme Pratique.

WALKING IN HIS FOOTSTEPS.

Wenceslaus of Bohemia was not only a great King, but also a great Saint. He found his chief delight in visiting Jesus in the most Holy

Sacrament; and not content with going there during the daytime, he would often rise from his bed at night, to adore his King and his Master in the holy tabernacle.

These pious pilgrimages he performed in secret; none knew about them, with the exception of one of his servants, whom he had chosen to accompany him, on account of his great piety, and on whose secrecy he knew he could depend. One night in the winter-time, when the rivers were covered with ice, and the snow lay deep on the roads, the King went out as usual to make his visits. His servant went with him.

As they were going along the road the poor man began to tremble on account of the intense cold. His feet were so benumbed that he could scarcely walk, although he had taken care to cover them with thick fur shoes. At length he complained to his royal master, and said that it would be impossible for him to go a step further, for he was nearly frozen.

The holy King answered: "Try, my dear friend, to walk in the prints my feet have made in the snow, and perhaps you will not feel the cold so much."

The servant did this, and, wonderful to relate, his feet immediately became warm; he no longer felt cold, and found no difficulty in accompanying his master to the different churches he visited, although the cold continued to be as intense as before.

Life of St. Wenceslaus.

If you walk in the footsteps of Jesus, my child, you will not find much difficulty in bearing the trials and afflictions of this life; for as virtue went forth from Him, when He was on this earth, to all those who approached Him, so also, if you keep near Him in spirit, you will find strength to bear these trials.

THE DOCTRINE THAT JESUS TAUGHT.

The whole of the teaching of Jesus Christ is contained in these two great virtues: the love of God and of our neighbor.

One day, a certain lawyer stood up tempting Him, and saying: "Master, what must I do to possess eternal life?"

But He said to him: "What is written in the law, how readest thou?"

He answering said: "Thou shalt love the Lord thy God with thy whole heart, and with thy whole soul, and with all thy strength, and with all thy mind, and thy neighbor as thyself."

And He answered him: "Thou hast answered right. This do, and thou shalt live" (St. Luke X. 25).

My child, what is the cause of all the evils that are in the world, and of all the crimes that people commit? It is because God is not loved as He ought to be, and because we do not love our neighbor as ourselves. If these two commandments were observed as they ought to be, this world would be like Heaven itself.

It was to put men in mind of these two commandments that Jesus Christ came to preach His Gospel. He had so great a desire to instruct them that He went about through the towns and villages, preaching in the synagogues and public places, by the wayside and everywhere. He spoke with so much sweetness that the people followed Him in crowds wherever He went.

In order that this heavenly doctrine might be handed down to all ages, He established His Church, and chose twelve Apostles, who were to go throughout the whole world and teach the things He had taught them. At the present day the Bishops and priests of the Church, who are the successors of the Apostles, teach us the same truths that Jesus preached long ago to the people of Judea.

THE MIRACLES OF JESUS CHRIST.

To prove that He was the true Son of God and the Messiah promised to redeem mankind, Jesus worked many miracles. A miracle is something that man cannot do, because it is beyond the power of human nature, but which is easy to God, Who can do all things.

With five barley loaves He fed more than five thousand persons. At His command Lazarus, who had been dead for four days, came forth alive from the tomb. One day He went to His disciples walking on the water as if He had been on dry land. With one word He calmed the sea in a terrible tempest, which threatened to destroy the ship in which He and His Apostles were. At the marriage feast of Cana in Galilee He, at the request of His Blessed Mother, changed water into wine. He cured the sick wherever He went, gave sight to the blind, and made the dumb speak, so that the people cried out: "This is of a truth the prophet that is to come into the world" (St. John VI. 14).

In sending His Apostles to preach His Gospel to all nations, He gave them power to do the things He Himself did. They also healed the sick, raised the dead to life, and performed many wonderful things, to show that it was God Who sent them.

But there was a difference in the way in which the Apostles and the Saints worked these miracles—they always did them in the Name of Jesus Christ. When St. Peter cured the lame man at the gate of the Temple of Jerusalem, he said to him: "In the Name of Jesus Christ of Nazareth, arise and walk."

But Jesus worked His miracles by His own power. He said to a certain man who was a leper: "I will; be thou made clean"; He said to Lazarus: "Come forth"; and to a young man who was dead: "Young man, I say to thee, Arise."

So, my child, Jesus Christ is really God, equal to His Father, since He has done those works which God alone can do. We must, therefore, believe in Him and be His true disciples by following the doctrine He has taught us.

2

JESUS IN HIS INFANCY TEACHES US HUMILITY

In His Divine Infancy, Jesus teaches you, my child, to be humble; for although He is the great and eternal God, He became for our sakes a poor, lowly child.

The Saints call humility the 'foundation of all other virtues,' and the reason of this is, because without it all other virtues would soon fade away or fall to pieces, just as a house, no matter how beautiful it may be, would fall to the ground unless it were built on a solid foundation.

THE GREATEST SINNER.

St. Francis of Assisi was one of those Saints whom God raised up to accomplish His greatest works. Every day of his life he became more and more holy, so that the fame of his sanctity was soon spread over the whole world.

One day God was pleased to show to one of the disciples of St. Francis the place He had prepared in Heaven for the great Saint. It was high above the angels, even among the Seraphim who are so near the throne of God.

Not long after this he met St. Francis, and said to him: "My Father, would you be pleased to tell me what opinion you have of yourself, and of the good you have done."

"My dear brother," he answered, "I believe that there is nowhere on the face of the earth so great a sinner as I am."

"But, beloved Father," answered the other, "how can you say that? Or how can that be true? Are there not murderers, and thieves, and other criminals in the world who have been guilty of enormous crimes; how can you say, then, that you are the greatest sinner on the face of the earth?"

The Saint answered: "Of one thing I am certain, that if these criminals of whom you speak had received from God the same graces as I have received, they would be infinitely more holy, and more grateful to God than I have been. And I am also certain that if God had for an instant left me to myself, I would have fallen into greater sins than they have committed, and would have become the greatest sinner in the whole world."

My child, what an example is that for you! When you are tempted to think well of yourself because you are better than others, you must remember that if it had not been for God's grace, you would not have been so good, and then you will thank God for being so kind to you.

"WHAT MUST I DO TO BE GOOD?"

The Blessed Curé of Ars was asked one day by one who had taken a firm resolution to serve God faithfully: "Father, what must I do to be good?"

"My child, you must love the good God."

"And what am I to do in order that I may love God?"

"Ah! my child, be humble," he answered. "Humility! humility! humility! It is our pride that prevents us from becoming saints."

ADVICE OF FATHER LEFEVRE.

A certain person went to Father Lefevre and said to him: "My Father, I am anxious to become a saint. Tell me what work of piety I ought to perform that I may reach the Kingdom of Heaven."

"I recommend you to prostrate yourself on the ground from time to time before your crucifix," answered the holy priest, "and say to Jesus Christ: 'O my Jesus, be Thou my model and the example of my life. Thou didst humble Thyself, even so far as to die on the cross for me, and I am so proud. Thou wert obedient even unto death, and I am always seeking my own will. Thou wert a 'Man of Sorrows' from Thy birth, and I am always afraid of suffering. O Jesus, teach me to be humble and obedient and patient, like Thee.'

The man followed this simple advice, and soon became very perfect.

IN THE CEMETERY.

One day St. Elizabeth of Hungary, when quite a young girl, was playing with her companions, who were all of the same age as herself. They began to show her their beautiful clothes and the precious ornaments they were wearing.

St. Elizabeth made no remark, but quietly taking them to a cemetery which was not far distant, she pointed to the tombs, and said: "The people who are buried there, beneath the ground, were once beautiful and young as we are. What are they like now? And what has become of all the fine apparel they wore? All gone! It is all over with them. One day it will be the same with us. Why, then, should we be proud, and occupy our minds with our bodies, and think so much of what we wear? Rather let us try to think of God, and speak of those things which we can take with us when we leave the world."

Many who have led holy lives for a long time, have in the end lost all the merits of their good works, and their souls also, because they allowed pride to enter their hearts.

THE SOLITARY WHO BECAME PROUD.

We read in the life of St. Pachomius and of St. Palemon that a certain solitary was favored by God with the gift of miracles on account of his holy life; he could even walk on burning coals without feeling pain.

But these extraordinary favors of Heaven were the cause of his great fall. For he began to think himself a great saint, and far superior to all the other monks of the desert.

St. Pachomius, seeing his great danger, often spoke to him of the necessity of watching, as he had not yet reached the Kingdom of Heaven, and might still not persevere to the end. But the unfortunate man was very angry at him for his advice, and instead of attending to it only became more and more proud.

In the end, what the Saint had foreseen came to pass: the man fell into a mortal sin, and died a miserable death.

Sometimes we read of kings and others in high positions performing the most humble works; they did this that they might keep themselves from falling into pride.

BLESSED AMADEUS, DUKE OF SAVOY.

Blessed Amadeus, Duke of Savoy, had a pious mother, who taught him to practice from his childhood the great virtue of humility.

When he succeeded his father, this virtue shone in him like a bright light on a mountain-top, and was seen by everyone.

Every day he fed a large multitude of poor people in his palace, and with his own hands served out food to them. Those amongst them who were the most decrepit and loathsome were the ones he loved best.

Some of his officers, and those in a high position in his household, once told him that although it was an excellent thing in a Prince to be charitable, he went too far in serving the poor with his royal hands. "Such an action," they said, "detracts from your dignity. It is a sufficient act of condescension on your part to be present when they receive their alms"; and they begged him not to continue any longer to serve them as he had hitherto done.

The Prince turned towards them with eyes filled with anger. "Do you believe the Gospel?" he said. "If Jesus Christ considers as done to Himself whatever we do to even the least of His disciples, what greater honor could be given to a Prince than to serve them?"

These words put an end forever to their complaints, and the good Prince continued as usual his pious work.

HUMILITY OF ST. ALOYSIUS.

When St. Aloysius was a student, he never sought to excuse himself when he was blamed for anything, whether he was guilty or not. If he was in the wrong, then he was justly found fault with; if he was blamed innocently, he said to himself: "I have certainly been wrong some other time, and I will accept this reproof for what I should have then received."

ST. ANTHONY'S SURPRISE.

One day St. Anthony had a vision, in which he saw the whole world covered with snares and nets which Satan had spread out to catch the souls of men. This sight filled him with great surprise and sadness. "O my God," he exclaimed, "who can ever hope to escape all these snares, for they are everywhere?"

He heard a voice which answered him: "The man who is humble."

SATAN HATES HUMILITY.

St. Macarius was once going to his cell with some palm-leaves with which he was accustomed to make mats. Satan appeared to him carrying a scythe, with which he tried to strike him. But he could not touch him.

"O Macarius," he said to him in a tone of great anger, "how

grieved I am that I cannot strike you. I can do the works you do better even than you are able to do them. You, indeed, sometimes fast, but I am always fasting: you sometimes watch when others sleep; I never sleep, I am always watching. But there is one thing that makes you stronger than I am, and that is your humility."

O my child, learn from the example of Jesus to be humble, and the enemy of your soul shall have no power to hurt you.

3

JESUS IN HIS CHILDHOOD TEACHES US TO LIVE WITH GOD

Jesus in His childhood gives us a beautiful example of detachment from the world and union with God. You also, dear child, must give yourself to God, even from your childhood, and during all your lifetime never cease to please Him.

ALWAYS GOD'S CHILD.

St. Euphrasia was only about seven years old when she felt within her soul a great desire to be always the child of her Father in Heaven.

So one day she went to her mother and said to her: "Oh, mother, I would like so much to be God's own child all my lifetime."

Her mother wept with joy when she heard these words. She pressed her darling to her bosom, and from her inmost heart thanked God for having put such a holy desire into the soul of her dear daughter.

When Euphrasia grew a little older, her mother took her to a convent, and placed her under the care of the holy nuns, because she knew they would teach her how to be always God's child according to her desire.

On the day when she went to the convent the Superioress gave her a little picture of the Holy Child Jesus. Euphrasia kissed it with the greatest devotion and said: "My dear Jesus, I am going to be your own child all my lifetime."

Before returning home, her mother led her into the chapel, where there was a statue of Our Divine Savior on a little altar. She knelt down before the altar, and, placing her little daughter in front of her, she prayed thus: "O Lord Jesus, take my dearest child under Your special protection. She loves You, and she desires nothing else in this world but to be Yours always."

Then, speaking to the child, she said: "My dearest child, since God has made the whole universe, and preserves it by His power, may He also enable you to persevere to the end of your life in loving Him as you do today."

When she had finished this prayer, she rose from her knees, and, leaving her little girl in the hands of the Superioress, left the convent, shedding many tears.

Some time afterwards, God took her from this weary world to go to pray for her dearest little one before His throne in Heaven.

Euphrasia never forgot her early consecration to God. Whenever the world tempted her by its vanities, or whenever the Devil tried to turn her thoughts away from God, she drove away the temptation, saying: "I promised my beloved Jesus when I was a child to be His all my lifetime, and that promise I will *never* break."

God rewarded her fidelity even in this world, for we read that He often made use of her to work His miracles. She is now in Heaven with Him; and so also, my child, will you be one day, if, like her, you be faithful to that promise you so often made to Him: "My Jesus, I am Thine and Thou art mine. Grant that I may love Thee always."

Catéchisme de Rodes.

"I AM JESUS OF NAZARETH."

St. Teresa was one day walking along one of the corridors of the convent in which she lived. Suddenly she met a little boy, very young, and very beautiful. She was astonished to see the child there, for no boy had ever been seen there before.

"Tell me, my child," she said, "who you are, and how you came here."

But the child did not answer her.

"What is your name?" St. Teresa asked. The child looked up into her face, and, with a heavenly smile upon his lips, said to her: "Tell me your name first, and then I will tell you mine."

St. Teresa answered: "Well, since you wish it, I will tell you: my name is 'Teresa of Jesus.'"

Then the little boy, in a voice of celestial sweetness, replied: "And my name is 'Jesus of Teresa.'" Saying these words, He disappeared.

It was Our Blessed Lord Himself, Who came to show His servant how much He loved her, because she loved Him and His holy Name so much.

From her Life.

O my child, love Jesus as St. Teresa did, and bear His holy Name in your heart. He may not come visibly and speak to you as He did to her, but you will certainly hear Him speaking to you in your heart, and there telling you that He loves you.

4

JESUS IN HIS PRIVATE LIFE TEACHES US OBEDIENCE

My child, of all the virtues God loves to see in a Christian child, there is not one that pleases Him so much as the virtue of obedience. It is also that virtue that brings us, even in this life, the greatest peace and happiness. Moreover, it is the one Jesus Himself practiced with the greatest perfection during the years of His private life. The Scripture says of Him: "And He went down with them" (Our Lady and St. Joseph), "and came to Nazareth, and was subject to them" (St. Luke II. 51).

"YES, FATHER, I WILL GO."

An old man some time ago told me the following story about what once happened to himself:

"One evening in the summertime as I was returning home after a hard day's work in the hayfield, tired and hungry, I met my father on the road to town. He said to me: 'I wish you would take this parcel to the village for me, James.'

"I was at that time a boy of twelve and, like other boys of my own age, I was more fond of play than of work. I was vexed that he should ask me to go to the village after my day's work, for it was about two miles distant. But I loved my father, and I showed my love for him by always obeying him at once; so I at once joyfully said: 'Yes, father, I will go.'

"'Thank you, James, my boy,' he said; 'I was going myself, but, somehow, I don't feel very well today. You have always been a good son to me, James.'

"I hurried into the town, and was soon back again. When I came near the house, I saw a crowd of people at the door. One of them came to me, the tears rolling down his face. 'Your father,' he said, 'fell dead just as he was entering the house; the last words he spoke were to you.'

"I am an old man now, but I have thanked God over and over again in all the years that have passed since that hour that these last words were: 'You have always been a good boy to me, James.'"

THE FOUR SOLITARIES AND THE ABBOT.

Four solitaries came one day to visit the great Abbot Pambo, to obtain his advice about the kind of life they ought to lead to please God with the greatest perfection.

One of them said that he fasted much; another said that he practised rigorous poverty; the third said he spent his time in works of charity; and the fourth that he had for the last twenty-two years lived in strict obedience to one whom he had chosen to guide him in the way of virtue and perfection.

When he had heard them all, the holy Abbot turned to the last one who had spoken, and said: "It seems to me, my brother, that what you do is more perfect than the good works of the others, because what they do is done by their own choice; but you, by practicing obedience, follow not your own will, but the will of another. Now, those who are obedient, and persevere in obedience to the end of their lives, are equal in merit before God to those holy ones who have confessed the faith of Jesus Christ at the risk of their lives, or who have laid down their lives in testimony of their faith."

ST. MARY MAGDALEN OF PAZZI'S OBEDIENCE.

When St. Mary Magdalen of Pazzi was a novice, her Superioress, knowing how much she loved prayer, gave her permission to spend more time at it than the other novices. "You can spend in the chapel at your prayers," she said to her, "the time in which the other religious are occupied in manual labor."

"Dear mother," replied the humble religious, "it is better that I should do as the others do, because if I fulfill these duties well in virtue of obedience, I know that I am doing the will of God; and, on the contrary, if I occupy my time with what I like myself, no matter how good the work may be, I am not seeking God's holy will so much as my own."

God loves to see this virtue of obedience, not only in your childhood, but throughout the whole course of your life, as He has often shown, even by miracles.

ST. FRANCES OF ROME.

Although St. Frances of Rome devoted her life to prayer and penance and good works, she never allowed anything to prevent her fulfilling her duties to her husband: she always obeyed his slightest wish, and never murmured at any interruption which he might cause her.

One day he sent for her when she was reciting the office of the Blessed Virgin. She went to him instantly, did what he required, and returned to her prayers. But soon another summons came, then another, and another. Four different times was she disturbed, and always for trifling reasons; but she obeyed with perfect good humor and returned to her office without having her peace of mind broken.

On taking up her book for the last time, she was surprised to see the words she had four times begun and left unfinished written in letters of gold; and her angel guardian whispered in her ear: "It is in this way that God rewards the virtue of perfect obedience." The golden letters remained in her book as long as she lived.

ST. BENEDICT AND THE LITTLE BOY MAURUS.

One day a monk named Placidus went to draw water from a lake near the monastery. In doing so, he fell into the lake and disappeared. St. Benedict, from his cell, saw the danger, and, calling the boy Maurus to his side, said to him: "Make haste; run to the lake, for Placidus has fallen into it. Go and save him."

The obedient boy knelt for the Abbot's blessing, and, thinking only of fulfilling the order he had received, ran to the lake and on to the water as if it had been solid ground, and, taking Placidus by the hair, brought him safely to the bank. It was then only that he observed that he had been walking on the water, and he was filled with amazement at it.

It was in this way that God rewarded him for his prompt obedience.

5

JESUS IN HIS PUBLIC LIFE TEACHES US TO BE MEEK

My child, when Our Lord went forth to preach His Gospel to the people, He taught them, not only by His words, but also by His example, how to reach the Kingdom of Heaven. The virtue of meekness is the chief one He proposes to us for our practice, and He esteems it so much that He promises the Kingdom of Heaven in a special manner to those who practice it. "Blessed are the meek, for they shall possess the land."

THE WAY TO PURCHASE HEAVEN.

St. Bernardine was one day, according to the rules of his Order, passing along the streets of Siena collecting alms for his monastery. He was accompanied by one of his brethren.

Some wicked men, who met the good religious, took up stones and threw them at them, wounding them on the feet. His companion was very much annoyed at this cruel treatment, and asked the Saint to speak to them so that they might go away.

But he gaily answered: "Oh no, my brother; let them torment us as long as they please; they are teaching us how to practice the great virtue of meekness, and are giving us an opportunity of gaining much merit for the Kingdom of Heaven by our patience."

WHAT I LEARNED AT SCHOOL.

A young man had been sent to a certain school at a distance from his native city, that he might receive an education in the higher branches of learning, for which that school was famous.

When his studies were ended he returned home. His father was very glad to see him, and asked him what progress he had made, and if he had gained many prizes.

The young man modestly answered: "My father, I hope to show you in a short time what I learned at school."

His father was not pleased with this answer, for he expected to hear that he had become a great scholar, and that he would be able to show him at once some of the things he had learned. So he became angry, and struck his son very cruelly, saying: "O wretched boy, you have lost all your time, and the great sums of money I have expended on your education have been thrown away."

The boy submitted without a murmur to the unjust chastisement of his father, and when his fury was exhausted he meekly said to him: "Now, my father, you see a part of what I learned at school, and you see that I have not lost my time, since I have learned the virtue of meekness, and since I have become a better boy than I was before you sent me to it."

My child, you may not be able to preach many eloquent sermons by your words, but when you are meek and gentle, your conduct has more effect on others than the most eloquent words you could utter.

ST. FRANCIS REGIS IN THE INN.

One Sunday morning, St. Francis Regis heard that in a certain hotel in the city where he dwelt, there was a large company assembled, and that they were quarreling and drinking to excess. He went at once to the place to try and put an end to the evil.

When he entered, the noise suddenly ceased. "My children," he said, with the utmost sweetness, "it is not thus that you should act. Cease, therefore, to offend God, and quarrel no more."

These words, instead of putting an end to their strife, only made them cry out the louder. They all rose up and ordered him to leave. One of them even struck him a blow on the face.

"Thanks, my dear brother," said the holy man, without any signs of anger; "if you knew me better, you would say I deserved even more than you have given me."

When the others heard this answer, and saw how far their companion had gone, they became ashamed of what they had done. They all begged his forgiveness, and immediately left the hotel in peace.

TWO LITTLE CHINESE CHILDREN.

Two little children in China—a brother and sister—were quarreling. The brother, being angry at something his little sister had done to him, raised his hand and struck her. She began to cry, but did not strike him in return, for, at that moment, the words of the "Our Father" came into her mind, and she meekly said, amidst her tears: "My dear brother, I forgive you, as I myself hope one day to be forgiven."

The brother, hearing these words, was very sorry for what he had done, for he also called to mind the lessons he had received, and the resolution he had taken to practice them. He had forgotten them at the moment that he had struck his sister; but when he heard her gentle words of forgiveness they came back to his mind, and he said: "My own little sister, it was very wrong in me to strike you; won't you try and forget that I did it, and I will never do it again?"

But she had already pardoned him. And so faithful to his promise was he that he was never after that time seen to be angry with anyone, or to say an angry word.

"JESUS SUFFERED MORE THAN I DO."

St. Vincent of Paul was frequently calumniated, but he never tried to justify himself.

One of the priests under his care said to him one day, when some person had spoken untruthfully of him: "Father, why do you not justify yourself, since you are so falsely accused?"

"My brother," was his reply, "I will try to justify myself by my works, but never by my words."

Another day, when he was speaking to the Queen, she told him that he had been accused to her of a certain fault of which she knew that he could not be guilty. The Saint, without the least sign of disappointment, said: "Madam, I know I am a great sinner."

"But you are innocent of this sin; why, then, do you not endeavor to justify yourself?"

St. Vincent answered: "Jesus Christ was calumniated more than I have been, yet He did not try to justify Himself, neither will I."

6

JESUS IN HIS SUFFERING LIFE TEACHES US HOW TO BEAR OUR CROSS

My child, Jesus in His suffering life teaches you that the royal road to Heaven is suffering patiently, through love for Him, all the crosses and trials of this short life, because it is His holy Will.

A GREAT SCHOLAR WHO COULD NOT LEARN ANYTHING.

Blessed Veronica of Binasco was the daughter of very poor parents, who had often great difficulty in procuring even the necessaries of life. So from her very infancy the child had to go to work, and received no education.

But she was a pious child, and very devout to Our Blessed Lady.

When she began to grow up, she had a great desire to learn to read. During the daytime she had no leisure for this, so she sat up at night when her parents had gone to rest, that she might learn to read. Still she made no progress, because she had no one to teach her.

One night, being very sad and weary, she asked Our Blessed Lady herself to come and teach her.

Mary appeared to her; but the poor child was terribly frightened when she saw her, and fell on the ground.

The Blessed Virgin said to her: "Don't be afraid, my child; I myself have come to teach you. There are just three letters you need to learn, and when you have learned them you will have learned enough."

The first one is white, the second black, and the third one red."

Veronica said to Our Lady: "O Mary, dearest Mother, teach me what these three letters mean."

Mary answered: "The white one means purity of heart; the black one means compassion for poor sinners (for whom my Son Jesus died) and zeal for their conversion; and the red one means devotion to the sufferings of Jesus. Study these three letters well, and it matters little whether or not you know anything else."

Saying these words, Our Lady disappeared

From her Life.

When a person keeps before his eyes all that Jesus said and did during His Sacred Passion, it will be easy for him to bear patiently the evils that come to him in this world.

"I AM NOT AFRAID."

There was once a pious young girl who wanted to be a nun. She went to a convent of the Carmelites and asked the Superioress to admit her into that convent.

"My child," said the Superioress, "our Order is a most severe one, and I am afraid that you would not be able to practice all the austerities which our rule enjoins. Come, and I will show you how severe is the life we lead."

So she led the young postulant through the convent and showed her the poor food, and the hard beds, and the silent and heavy work which was the portion of all those who dwelt within the convent walls. She did this on purpose to try her. But nothing that she saw seemed to frighten her; on the contrary, she seemed to view everything with calm serenity.

After showing her all these things, and describing to her all she would have to suffer if she became a Carmelite nun, she said to her: "Now, my child, tell me, how could you bear that hard and trying life?"

"Reverend mother," she replied, "may I ask you one question?"

"Certainly, my child."

"Are there any crucifixes in the convent?"

"Yes, there is one in every room, as you must have seen."

"Ah, then, do not be afraid of me, for if there is a crucifix in my cell where you say my hard bed will be, and in the place where I will receive such poor food, and in the church where I will have to spend so much time in prayer, I will not find any difficulty in bearing with all you have described to me; the sight of my dear Jesus on the cross will give me strength and courage to surmount them all."

The Superioress at once consented to admit her, and she became a model of piety and fervor to all the other nuns.

Catéch. en Exemples.

THE LADY'S CROSS.

There was a pious lady who lay on her bed of sickness, enduring great pain. One day a friend came to visit her. When she saw the awful sufferings the good lady was enduring, she pointed to a crucifix which stood on a table near the bed, saying: "Let us ask our dear Lord to free you from these cruel pains, and I am sure He will not refuse to hear us."

But the other answered: "What do you say? How can you keep your eyes on the cross and advise me to do that? It is just the sight of Jesus nailed to the cross that tells me that I also must remain nailed to my cross."

"Ah!" replied her friend, "I see now where you obtain that courage which makes you suffer so patiently; but do you not sometimes wish that God would free you from your pains?"

"It is true," she replied, "sometimes the pain seems almost more than I can bear, but then I think of Jesus on His cross, and I say to myself: 'Jesus suffered for me more than I am suffering for Him, and He did not complain,' and thus I feel encouraged to suffer still more. I do not wish to be like the bad thief who desired to be taken off his cross, but rather like the good thief who wished to remain upon it; and like him I pray to Jesus to remember me now that He is in His heavenly kingdom."

Rep. du Catéch.

"I AM INNOCENT."

St. Peter of Verona, one of God's holy martyrs, was falsely accused of a great crime, and in punishment for it was banished to a lonely spot far away from all who knew him.

For a long time he bore this heavy cross with joy and patience, but as years rolled on he began to feel weary. One day as he was praying before the great crucifix in the church, he complained to Our Lord: "O my God," he said, "You know I am innocent of the crime of which I was accused, and that I am suffering this punishment without having merited it."

But Our Lord answered him: "And I also, Peter, was innocent. Did I deserve to receive all the injuries and insults and sufferings men heaped upon Me in My passion? Learn, then, from My example to suffer with joy the greatest punishments even for crimes which you have never committed."

These words of Jesus consoled him. From that time he felt great joy in suffering, and nothing gave him so much consolation as to suffer humiliation for the love of God.

God in His own good time showed the innocence of His servant, and he was not only restored to his former position, but loaded with greater honor and glory than before, according to the words of Our Blessed Lord, "He that humbleth himself shall be exalted."

THE COUNT ELEAZAR.

The Count Eleazar was one of those few men who, living in the world and occupying a high position in society, had his whole soul with God in Heaven.

But he had many crosses to bear—he could not have become a saint without them. People said many things about him which were not true, and blamed him for many things of which he was altogether innocent. He heard all these calumnies without so much as appearing to hear them, and even sometimes smiled.

His wife Delphina, although also very virtuous, did not understand how he could bear so patiently all the cruel things that were said about him. One day, when he had been accused of something worse than usual, she said to him: "I am astonished you can bear all these evil words so patiently."

He answered: "My dear wife, of what use would it be for me to get angry? It would not make the case any better, neither would it silence my enemies. But I will tell you my secret.

"Every time I meet with any humiliation, I think of my Divine Lord standing before Pilate, and that I hear Him accused by false witnesses, calumniated by his enemies, ill-treated by the soldiers, despised and insulted by the Jews, on whom He had conferred so many blessings, and who, only a few days previously, had hailed Him with shouts of 'Hosanna!' Finally, I think I see Him innocently condemned to death by His most unjust judges.

"Then I say to myself: 'What comparison does the little injury I am receiving bear to the cruel treatment and the insults the most innocent Jesus had to endure? And all this, too, for my sake.' This thought, my dearest wife, makes me calm, and keeps down the angry thoughts when they begin to rise within me."

Rep. du Catéch., II. 92.

BROTHER JUNIPER'S PRECIOUS JEWELS.

Among the companions of St. Francis there was one who was remarkable for his great simplicity. He was called Brother Juniper. No one ever saw him angry, and if anyone desired to see him at the height of his joy, he had only to call him names and laugh at him.

One day he was passing through the streets along with St. Francis, when he met a person who had been a great companion of his in his boyhood, but who had grown up without any fear of God.

As soon as this man saw Brother Juniper, he began to call him a fool for having deserted the world and its pleasures. But as these words only made the good brother laugh, he became very angry, and uttered every abusive word that his memory could suggest.

Brother Juniper was only the more pleased at this, and taking up the ends of his tunic, as people are accustomed to do when they are going to carry something, he said: "Come, don't be so sparing with those precious stones; throw me some more of them."

This was the name he gave to all the injuries and insults people gave him.

St. Francis, who heard these words, said to those who were with him: "I wish we had a whole forest of such Junipers as this one."

Yes, God will one day gather up each one of the trials and affronts we have suffered lovingly for Him, and will place them like precious jewels in the crown which He will give us in Heaven.

BROTHER BERNARD'S GREAT JOY.

"What is it that gives you so much joy today, Brother Bernard?" said one of his companions to him.

He answered: "I have received today something brighter even than the purest gold; something greater than the highest honor on earth."

"And what is it?" asked the other.

"The Cross," said the Saint. "Today a heavy trial has come upon me, and the world has said much against me. Today I have indeed found a pearl of great price."

It was in this way the Saints spoke of affliction. It made them happy, because it made them throw themselves on God, and think of their home in Heaven.

THE PATIENCE OF ST. NORBERT.

St. Norbert was once trying to make some people change their lives. They had for a long time been accustomed to live in a very careless manner, and no one had the courage to correct them.

St. Norbert's words were far from being pleasing to many of them. Some even went so far as to openly insult him, and one of them, more rude than the rest, went up to him and spat on his face, and would have done even more had he not been prevented by those who were present.

The insult was indeed a most shameful one, but the Saint tried to excuse the man, and in his heart thanked God for having given him a share in the ignominies of His sacred Passion, and an occasion of doing penance for his sins.

Learn, then, my child, to bear patiently, as the Saints did, the crosses and trials which meet you every day, and keep in mind that God sends them to you that you may gain merit for Heaven.

ST. ROSE OF LIMA'S PATIENCE.

When St. Rose of Lima was only a very young child, it happened that someone thoughtlessly pinched her thumb by shutting the lid of a box hurriedly. The pain was very great, but she tried to conceal it. Her mother, who was soon told of what had occurred to her child, ran at once to help her; but Rose hid her finger, and did not let it appear that there was anything the matter with her.

THOSE WHOM JESUS LOVES BEST.

Jesus Christ one day appeared to St. Teresa and told her that the souls who were dearest to His Father were those who suffered most, especially when they accepted their sufferings with love.

From that moment the Saint endured her sufferings with the greatest joy, because she knew that at that moment she was the most pleasing to her Father in Heaven, and used to say that she would not exchange her sufferings for all the treasures of the world. Her maxim was this: "To suffer or to die."

BLESSED ANGELA ON JOY IN SUFFERINGS.

One day Blessed Angela of Foligno was asked how she could suffer so much and be at the same time so full of joy and happiness.

She answered: "Believe me, we do not know the real value of sufferings, for, if we really knew their value, instead of repining when under pain or suffering, we would rather rejoice, and would always be happiest when we had most to suffer."

ST. FRANCIS' PRAYER.

St. Francis of Assisi was once suffering the most acute pain; he seemed to all who saw him to be in intense agony. One of the brethren, filled with compassion at his condition, begged him to pray to God that He would take away from him at least part of the pain, since it was so exceedingly great.

The only answer the Saint made was this: "O Lord, my God, I return Thee most fervent thanks for the sufferings Thou hast been pleased to send me, and I beseech Thee to increase rather than diminish them."

It was in this way that the Saints showed their esteem for sufferings.

SAYINGS OF SOME OF THE SAINTS ABOUT SUFFERINGS.

St. John of the Cross said that if the choice were given to him to be placed in Heaven along with the angels, or to be sent to prison with the Apostle St. Paul, he would prefer to go to prison rather than into Heaven, because in prison he would be able to gain more glory for paradise.

St. Louis of France, while speaking to the King of England on the immense sufferings he had to endure when he was in captivity, said to him: "I thank God with my whole heart for the misfortunes that befell me at that time; I am filled with more joy at the thought of the patience that God then granted me, than if He had made me master of the world."

A certain holy man, who had passed a whole year without being sick or suffering any pain, lovingly complained of it to God, saying: "O my God, Thou hast surely forsaken me this year, since Thou hast not sent me any infirmity."

A servant of God who was suffering great pain from a malady with which he was afflicted, said this prayer to God: "O my God, if Thou wishest to increase my sufferings, be pleased also to increase my patience." Then, speaking to himself, he said: "O my soul, take courage now; just have a little patience for a short time longer, and, like the good thief, you will pay all the debts due by your sins and gain eternal rest in Heaven."

When the Apostle St. Andrew was being led to the place of his death, he saw at a distance the cross on which he was to die. As soon as he beheld it he exclaimed in a transport of joy: "O good cross, so many years desired, and now at length granted to my longing soul; with confidence and great joy I come unto thee. Do thou in like manner rejoice and be glad at receiving a disciple of Him Who hung upon thee."

ST. VINCENT OF PAUL IN HIS SUFFERINGS.

When St. Vincent of Paul was a young man, he was afflicted with so much pain that sometimes he could not get any rest night or day. But in the midst of all this pain, his countenance was always serene and joyful, as if he was enjoying perfect health. Never was there heard to come forth from his mouth a complaint of any kind, and he was always blessing and praising God for His goodness to him. He looked on his sufferings as so many special blessings from God; and when at any time the severity of the pain brought a sigh to his lips, he immediately turned towards the crucifix, where he always found new courage. "I am suffering very little indeed," he used then to say, "in comparison with the inconceivable pain which Jesus Christ suffered for love of me."

One of his priests having one day seen that his legs were swollen to a great extent and were full of sores, said to him in a tone of compassion: "O my Father, the pain you suffer from these sores must surely be insupportable."

The Saint immediately answered: "What do you say? How can you say that anything that God sends to us is insupportable? May God forgive you for what you have said. It is not in that manner that one ought to speak of what Jesus Christ ordains. Besides, is it not just that God should chastise with severity those who have offended Him as I have done? And do we not entirely belong to God, and cannot He do with us whatever He likes?"

THE KNIGHT HILDEBRAND.

Long ago a certain knight called Hildebrand had received a great insult from another nobleman, who had an ill-will towards him. Hildebrand felt the insult so keenly that he determined to be revenged.

Accordingly he sent a challenge to his enemy, and appointed the time and the place where they would meet and fight a duel, for in those days it was supposed that blood alone could wipe out injuries of this kind.

When the day came, Hildebrand rose early and prepared for the combat. As he was going towards the place appointed, he had to pass by a chapel, and as the hour of meeting had not yet come, he thought he might go into the chapel to wait.

So he entered. He began to walk around the chapel, and to examine the pictures that hung upon the wall. The first one he looked at represented Our Divine Savior being clad in a fool's garment by Herod, and underneath he read those words: "He rendered not evil for evil."

After looking at this one for a few moments, he went on a little further, and stood before another, representing the scourging of Our Lord at the pillar. Below this picture were the following words: "When He suffered He threatened not." Near this one hung another. It was the death of Jesus on the Cross. The inscription on this picture was the dying prayer of Jesus to His Heavenly Father for His murderers: "Father, forgive them, they know not what they do."

It was not by chance that Hildebrand had gone into this church: God, who desired earnestly his conversion, had led him in, and now His grace spoke to him by these pictures. As the ice melts away before the heat of the sun, so did his anger melt away at the sight of these holy pictures. He threw himself on his knees and began to pray. He prayed for pardon for himself and pardon for the one who had injured him.

The hour came for the contest to begin. Hildebrand rose from his knees to go and meet his enemy, who was awaiting him. But what was the surprise of the latter to see the knight walk up to him, take him by the hand, and ask his forgiveness. "Jesus forgave His enemies and prayed for them; let us do the same," he said.

The other willingly acceded to his request, and from that day forward they became the greatest friends.

Catéchism en Exemples.

Since every little pain or trouble in this world will have its special reward in Heaven, if we bear it patiently for God's sake, you ought, my child, to be glad when God gives you an opportunity of gaining this reward.

7

JESUS IN HIS GLORIOUS LIFE TEACHES US TO DESIRE HEAVEN

Lastly, Jesus teaches us by His resurrection and ascension into Heaven, to despise this world, and to fix all our thoughts in Heaven, which is our eternal home.

THE DEATH OF ST. JEROME.

When the friends of St. Jerome saw him lying in a burning fever, which was so soon to prove fatal, they were filled with grief, but not one of them had the courage to tell him of his danger. As they stood around his bed, tears fell from their eyes, but no one spoke.

"My children," he said, "why do you weep? I know the news you wish to give me. These tears tell me there is no longer any hope of recovery."

"Alas, Father, it is too true!" they replied. "The physician has just told us plainly that you are going to leave us."

"Oh! what joyful news you have brought me, my children; may God reward you. The time is at length come when I shall enter into the presence of my God in Heaven, there to be filled with eternal joy! O my children, weep not, but rather rejoice with me at this happiness."

From his Life.

PART VI
JESUS CHRIST OUR JUDGE

1

THE GENERAL JUDGMENT

My child, when you are asked the question, "Will Christ come again?" you immediately answer: "Yes, Christ will come again at the last day to judge all men;" and when you are asked: "Shall not every man be judged at death?" you answer: "Yes, everyone shall be judged at death, as well as at the last day." The former is called the general judgment, and the latter the particular judgment.

Of all the things that can happen to us, there is nothing so terrible as these two judgments of God, because our happiness or misery in the life to come depends upon the sentence we shall then receive. We should often, then, think of these judgments of God. We shall consider, in the first place, the General Judgment—that judgment which will take place when time is over and the "world shall be no more."

It is Jesus Christ Himself Who gives us an account of the terrible Day of Judgment.

THE END OF JERUSALEM, AND THE LAST JUDGMENT.

"When you shall see the abomination of desolation," said Jesus to His disciples, "which was spoken of by Daniel the prophet, standing in the holy place: he that readeth, let him understand. Then they that are in Judea, let them flee to the mountains, and he that is on the house-top, let him not come down to take anything out of his house: and he that is in the field, let him not go back to take his coat. And woe to them that are with child, and that give suck in those days. But pray that your flight be not in the winter, or on the Sabbath.

"For there shall be then great tribulation, such as hath not been from the beginning of the world until now, neither shall be. And unless those days had been shortened, no flesh should be saved: but for the sake of the elect those days shall be shortened. Then if any man shall say to you: 'Lo here is Christ, or there,' do not believe him. For there shall arise false Christs and false prophets, and shall show great signs and wonders, insomuch as to deceive (if possible) even the elect. Behold I have told it to you beforehand.

"If therefore they shall say to you: 'Behold He is in the desert;' go ye not out: 'Behold He is in the closets;' believe it not. For as lightning cometh out of the east, and appeareth even into the west: so shall also the coming of the Son of Man be. Wheresoever the body shall be, there shall the eagles also be gathered together.

"And immediately after the tribulation of those days, the sun shall be darkened, and the moon shall not give her light, and the stars shall fall from Heaven, and the powers of Heaven shall be moved. And then shall appear the sign of the Son of Man in Heaven: and then shall all the tribes of the earth mourn: and they shall see the Son of Man coming in the clouds of Heaven with much power and majesty.

"And He shall send His angels with a trumpet, and a great voice: and they shall gather together his elect from the four winds, from the farthest parts of the Heavens to the utmost bounds of them.

"And from the fig-tree learn a parable: when the branch thereof is now tender, and the leaves come forth, you know that summer is nigh. So you also, when you shall see all these things, know ye that it is nigh even at the doors. Amen I say to you, that this generation shall not pass, till all these things be done. Heaven and earth shall pass, but My words shall not pass. But of that day and hour no one knoweth, no, not the angels of Heaven, but the Father alone. And as in the days of Noe, so shall also the coming of the Son of Man be. Watch ye therefore, because you know not what hour your Lord will come."

St. Matthew XXIV. 15 *et seq.*

THE "COMING OF THE SON OF MAN."

"And when the Son of Man shall come in His majesty, and all the angels with Him, then shall He sit upon the seat of His majesty; and all nations shall be gathered together before Him, and He shall separate them one from another, as the shepherd separates the sheep from the goats: and He shall set the sheep on His right hand and the goats on His left.

"Then shall the King say to them that shall be on His right hand: 'Come, ye blessed of my Father, possess you the kingdom prepared for you from the foundation of the world. For I was hungry, and you gave me to eat: I was thirsty, and you gave me to drink: I was a stranger, and you took me in: naked, and you covered me: sick, and you visited me: I was in prison, and you came to me.' Then shall the just answer Him, saying: 'Lord, when did we see Thee hungry, and fed Thee; thirsty, and gave Thee drink? And when did we see Thee a stranger, and took Thee in? or naked, and covered Thee? Or when did we see Thee sick or in prison, and came to Thee?'

"And the King answering, shall say unto them: 'Amen I say to you, as long as you did it to one of these my least brethren, you did it to Me.'

"Then He shall say to them also that shall be on His left hand: 'Depart from Me, you cursed, into everlasting fire which was prepared for the devil and his angels. For I was hungry, and you gave Me not to eat; I was thirsty, and you gave Me not to drink; I was a stranger, and you took me not in; naked, and you covered Me not; sick and in prison, and you did not visit me.'

"Then they also shall answer Him, saying: 'Lord, when did we see

Thee hungry, or thirsty, or a stranger, or naked, or sick, or in prison, and did not minister to Thee?'

"Then He shall answer them, saying: 'Amen I say to you, as long as you did it not to one of these least, neither did you do it to Me.'

"And these shall go into everlasting punishment: but the just into life everlasting."

St. Matthew XXV. 31 *et seq.*

THE REMORSE OF THE WICKED.

The Holy Ghost in the Sacred Scriptures tells us of the terrible remorse of the wicked when they shall see themselves condemned to a miserable eternity at the Day of Judgment.

"Then shall the just stand with great constancy against those who have afflicted them, and taken away their labors: these seeing it shall be troubled with terrible fear, and shall be amazed at the suddenness of their unexpected salvation; saying within themselves, repenting, and groaning for anguish of spirit: 'These are they, whom we had some time in derision, and for a parable of reproach. We fools esteemed their life madness, and their end without honor: behold how they are numbered among the children of God, and their lot is among the Saints.'

"'Therefore we have erred from the way of truth, and the light of justice hath not shined unto us, and the sun of understanding hath not risen upon us. We wearied ourselves in the way of iniquity and destruction, and have walked through hard ways, but the way of the Lord we have not known.

"'What hath our pride profited us? or what advantage hath the boasting of riches brought us? All those things are passed away like a shadow, and like a post that runneth on, and as a ship that passeth through the waves, whereof when it is gone by, the trace cannot be found, nor the path of its keel in the waters; or as when a bird flieth through the air, of the passage of which no mark can be found, but only the sound of the wings beating the light air, and parting it by the force of her flight; she moved her wings and hath flown through, and there is no mark found afterwards of her way: or as when an arrow is shot at a mark, the divided air presently cometh together again so that the passage thereof is not known: so we also being born forthwith ceased to be: and have been able to show no mark of virtue but are consumed in our wickedness.'"

"Such things as these the sinners said in hell."

Wisdom V. I et seq.

ST. EPHREM'S SERMON ON THE GENERAL JUDGMENT.

St. Ephrem, who glorified the Church by his piety and learning in the fourth century, was frequently obliged to cease speaking when preaching to the people, because of the abundance of tears he shed.

On one occasion he was preaching on the General Judgment. "Give an attentive ear," he said, "to what I am going to tell you about the second coming of Our Lord. But who is able to describe these terrible things? Where can we find the tongue that can explain them? The King of kings, seated on a great, resplendent throne, will command all the people of the earth to appear before Him. At the thought of this my eyes are filled with tears, my voice trembles, my tongue adheres to my palate, and I can scarcely utter a word.

"Then, the great King having given this order, the earth and the sea will become troubled, and will give up the dead that are hidden in them, and all will stand before His awful tribunal. Then they shall say to the mountains and the rocks, 'Fall upon us, and hide us from the face of Him that sitteth upon the throne, and the wrath of the Lamb, for the great day of their wrath is come, and who shall be able to stand?'" (Apoc. VI. 16).

"The Lord shall then command the book of the living and of the dead to be opened: and then, oh! the tears that shall be shed." But here the holy man ceased to speak, interrupted by his sighs and great weeping.

"Oh, continue!" cried out the people; "continue, O Father, thy discourse, and speak to us of what shall then take place."

"Beloved of Jesus Christ," broke forth the Saint, "then shall the Judge look upon all Christians who are there, and search for the character of the Faith received in Baptism, when they renounced the devil, the world, and the flesh. Happy then shall those be who have preserved it inviolate to the end of their lives.

"Then shall come the great separation. Husbands and wives shall be separated, children and parents shall be separated, friends and friends shall be separated. And when the good have been placed on the right side, and have received the reward of their good works, and when the wicked shall have been placed on the left hand, and have received the fatal sentence of eternal condemnation, then shall the philosophers, and the wise ones of the world, and those who did not fulfill the Will of God while on earth, raise up their sorrowful eyes to those whom they shall never see again: 'Farewell forever, ye Saints and servants of God: farewell, ye prophets, apostles, and martyrs; farewell, thou most holy Virgin and Mother of God our Savior; you all prayed for our salvation, and we would not be saved. Farewell, also, O holy Cross, on which our Savior died for us: farewell forever, O Paradise of delights, for which we were made, the eternal kingdom, the heavenly Jerusalem. Farewell to you all; never, never shall we see you again, but forever and ever shall we be plunged into an abyss of torments which will never end. Farewell, farewell."

Guill., p. 600; 5th edit.

2

EXAMPLES OF THE TERROR OF EVEN THE THOUGHT OF THE LAST DAY

God has been pleased to give us some idea of the terror which, at the last day, will come upon those who have not loved Him during the time of their life on earth.

ST. CEDDA IN A THUNDERSTORM.

In the days when our holy Faith flourished in our own country, the diocese of London was governed by a holy Bishop whose name was Cedda.

Venerable Bede tells us that whenever that holy man heard the thunders rolling in the heavens, he used to throw himself upon the ground, and call on God to have mercy on him. And when he saw the lightning flash around him, he would tremble from head to foot, and run to the church, where he would lean against the altar, and pray with tears in his eyes till the storm had come to an end.

Some people who saw him on these occasions thought within themselves that to act in this way was the mark of a fear which they did not expect to see in one who was their pastor and Father. They told him this one day.

"O my children," he answered, "it is not the storm that makes me afraid, but every time I hear it burst forth, I think of the terrible Day of Judgment. The howling of the tempest puts me in mind of the cries of despair of poor sinners on that day. When I see the lightning, I think of the anger of Jesus Christ against those who have offended Him; and when I hear the thunder, I think I hear the terrible voice of Jesus Christ pronouncing the awful sentence of condemnation against them. If I tremble now even at the thought of these things, how much more will I tremble when I really see them!"

From his Life.

KING PHILIP AND HIS TWO NOBLES.

Philip II, King of Spain, was at Mass in the chapel attached to his palace; many of the nobles were also present.

During the time of the holy Sacrifice the King noticed that two of them, forgetting the sanctity of the place, were behaving in a very disrespectful manner in the presence of God. He said nothing to them at the time, but when Mass was ended, and they had left the chapel, the King sent for them. When they came into his presence they saw at once by the severity of his countenance that he was very angry.

"I observed today," said the King, "the unworthy manner in which you conducted yourselves in the chapel at Holy Mass. For that sin I banish you both from my presence forever. I cannot allow anyone to live with me who behaves so disrespectfully in the presence of God. Do not dare, so long as you live, to enter my palace again."

These words, pronounced in a tone of severity, made such an impression on the two nobles that one was struck with apoplexy, and died on the spot; the other soon afterwards lost his reason, and remained insane during the rest of his life.

If the words of a King in this world had such an effect on those who had offended him, how terrible will be the effect of those words of the Eternal King of Heaven upon those who are lost: "Depart from me, ye accursed, into everlasting fire, prepared for the devil and his angels!"

THE PICTURE OF THE LAST JUDGMENT.

Peter of Arezzo was one who feared neither God nor man. If anyone spoke to him of the punishments of sin, or of the Last Judgment, he only laughed at him.

One day he went to see a great picture in a church in Rome. It was a picture of the Last Judgment. He looked at it for a long time in silence, and then went away. People wondered where he was going so silently, and watched him. They saw him kneel down to say his prayers. The sight of the picture had changed his heart. He said, "If I am so frightened by the sight of a picture of God's judgment, what will become of me when that judgment itself really comes?" And so he became good, and remained good as long as he lived.

The Holy Ghost says in the Scriptures, "Remember thy last end, and thou shalt never sin."

"IF MEN BUT ONLY KNEW..."

St. John Climacus relates the following incident, of which he himself was an eye-witness.

There was in the deserts of Egypt a solitary, who for a long time lived a careless life, neglecting to aspire after the perfection of his state, and thought but little of the judgments of God.

In course of time he became ill, and was soon at the point of death. When he appeared to those around him to be in his agony, God was pleased to show him in a vision the state of his soul. During one whole night he seemed to lie unconscious, and it was then that he saw how God, in His mercy, had given him the grace of seeing how terrible are His judgments on those who do not serve Him.

When in the morning he regained his senses, the thought of what he had seen so filled his soul with fear that he resolved to spend the rest of his life, if God would yet spare him for a time, in doing the most rigid penance for his past negligences.

His first words to those who had silently witnessed the terrible agony of that night, among whom was St. John Climacus himself, were: "My brethren, depart from me; leave me alone." Then, rising from his bed, weak though he was, he closed the entrance to his cell, which he was resolved never to leave till the hour of his death.

For twelve years he lived there enclosed without speaking to anyone, subsisting on bread and water which the brethren brought him. He sat on the ground in silence, meditating continually on what he had seen; he never moved from that posture day nor night, and kept his eyes continually fixed on the heavens above him, while shedding abundance of tears.

When at length it was evident that his last hour was near, the brethren of the monastery broke open the door, and stood before him. Then, as was the custom among them when death came to visit one of their number, they besought him to say to them some words of edification which they might afterwards call to mind. For a long time he begged to be excused, but at length, yielding to their continued pleadings, he said: "Forgive me, my brothers, if I say to you only one word. Amen, amen I say to you, if men only knew how terrible are the judgments of God, they would never, never sin."

Having said these words, he calmly expired, leaving the solitaries penetrated with great fear.

DE BUSSI: *Nov. mois de Marie.*

THE PARTICULAR JUDGMENT.

Besides the General Judgment at the Last Day, there is also the particular judgment which takes place at the moment of our death. The Catechism tells us that "Every one will be judged at death as well as at the Last Day"; for "it is appointed unto men once to die, and after this the judgment" (Heb. IX. 27).

We shall then have to give a strict account of every thought, word, action, or omission of our whole lives, and the sentence of the just or of the wicked shall then be pronounced on us, which will infallibly fix our fate for all eternity. If the just Judge finds that you have done the work your Heavenly Father placed you in this world to do, my child, He will reward you for it in Heaven; but if you have neglected it, you will be sent to Hell forever.

THE HOUSE NOT BUILT.

There was a rich man who sent one of his servants into a distant country to build a new house for him on a property which he had bought.

He gave him the plans of the building, and also furnished him with the money that would be required to build it.

"I cannot tell you," he said to him, "when you may expect me to go to take possession of my new house, but I will give you sufficient time to finish it, and when I think that you have completed it, you may expect to see me."

The servant was pleased with the confidence his master had in him, and immediately departed.

When he reached the place to which he had been sent, instead of beginning at once, as he ought to have done, to execute the orders he had received, he amused himself by traveling through the country. He took up his attention with its curiosities, studying the manners and customs of the people which were so new to him, and forming the acquaintance of some of the inhabitants, with whom he spent the greater part of the day.

From time to time, it is true, he went to the overseers, and spoke with them about commencing the new building, but very little was done, and the work progressed but slowly. One day it was a party of pleasure that he had to attend; another, it was an excursion he had promised to make; at another time it was an amusement of which he had the principal part, or some other similar reason that made him neglect his master's work.

One morning he received a letter from his master; this letter was to tell him that he might expect him in a few days.

This news filled him with dismay. He saw that there was now an end to all his pleasures, and the amusements which had taken up so much of his time and attention. He foresaw also that the meeting with his master would be a very unpleasant one, for he knew that he had neglected his work, and he feared the consequences.

The first words his master said to him on his arrival were: "I hope the house I sent you to build is now quite finished, for you have had sufficient time to do so."

The servant hung down his head, and replied that he was sorry to say it was little more than begun.

"And what have you been doing all the time?"

He tried to excuse himself by saying that he had been very busy, that he had made many excursions through the country to study the customs of the people, and to learn all about its products and manufactures.

His master interrupted him, and said in an angry tone, "It was not for that purpose I sent you here. I sent you to build a house for me. What do all these things you mention matter to me? You have neglected the only thing I wanted done—the only thing I sent you to attend to."

He tried to excuse himself, saying, "I had the intention all the time of accomplishing the work. I thought I would have had plenty of time to attend to it, but you have come at the moment I least expected you."

"Did I not tell you when I sent you here," said the master, "that I would come when I thought you would have had sufficient time for the work? You ought to have begun at once. If you had done so, the house would have been finished before now."

The end of the matter was that the unfaithful servant was not only dismissed from his employment, but severely punished for having misspent his master's time, and for having squandered the money he had received for his master's work.

Catéch. de Rodez.

THE EMPEROR AND HIS FAVORITE.

The Emperor Charles V was standing at the bedside of one of his most faithful servants who was dying. He had always had a special affection for this man because he had served him from his infancy with the greatest fidelity, and when he saw him so ill he was filled with sincere grief.

"My dear friend," the Emperor said to him, "you have ever been a faithful servant to me, and I am sorry to see you now lying there suffering so much. Ask of me, then, whatever you like—any favor you please—and I will give it to you."

"Ah, sire," said the dying man, "there is one great favor which I will ask you to give me."

"What is it? Tell me," said the Emperor eagerly.

"Give me, then, one day more of life—just one day more."

"Alas, my friend!" he replied, "you ask of me what is beyond my power to give; the most powerful monarch on the face of the earth cannot add even one hour to a man's life when God's time has come."

At these words the nobleman raised his dying eyes to Heaven, and sighed.

"O foolish man that I have been!" he cried out. "I have spent my whole life in the service of my King; and now when I ask him for a little longer time to live he cannot grant me even one hour. Oh! If I had only served my God, my Heavenly King, as faithfully as I did my earthly master, how happy would I be at this moment! But, alas! I did not do that, and now I die in fear and trembling at the terrible judgment that awaits me."

These were his last words.

Catéch. de Persévérance.

3

THE SAINTS AND GOD'S JUDGMENTS

The Saints of God, who knew better than others the great evil of sin, kept the thought of God's judgment always before their eyes. It was chiefly this thought that made them overcome all their temptations.

But even some of the Saints themselves, when the hour of death came, were afraid of the judgments of God. Read, my child, the following examples; they will show you how strict are the judgments of God.

"NO ONE CAN IMAGINE."

There lived long ago in one of the monasteries belonging to the Cistercian Order, two holy monks who had a great affection for one another, and who seemed to lead unblemished lives.

One of them died. Soon after his death he appeared to his friend whom he had left behind, while he was offering up prayers for the repose of his soul.

As soon as he saw him, and perceived that his face bore marks of suffering, he asked him how he came to be in that state. The deceased monk answered, saying three times these words: "No one can imagine —no one can imagine—no one can imagine—"

"What do you mean," said the other, "by these strange words?"

The dead religious answered: "No one can imagine how severe are the judgments of God, and how terrible are His punishments."

Saying this he disappeared, leaving the religious full of fear.

Jac. a Paradiso.

THE HOLY MONK AGATHO.

When the holy monk Agatho was near the end of his life, he was seen to keep his eyes fixed on Heaven. The brethren around him asked him: "What are you gazing at so earnestly, Father?"

"I am in the presence of God, waiting for the judgment to begin."

"But you have, as we all know, lived a life of the utmost purity for so many years; of what, then, are you now afraid?"

"It is true, my brothers," he replied; "I have tried as far as I was able to keep the commandments of God, but how am I to know whether or not my actions have been pleasing to Him? The judgments of God are so different from those of men, and no one can tell whether he is deserving of God's love or hatred. I know that I have sinned, but I do not know if God has pardoned me."

These were his last words.

RUFFIN: *Vie des Saints,* III.

THE DYING MONK.

St. John Climacus, who lived in the sixth century, tells us that there was once a holy man called Stephen, who lived to a very old age. He had even from his youth lived for God alone, and had served Him with the greatest care all that time.

But he fell sick, and it was evident to everyone that he must soon die.

A few hours before his death he appeared to be, as it were, out of his senses. He cast his eyes from one side to the other, and seemed to be in a state of great fear. Those around his bed could not imagine what was the matter, and thinking that the Devil was tempting him with some terrible temptation, as he often does those who are dying, they began to pray for him.

Suddenly they heard him speak; they listened to the words that fell from his lips, and they knew that he imagined himself to be standing before the judgment-seat of God.

"It is quite true," they heard him say; "I did commit that sin; but to obtain pardon for it, I fasted three years on bread and water."

Again he said: "That is also true; but I confessed it and did penance for it."

"No," he said, as if answering another accusation. "No, I did not do that sin. I never committed a sin like that; so that is false."

"Alas!" he said, after a pause, "I have no excuse for that sin. I must acknowledge that I committed it, and all I can do now is to throw myself on God's infinite mercy."

After this the holy man expired; and the religious who saw the terror that was on his countenance, and heard the words he had said, trembled with fear. They said one to another: "If this man, whom we all looked upon as a Saint, had to undergo such a terrible judgment, what will become of us?"

Catéch. de Rodez.

My child, you may say the same to yourself. You have indeed sinned, but what penance have you done for your sins?

BROTHER MORICO'S FEARS DISPELLED.

When Brother Morico of the Order of St. Francis was at the point of death, he had a terrible vision which frightened him. He thought he was standing at the tribunal of Jesus Christ, who was asking of him a rigorous account of every thought, word, and deed of his life. Despair began to seize upon him, and he began to cry out with all his strength: "I am lost! I am lost forever!"

When the religious heard his cries, they ran to his bedside and asked him what was the matter. But he heeded them not, and continued to cry out louder still: "It is all over with me; I am lost—lost for all eternity."

The brethren of the monastery, who knew how good he had been all his lifetime, saw that this was a temptation of the Devil; so they asked him to hope in Jesus Who died for him, and to put himself under the protection of Mary, whom he had ever so ardently loved.

For a quarter of an hour Morico was silent, then he suddenly began to sing a hymn of praise to the holy Name of Jesus. Two of the monks who knelt in prayer by his bedside, amazed at the sudden change from intense despair to great joy, asked him the reason of it.

"When I cried out so loudly," he said, "I imagined I was at the dread tribunal of God, Who commanded me to give Him an account of my whole life. Although I was not conscious to myself of any grievous sin, yet so strict was the examination that I thought there was no hope for me, and that I was surely lost. But at that terrible moment I imagined I saw Our Blessed Lady, who came to console me, and she said to me: 'My child, say one hundred times the most holy Name of Jesus, and you will obtain pardon for the faults you have done.' I said that blessed Name one hundred times, and I know that Jesus, the Lamb of God Who takes away the sins of the world, has had mercy on me." Soon after this he died in peace.

4

HOW STRICT ARE THE JUDGMENTS OF GOD

The judgments of God are not like our judgments; He often sees faults where we think there are none. Perhaps you, my child, may not be conscious to yourself of much sin; yet do not be too confident, and often pray as the prophet David did, "From my hidden sins deliver me, O Lord."

GOD'S JUDGMENTS NOT LIKE THOSE OF MEN.

There lived in the convent over which St. Gertrude presided, a young religious, for whom the holy abbess had a singular affection, on account of her zeal for the practice of virtue, and her earnest piety.

God was pleased to take her out of this world at a very early age.

St. Gertrude wept much for the dear sister whom she had so tenderly loved, and prayed for the repose of her soul with great fervor.

One day, while thus praying for the departed nun, she had a vision. She saw her before the throne of God, all surrounded with a bright light, clad in beautiful garments, and wearing costly jewels. Yet there seemed to be on her countenance marks of sorrow; for her eyes were cast down, and she seemed to be afraid to look upon the face of the adorable majesty of God; she even seemed to try to turn away from Him.

Gertrude was afflicted when she saw her spiritual daughter thus trembling before Jesus her Spouse; so she said to Him: "O most sweet Jesus, why do You not, in Your infinite bounty, call upon her, who loved You so much on earth, to enter at once into the joys of Paradise? Why do You not take her into Your arms? Why do You leave her there by herself sad and sorrowful?"

Jesus turned towards the religious, and with a smile on His countenance, made a sign to her to approach.

But instead of doing so she became only more and more troubled. She began to tremble, and turning away from Jesus altogether, she left the place. The astonishment of St. Gertrude was now increased. She followed the sister and said to her:

"My daughter, why did you turn away from Jesus Who called on you to go near Him? You were on the point of entering into the possession of Heaven, which you desired all your lifetime to obtain; and now, when your beloved Spouse asked you to go in, you refused to go, and turned away. Do you not see that at this moment Jesus is calling you?"

The religious answered: "Ah! My mother, I am not yet worthy to approach the Immaculate Lamb of God: there are yet some stains on my soul. To enter into the presence of Him Who is the Sun of Justice one must be more pure than light itself, and I have not yet that perfect purity. Even if I saw the gate of Heaven open to let me in, I would not enter till I had wiped out even the smallest of my sins, for I know that the choirs of Holy Virgins, who follow Him wherever He goes, would not admit me amongst their number."

"And how can that be, since I see you surrounded with glory and light?"

"My mother," she replied, "all that you see is but a shadow of the beauty of God's elect in Heaven. It will be quite another thing altogether, when I will see God and live in God, and enjoy His presence for all eternity. But to enjoy that happiness I must be free from every stain."

LOUIS DE BLOIS: *Mon. Spir.* XIII.

ST. STEPHEN OF CITEAUX.

In the days of the great St. Bernard there lived a holy monk called Stephen. He had spent a long life in the service of God, and had shone as one of the brightest lights of the Order of Citeaux from his early youth. He was called the patriarch of that Order, and everyone looked up to him as to a living Saint.

When he had reached a good old age, he prepared for death, for he knew it would soon come. It is in the following words that his historian gives us an account of it:

"The time had come when the holy man was to receive the reward of the many labors he had accomplished in the service of Jesus Christ, and to pass from the poor and humble state he had chosen, after the example of Jesus Christ, to go to His eternal home in Heaven.

"Then the abbots of his order, to the number of twenty, met together at Citeaux. They wished to be present to witness his happy death, and aid him with their prayers.

"When he was in his agony, and seemed to have expired, they were speaking together of the holy life he had led, and of the great reward God must have in store for him in the home to which he was going. They said one to another how happy must he now be, at the thought of having done so much good to the Church of God: how full of hope and confidence he must be of a happy judgment from Jesus Christ, Whom he has served so well.

"At these words, which the dying monk overheard, he roused himself, and collecting all his strength, said: 'My brethren, what did you say? I protest that I go to the judgment-seat of God with as much fear as if I had never done any good at all. For if, by the help of Jesus Christ, some little good may have been done through me, I am afraid that I may not have done all that was required of me, and that I did not correspond with the graces of God as I ought to have done.'

"Upon this," continues the narrator, "the holy man breathed forth his last sigh, passed out of this world, and reached the kingdom of peace, which had always been the only object of his desires."

Life of St. Bernard, p. 220.

A YOUNG MAN CONVERTED.

St. Vincent Ferrer tells us of a young man who, in a vision, was taken before the judgment-seat of Jesus Christ.

The sight that met his eyes as he stood there to be judged, the majesty of the Sovereign Judge, the different questions that were put to him which he could not sufficiently answer, frightened him so much that on his awakening he was trembling from head to foot, and covered over with a cold sweat.

"Thanks be to God," he cried out as soon as he had recovered from his surprise, "what I have seen was, after all, only a dream. Yet one day it will really take place, and it may be very soon, even this very night, perhaps."

He at once arose from his bed, and, falling on his knees, took the resolution that from that moment till the end of his life he would never offend God even by the smallest sin, and would spend the rest of his life in doing penance. So great was the fear of God's judgment that his hair became white from the effects of it, even in his youth.

Noël: *Catéch. de Rodez.*

THE HOLY MAN NILUS.

There was a young man whose name was Nilus. He was clever and cheerful, and his countenance was pleasing. People spoke about the talents he possessed, and praised and flattered him even from his boyhood.

He had received from his parents a Christian education, but the attractions of the world deceived him, and he would not believe those who told him of the terrible end to which they would bring him. Day by day he became more and more worldly; gradually his practices of piety became fewer, and finally he neglected them all. He was now what people had told him he would soon become—a youth who had abandoned his Creator to serve the creature.

But although he had abandoned his God, God had not forsaken him. He became very ill, and the doctors gave him but little hope of recovery.

"What will become of me?" he said to himself during one of these hours he had to pass alone in bed. "What will become of me? I have given myself to the world to please it, and now it can do nothing for me; it leaves me alone in the arms of death as if it had never known me, and when I die it will forget me altogether. I have turned my back upon my God, for Whom alone I ought to have lived, and how can I expect Him to receive me now? And yet I cannot escape him. I will soon have to appear before Him to be judged, and what sentence can I expect to receive? If I had loved and served Him, as my parents told me so often to do, I would now have some confidence to expect the sentence of the elect. But I did not do that; and I can look for nothing from my Judge but the sentence of the wicked, whose example I followed.

"O my God," he prayed, "make me better, and I will be one of Your most faithful servants."

God in His mercy heard his prayer. His sickness gradually left him, and he was soon able to rise and walk about.

A few days after he had risen from his sick-bed, and while he was still very feeble, he disappeared from his parents' house. He had taken the resolution to leave the world which had been his ruin, and seek shelter amongst those men who had left all things to follow Christ.

On his way he was met by a Saracen, who asked him whence he came and whither he was going.

"I am going to a monastery to serve God for the rest of my life, and so save my soul."

The Saracen, looking at his youthful countenance and the rich clothes he wore, said to him, "That is indeed a strange notion you have taken into your head; but I think you might at least have waited till you had become an old man before you adopted that kind of life."

But Nilus answered: "Oh, sir, the advice you give me is a very wrong one; you say I ought to wait till I become old before I give myself to God! Do you think that it would be just to give to God only the dregs of a life which belongs to Him from the beginning, and to give the best and most beautiful part of it to His enemy? Oh no!"

The Saracen was moved by this answer, and encouraged him to persevere in his good resolution. Nilus did so, and by his fervor blotted out the sins of his youth, and became eminent for sanctity.

Like Nilus, we may have already turned from God to serve the world. We must at least confess that we have not been so fervent as we ought to have been. Let this example move us to begin now, and for the time to come to serve God with our whole strength.

5

SIN THE ONLY CAUSE OF FEAR AT THE DAY OF JUDGMENT

My child, it is sin alone that will make God pass the sentence of eternal death upon the wicked. If you live without sin and die without sin, God will most certainly take you to Heaven.

WHAT ST. JOHN CHRYSOSTOM WAS AFRAID OF.

St. John Chrysostom had the greatest horror of sin, because he knew that sin was the only thing that could keep him out of Heaven on the Day of Judgment.

The Emperor of Constantinople was a haughty and proud man, and could not bear to be reproved.

St. John was the only one who had the courage to tell him that he was doing wrong. In consequence of this, he bore an ill-will towards the Saint, and one day he said to his nobles around him, "I wish some of you would find a way to get rid of that Bishop."

Four or five of them who also hated the Saint for having rebuked them for their misdeeds, gave their opinions.

One said, "Send him into exile into a far-off country, and he will not trouble you any longer."

Another said, "Take from him everything he has; that will make him less arrogant."

A third said, "Put him into prison, and load him with heavy chains."

The fourth said, "Are you not his master? Put him to death; that is the simplest way to get rid of him."

The fifth, who seemed to be deep in thought for a few moments, said, "You are all wrong; none of the ways you have suggested will do, if you want to be avenged on him. It is of no use to send him into exile, for one part of the earth is as agreeable to him as another. By depriving him of his worldly goods, you do not injure him so much as the poor, among whom he distributes all he possesses. Then, if you put him into prison and load him with chains, you will give him what he esteems above all things else— an occasion of suffering for the love of God. If you condemn him to death, you only send him the sooner to Heaven. No, O prince; if you wish to be avenged of your Bishop, force him to commit sin. I know him well, and I know, moreover, that there is but one thing that he is afraid of in this world, and that is sin. He is not afraid of exile, nor loss of goods, nor imprisonment, nor death; he is afraid only of sin."

This was confirmed on another occasion, when a messenger came to the Saint from the Empress, threatening him with great penalties if he did not grant her a request which his conscience would not allow him to grant.

"Go and tell the Empress," he said, "that John Chrysostom fears only one thing—that is sin."

Life of St. John Chrysostom.

"MY JESUS, MERCY!"

A young man, who had allowed himself to be carried away by the seductive words and example of wicked companions, soon forgot the maxims of our holy Faith in their wicked company.

A virtuous mother had neglected nothing in his tender years that would inspire him with the love of God and of the things of Heaven, and it was to this Christian education which he had received at her knees that, although he had lost his piety and virtue, he had been able to preserve his Faith.

One night which followed a day in which he had given way to many and grievous sins, he had a terrible dream. He imagined that he had been struck by the hand of death, and that he had already stood before the dread tribunal of God. No one can ever describe what must have been his confusion, his fear, and his terrible agony at that moment; for when he awoke he lay as if in a burning fever, covered with sweat, and trembling from head to foot; his hair also had during that night become white as snow.

"Leave me alone," he said to those who in the morning discovered him in this terrible condition; "leave me alone! I have seen my Judge; pardon, O my God! My Jesus, mercy!"

The young men who had led him astray, hearing that he was ill, and his mind apparently deranged, went to visit him, and offer such condolence as is usually given on these occasions. On seeing them enter, he cried out: "Begone, all of you! No longer shall you be my friends; I will never more see you. I have this night seen my Judge. Oh, what majesty, what severity shone upon His angry countenance! Oh, what accusations He made against me! What interrogations He made, to which I could answer nothing! All my sins were written down in a great book, and I read them. I saw the enormous number I had committed, and their greatness. The devils were standing near waiting for the signal from the terrible Judge to drag me into hell-fire. I trembled then, and I tremble still; as long as I live in this world, so long will I tremble. False friends, begone; go away from me forever. Oh, happy indeed would I be if I only could know that I had appeased my terrible Judge, even by a life of the most rigorous penance! I now from this instant consecrate my life to this. Alas! I must most certainly very soon really appear before that tribunal which I have seen in my dream, perhaps even this very day.

"Oh, pardon me, my God," he continued; "I will from this moment never cease to cry to You for pardon and mercy. O my Jesus, mercy! O my Jesus, pardon!"

LASAUSSE: *Explication du Catéchisme*

6

HOW BEST TO SECURE THE SENTENCE OF THE ELECT

One of the best ways to secure for ourselves the sentence of the blessed when the Day of Judgment comes is to do all the good we can to our neighbor; for Jesus Christ expressly says that at the Day of Judgment He will consider as done to Himself whatever we do to them.

"I AM PREPARING FOR JUDGMENT."

Among the Saints of the Middle Ages there is no one better known or better loved than St. Elizabeth of Hungary. The people used to call her the "dear St. Elizabeth," because she was so charitable to the poor, and was so kind to all who were in affliction.

Of all the works of charity she performed, that of visiting the sick in the hospitals and the poor in their homes was the one she loved most. She would watch by their sick-bed; and give them their food, and perform for them the menial duties of a sick- nurse, with the same care and diligence as if she had been hired for that purpose.

The ladies of her household, who did not care for this kind of employment, used to try to persuade her that it was beneath the dignity of her position to perform such things.

"It will be enough for you," they said, "to speak to them, and give them words of consolation; let others attend to their wants."

Elizabeth answered, "I am preparing for the Day of Judgment. On that day Jesus will ask me for an account of the good works I have done for Him, and I desire to be able to say to Him, 'You see, O Lord, when You were hungry, I gave You to eat; when You were thirsty, I gave You to drink; when You were naked, I clothed You; when You were sick, I visited You; because You said that in doing these things to the poor, I did them for Yourself. I beseech You be indulgent, therefore, to me in the sentence You are to pass upon me.'"

Life of St. Elizabeth.

WHY GOD HAS GIVEN US TIME.

Father Peter, a priest in the monastery of St. Sabas, tells us of a holy man who had spent sixty years in serving God. He began to do so when he came to the use of reason, and he continued without intermission till he had reached old age, weeping and doing penance.

One who happened to visit him, and who knew his holy life, asked him why he, who had always been so good, should live a life of such penance. "My father," he replied, "God has given us the present time that we may do good in it, and perform works of penance. Oh, what a terrible account shall we have to give to Him if we neglect to make good use of that time which is so short, yet so important."

7

THE TERRIBLE JUDGMENT OF THE REPROBATE

What a terrible moment shall that of the Particular Judgment be to one who has died in sin. God forever lost, Heaven forever forfeited, Hell his eternal portion. O my child, serve God faithfully now, that such a judgment may never come upon you when you die.

THE THREE TERRIBLE WORDS.

King Baltassar gave a great feast to a thousand of the great men of his kingdom. He commanded for this feast that all the gold and silver vessels which his father Nabuchodonosor had taken from the Temple of Jerusalem, should be placed upon the table, that out of them his wives and his evil friends might drink. He did this out of contempt for the God of Israel, and that he might show all the people how weak the God of Heaven was, and how powerless to avenge Himself on those who rebelled against Him.

Suddenly, in the midst of the enjoyments of the feast, the King was seen to become pale, and to tremble. His eyes were fixed upon the wall opposite to the place where he sat upon his throne, in all the glory of his majesty and the magnificence of his royal pomp. He saw there the fingers of a man's hand writing, and the words that these fingers wrote were these: "Mane, Thecel, Phares."

At that same moment his body seemed fixed to the throne on which he sat, and his knees to strike one against the other, and his feet became unmovable. When he was able at length to speak, he gave orders that all the wise men of his kingdom should hasten to his presence, and he promised magnificent rewards to the one who should tell him what these words meant. But no one was able to do so, and this increased the King's dismay more and more.

Then the Queen, his mother, told him of one of the Jewish captives whose name was Daniel, who was renowned for the gift of unraveling unknown mysteries. Daniel was immediately sent for, and explained to the King the meaning of the mysterious words he had seen, in the following manner: *"Mane:* God has numbered the days of thy reign, and that number is now filled. *Thecel:* thou hast been weighed in the balance, and art found wanting. *Phares:* thy kingdom shall be divided and given to the Medes and Persians."

This prediction was immediately accomplished. That same night Babylon was captured, and Baltassar was put to death.

The Prophet Daniel.

So, my child, a terrible day will most certainly come to those who have not served God, in which these three words will be accomplished in them also. When their last hour comes, the Sovereign Judge will say to them: "*Mane:* the number of the days given you on earth in which to save your soul is filled up. *Thecel:* You have been weighed in the balance of God's justice and you are found wanting in good works and laden with sins. *Phares:* the Kingdom of Heaven, with the throne of glory destined for you there, has been taken from you to be given to others whose lives you have despised." Oh, let us endeavor not to be of that number on the day when we shall be called to Judgment.

A MAN WHO DID NOT SERVE GOD JUDGED.

St. Bridget relates a vision she had of a soul at the Judgment-seat, who, while on earth, had not loved and served God.

The angel guardian of that soul spoke to God, the Eternal Judge, and said: "O great Judge, this soul had three great defects: it did not live a life of Faith; it considered what it heard of Your judgments as exaggerated or untrue, and was incredulous of Your great mercy to sinners.

"He was married while on earth, and lived faithfully indeed in that state, not for the love of God, but for that of his wife. He went to Church regularly as others did, not to please God, but that he might appear religious in the eyes of the world, and thus favor his temporal interests.

"O Lord, You have already given him his reward: beautiful children, health, and riches; moreover, You have preserved him from all the dangers he so much feared. But he has no good works to show to You; hence I deliver him up to Your justice."

That soul answered: "I would prefer to go eternally to Hell rather than to Heaven, in order that God might have no pleasure in me, for now He is for me an object of hatred and aversion."

The Lord then said: "You have yourself pronounced your sentence; go into everlasting fire prepared for the Devil and his angels."

Then, turning to the Devil, ready to receive that soul, he said: "If that soul, before leaving the body, had only had sincere contrition, and had asked My forgiveness, it never would have fallen into your hands. But it served you while on earth faithfully unto the end, it is therefore only just that it should forever belong to you."

Then, turning towards St. Bridget, Our Lord said to her: "All that you have seen and heard in this vision passed in the twinkling of an eye; but as you could not perceive these spiritual things as those do who have gone forth from the world, but only by images and symbols, I have permitted you to be present at the Judgment-seat as it would appear to human eyes in order that you might know My mercy for the good, and My severity towards the wicked.

Revelations of St. Bridget

PART VII
THE HOLY GHOST

1

WHO IS THE HOLY GHOST?

"I believe in the Holy Ghost." The Holy Ghost is the Third Person of the Blessed Trinity. He proceeds from the Father and the Son, and is equal to Them in all things.

JESUS PROMISES TO SEND THE HOLY GHOST.

In Jesus Christ's discourses to His Apostles, after His Last Supper, He said to them: "I will ask the Father, and He shall give you another Paraclete, that He may abide with you forever. The Spirit of truth, Whom the world cannot receive, because it seeth Him not, nor knoweth Him; but you shall know Him, because He shall abide with you, and shall be in you.

"The Paraclete, the Holy Ghost, Whom the Father will send in My Name, He will teach you all things, and bring all things to your mind, whatsoever I shall have said to you... When the Paraclete cometh Whom I will send you from the Father, the Spirit of truth, Who proceedeth from the Father, He will give testimony of me..."

St. John **XIV.**

KING LEOVIGILD AND ST. GREGORY OF TOURS.

There once lived in Spain a King whose name was Leovigild. Although professing the Catholic Faith, he gave ear to heretical teachers, who tried to lead him away from the revealed truths of our holy Faith. Among other things, he embraced the error of those who, although acknowledging the divinity of the Father and the Son, refused to believe in that of the Holy Ghost.

St. Gregory of Tours was informed of this by certain deputies whom Chilperic, King of France, had sent to that King, and who, on their return, had paid a visit to that holy Bishop. He, on his part, ever anxious to maintain the teaching of the Church, sent messengers to the King in Spain to ask him this question: "O King, since you refuse to believe in the divinity of the Holy Ghost, and will not acknowledge Him to be one God with the Father and the Son, would you be pleased to inform me how St. Peter could have said with truth to Ananias, 'Why hath Satan tempted thy heart, that thou shouldst lie to the Holy Ghost? Thou hast not lied to men, but to God.'"

The King, who held the Word of God in the highest esteem, was struck by these words, and after meditating on them for a time, saw how he had been deceived by the fallacies of the teachers to whom he had listened, and instantly professed aloud his adherence to the doctrines contained in the Holy Scriptures, and taught by the living voice of the Church; and not only he himself, but those who had been misled as he had been, joined him in the profession of the Catholic Faith in this mystery.

HAUTRIEVE, IV. 207.

2

THE WORKING OF THE HOLY GHOST IN THE BEGINNING OF THE CHURCH

The Holy Ghost came down on the Apostles on Pentecost Sunday, to confirm them in their faith, to sanctify them, and to enable them to found the Church.

THE DAY OF PENTECOST.

Ten days after the Ascension of Our Lord into Heaven the Holy Ghost came down upon the Apostles in the likeness of fiery tongues.

Just before leaving them, Jesus told them that they should not depart from Jerusalem, but should wait there until they should receive the Paraclete, Whom He promised to send them from Heaven.

St. Luke tells us that they did so. "And when they were come in," he says, "they went up into an upper room; and they were persevering with one mind in prayer with the women, and Mary the Mother of Jesus, and with His brethren.

"And when the days of Pentecost were accomplished they were all together in one place.

"And suddenly there came a sound from Heaven as of a mighty wind coming, and it filled the whole house where they were sitting.

"And there appeared to them parted tongues, as it were of fire, and it sat upon every one of them; and they were all filled with the Holy Ghost, and began to speak with divers tongues, according as the Holy Ghost gave them to speak.

"Now there were dwelling at Jerusalem Jews, devout men out of every nation under Heaven; and when this was noised abroad, the multitude came together, and were confounded in mind, because that every man heard them speak in his own tongue.

"And they were all amazed, and wondered, say-ing: 'Behold, are not all these that speak Galileans? And how have we heard every man our own tongue wherein we were born?' And they were all astonished, and wondered, saying one to another: 'What meaneth this?'

"But others, mocking, said: 'These men are all full of new wine!'

"But Peter, standing up with the eleven, lifted up his voice, and spoke to them: 'Ye men of Judea, and all you that dwell in Jerusalem, be this known to you, and with your ears receive my words; for these are not drunk, as you suppose, seeing that it is but the third hour of the day.'"

And he showed them in a beautiful discourse that Jesus, Whom a short time before they had put to death, was their Savior and the Eternal Son of God; that He had risen from the dead, and had ascended into Heaven; that from Heaven He had sent down the Holy Ghost upon them that day; and that by the power of that Divine Spirit the wonders they had just seen had been accomplished.

When they heard these things the grace of the same Holy Ghost touched their hearts, and about three thousand of them were at once converted.

Acts of the Apostles II.

SAUL AND BARNABAS SENT FORTH BY THE HOLY GHOST.

"Now there were in the Church which was at Antioch prophets and doctors, among whom was Barnabas, and Simon who was called Niger, and Lucius of Cyrene, and Manahen, who was the foster-brother of Herod the Tetrarch, and Saul. And as they were ministering to the Lord and fasting, the Holy Ghost said to them: 'Separate Me Saul and Barnabas for the work whereunto I have taken them.'

"Then they, fasting and praying, and imposing their hands, sent them away. So they, being sent by the Holy Ghost, went to Seleucia, and from thence they sailed to Cyprus....

"But the next Sabbath Day the whole city almost came together to hear the Word of God. And the Jews, seeing the multitudes (who were Gentiles), were filled with envy, and contradicted those things which were said by Saul (now Paul), blaspheming.

"Then Paul and Barnabas said boldly: 'To you it behooved us first to speak the Word of God, but because you reject it, and judge yourselves unworthy of eternal life, behold we turn to the Gentiles, for so the Lord hath commanded us.'...

"And the Gentiles, hearing it, were glad, and glorified the Word of the Lord, and as many as were ordained to life everlasting believed. And the Word of the Lord was published throughout the whole country....

"And the disciples were filled with joy and with the Holy Ghost."

Acts of the Apostles XIII.

CORNELIUS THE CENTURION IS RECEIVED INTO THE CHURCH.

"There was a certain man in Caesarea named Cornelius, a centurion of that which is called the Italian band, a religious man, and fearing God with all his house, giving much alms to the people, and always praying to God.

"This man saw in a vision manifestly, about the ninth hour of the day, an angel of God coming in unto him, and saying to him: 'Cornelius.'

"And he, beholding him, being seized with fear, said: 'What is it, Lord?'

"And he said to him: 'Thy prayers and thy alms are ascended for a memorial in the sight of God. And now send men to Joppe, and call hither one Simon, who is surnamed Peter: he lodgeth with one Simon a tanner, whose house is by the seaside: he will tell you what you must do.'

"And when the angel who spoke to him was departed, he called two of his household servants, and a soldier who feared the Lord, of them that were under him, to whom, when he had related all, he sent them to Joppe.

"And on the next day, whilst they were going on their journey, and drawing near to the city, Peter went up to the higher parts of the house to pray about the sixth hour. And being hungry, he was desirous to taste somewhat. And as they were preparing, there came upon him an ecstasy of mind, and he saw the Heaven opened, and a vessel descending, as it were a great linen sheet let down by the four corners from Heaven to the earth, wherein were all manner of four-footed beasts, and creeping things of the earth and fowls of the air.

"And there came a voice to him: 'Arise, Peter, kill and eat.'

"But Peter said: 'Far be it from me; for I never did eat anything that is common or unclean.'

"And the voice spoke to him again the second time: 'That which God hath cleansed do not thou call common.'

"And this was done thrice, and presently the vessel was taken up into Heaven.

"Now whilst Peter was doubting within himself what the vision he had seen should mean, behold, the men who were sent from Cornelius, inquiring for Simon's house, stood at the gate. And when they had called, they asked if Simon, who is surnamed Peter, were lodged there.

"And as Peter was thinking of the vision, the Spirit said to him: 'Behold, three men seek thee. Arise, therefore, and get thee down, and go with them, doubting nothing, for I have sent them.'

"Then Peter, going down to the men, said: 'Behold, I am he whom you seek. What is the cause for which you are come?'

"Who said: 'Cornelius, a centurion, a just man, and one that feareth God, and having good testimony from all the nation of the

Jews, received an answer of an holy angel to send for thee into his house, and to hear words of thee.'

"Then, bringing them in, he lodged them. And the day following he arose and went with them, and some of the brethren from Joppe accompanied him. And the morrow after he entered Cesarea. And Cornelius waited for them, having called together his kinsmen and special friends.

"And it came to pass that, when Peter was come in, Cornelius came to meet him, and falling at his feet, adored.

"But Peter lifted him up, saying: 'Arise, I myself also am a man.' And talking with him, he went in, and found many that were come together.

"And he said to them: 'You know how abominable it is for a man that is a Jew to keep company or to come into one of another nation: but God hath showed to me to call no man common or unclean. For which cause, making no doubt, I came when I was sent for. I ask, therefore, for what cause you have sent for me.'

"And Cornelius said: 'Four days ago, unto this hour, I was praying in my house at the ninth hour, and behold, a man stood before me in white apparel, and said: 'Cornelius, thy prayer is heard, and thy alms are had in remembrance in the sight of God. Send, therefore, to Joppe, and call hither Simon, who is surnamed Peter: he lodgeth in the house of Simon a tanner by the seaside.' Immediately, therefore, I sent to thee, and thou hast done well in coming. Now, therefore, all we are present in thy sight to hear all things whatsoever are commanded thee by the Lord."

"And Peter, opening his mouth, said: 'In very deed I perceive that God is not a respecter of persons, but in every nation he that feareth Him and worketh justice is acceptable to Him.'...

"While Peter was yet speaking these words the Holy Ghost fell on all them that heard the word. And the faithful of the circumcision who came with Peter were astonished, for that the grace of the Holy Ghost was poured out upon the Gentiles also, for they heard them speaking with tongues, and magnifying God.

"And Peter answered: 'Can any man forbid water, that these

should not be baptized, who have received the Holy Ghost as well as we?'

"And he commanded them to be baptized in the name of the Lord Jesus Christ. Then they desired him to tarry with them some days."

Acts of the Apostles X.

THE COUNCIL OF JERUSALEM.

"And some, coming down from Judea, taught the brethren: 'That except you be circumcised after the manner of Moses you cannot be saved.'

"And when Paul and Barnabas had no small contest with them, they determined that Paul and Barnabas, and certain others of the other side, should go up to the Apostles and priests to Jerusalem about this question....

"And when they had come to Jerusalem, they were received by the Church and by the Apostles and ancients, declaring how great things God had done with them....

"And the Apostles and ancients assembled to consider this matter. And when there had been much disputing, Peter rising up said to them: 'Men, brethren, you know that in former days God made choice among us that by my mouth the Gentiles should hear the Word of the Gospel, and believe. And God, Who knoweth the hearts, gave testimony, giving unto them the Holy Ghost as well as to us, and put no difference between us and them, purifying their hearts by faith. Now, therefore, why tempt you God, to put a yoke upon the necks of the disciples which neither our fathers nor we have been able to bear? But by the grace of the Lord Jesus Christ we believe to be saved, in like manner as they also.'

"And all the multitude held their peace....

"And after they had held their peace, James answered, saying: 'Men, brethren, hear me. Simon hath related how God first visited to take of the Gentiles a people to His name.... To the Lord was His own work known from the beginning of the world, for which cause I judge that they who from among the Gentiles are converted to God are not to be disquieted.'

"Then it pleased the Apostles and ancients, with the whole Church, to choose men of their own company, and to send to Antioch with Paul and Barnabas... writing by their hands: 'The Apostles and ancients, brethren, to the brethren of the Gentiles that are at Antioch and in Syria and Cilicia, greeting. Forasmuch as we have heard that some going out from us have troubled you with words, subverting your souls, to whom we gave no commandment, it hath seemed good to us, being assembled together, to choose out men, and to send them unto you with our well-beloved Barnabas and Paul, men that have given their lives for the name of Our Lord Jesus Christ. We have sent, therefore, Judas and Silas, who themselves also will by word of mouth tell you the same things.

"'For it hath seemed good to the Holy Ghost and to us to lay no farther burden upon you than these necessary things: that you abstain from things sacrificed to idols, and from blood, and from things strangled, and from fornication: from which things keeping yourselves you shall do well. Fare ye well.'

"They, therefore, being dismissed, went down to Antioch, and gathering together the multitude, delivered the epistle, which when they had read they rejoiced for the consolation; but Judas and Silas, being prophets also themselves, with many words comforted the brethren, and confirmed them."

Acts of the Apostles XV.

3

FIRST GIFT OF THE HOLY GHOST—WISDOM

When you received the Sacrament of Confirmation, the Holy Ghost bestowed on you His graces more abundantly, so that you might be able more easily to overcome the enemies of your salvation, and lead a life pleasing to God.

You are now to see what these gifts are, and how the Saints made use of them, that you, by imitating them, may obtain the same reward which they have now obtained in Heaven.

The first gift of the Holy Ghost is that of Wisdom. By this gift we are able to keep before our minds our last end, which is to be with God in Heaven forever, and to live in such a way while we are in this world as to secure that happiness.

THE YOUNG HERMIT AND THE ABBOT.

A young hermit one day came from a distant desert to visit the great Abbot Pambo, who was renowned throughout the whole country for his wisdom and knowledge.

The Abbot received him with great kindness, and told him to sit down by his side.

The young man then began to ask him many questions on the

most difficult points of the Holy Scriptures, and asked him to explain to him certain mysteries which even the most learned theologians could not explain without difficulty.

To all his questions the holy man answered nothing, so that the hermit was disappointed. He at last rose up and left the cell in disgust.

When he went out he met a disciple of St. Pambo, to whom he said: "I might have spared myself the trouble of this long journey, for your Abbot seems to know nothing. He could not give me an answer even to one of the questions I put to him."

"My dear brother," answered the other, "our holy Abbot does not spend his time in searching into the hidden things of God, which our poor limited understandings cannot comprehend. What he does know is how to lead a holy life on earth, that we may one day be worthy of seeing God in Heaven."

These words made him reflect a little. He at once went back to the cell of the Abbot, and said to him: "My Father, perhaps you will tell me what I have to do to lead a holy and pious life, and so one day get to Heaven."

St. Pambo, hearing this question, looked up; there was a smile on his countenance. "Now," he said, "your questions begin to please me, and now I shall be able to answer you."

The holy man then spoke to him of the great love of God in sending His only-begotten Son from Heaven that we poor sinners might one day be able to reach it, of our eternal home there, and of the sufferings of our Blessed Redeemer. The young man returned homeward, knowing now that true wisdom was only to be found in the love of God and the science of the Saints.

Lives of the Fathers of the Desert.

4

SECOND GIFT OF THE HOLY GHOST —UNDERSTANDING

The second gift of the Holy Ghost is Understanding. This gift enables us to know more perfectly the mysteries of our holy religion.

THE PIOUS MOTHER OF THE MACHABEES.

In the Sacred Scriptures we read of a mother who had seven sons whom she brought up from childhood to serve and love God. It happened that the tyrant Antiochus, who hated God and His holy religion, and who wished to root out of the Jewish nation the worship of the one true God, came to know of this family. He thought that as the children were as yet young, and had only their mother to watch over them, they would easily be brought to yield to his impious desires. But he forgot that that mother had brought up her little ones in the fear of God. It was this education that procured for them the victory in the day of trial.

When Antiochus asked the eldest son to obey his wicked command, this was the answer he received: "We are ready to die rather than transgress the laws of God received from our fathers."

And when he asked the next in age, whom already he had caused to be inhumanly tortured, if he would renounce the practices of his religion, he answered: "I will not do it." And when he was at the point of death, he said to the King: "Thou, indeed, O most wicked man, destroyest us out of the present life; but the King of the world will raise us up who die for His laws in the resurrection of eternal life."

"After him," says the Holy Scripture, "the third was made a mocking-stock, and when he was required he quickly put forth his tongue and courageously stretched out his hands, and said with confidence: 'These I have from Heaven, but for the laws of God I now despise them, because I hope to receive them again from Him.' 'So that the King and they that were with him wondered at the young man's courage, because he esteemed the torments as nothing.

"And after he was thus dead, they tormented the fourth in the like manner. And when he was now ready to die, he spoke thus: 'It is better, being put to death by men, to look for hope from God, to be raised up again by Him; for as to thee, thou shalt have no resurrection unto life.'

"And when they had brought the fifth they tormented him; but he, looking upon the King, said: 'Whereas thou hast power among men, though thou art corruptible, thou dost what thou wilt; but think not that our nation is forsaken by God, but stay patiently a while, and thou shalt see His great power, in what manner He will torment thee and thy seed.'

"After him they brought the sixth, and he, being ready to die, spoke thus: 'Be not deceived without cause, for we suffer these things for ourselves, having sinned against our God, and things worthy of admiration are done to us. But do not think that thou shalt escape unpunished, for that thou hast attempted to fight against God.'

"Now Antiochus, thinking himself despised... when the youngest was yet alive, did not only exhort him by words, but also assured him with an oath that he would make him a rich and a happy man, and if he would turn from the laws of his father, would take him for a friend, and furnish him with all things necessary. But when the young man was not moved with these things, the King called the mother, and counseled her to deal with the young man to save his life. And when he had exhorted her with many words, she promised that she would counsel her son.

"So, bending herself towards him, she said in her own language: 'My son, have pity upon me that bore thee nine months in my womb, and gave thee suck three years, and nourished thee and brought thee up unto this age. I beseech thee, my son, look upon Heaven and earth and all that is in them, and consider that God made them out of nothing, and mankind also. So thou shalt not fear this tormentor, but, being made a worthy partner with thy brethren, receive death, that in that mercy I may receive thee again with thy brethren.'

"And while she was yet speaking the young man said to the King: 'For whom do you stay? I will not obey the commandment of the King, but the commandment of the law which was given us by Moses.

"'But thou that hast been the author of all mischief against the Hebrews shalt not escape the hand of God. For we suffer for our sins, and though the Lord is angry with us a little while for our chastisement and correction, yet He will be reconciled to His servants....'

"Then the King, being incensed with anger, raged against him more cruelly than all the rest, taking it grievously that he was mocked. So this man also died undefiled, wholly trusting in the Lord. And last of all, after the sons, the mother also was consumed."

2 *Machabees* VII.

Thus did the Holy Ghost in the Old Law, as in the New, speak through the lips of those who were faithful to the holy Law of God, and by the words of His Wisdom bring to naught the wisdom of the great ones of this world.

5

THIRD GIFT OF THE HOLY GHOST—COUNSEL

The third gift of the Holy Ghost is Counsel. Counsel leads us to make a right choice in things relating to our salvation. It helps us also to avoid the deceits of the Devil.

THE BETTER PART CHOSEN.

When St. Maurus went into France to establish there the monastic life, he was kindly received by a rich and powerful nobleman named Florus. This man was so edified by the conduct of the Saint, and those who accompanied him, and was so moved by their pious exhortations, that he felt in his soul a great desire to be like them.

When the Saint asked him for a piece of ground whereon he might build a monastery for himself and his monks, Florus gave it to him with the greatest joy; and when the building was finished, he requested the holy abbot to allow him to become a member of his happy family.

St. Maurus thanked God for granting him this great grace, and gladly consented to receive him.

But before renouncing the world, Florus went to the King, who had for him the greatest esteem and love, to tell him of his intention.

"My liege," he said, "grant me leave to forsake the world, and to go into the monastery which the holy Maurus has built, that I may do penance for the sins I have committed in Your Majesty's service."

The King was filled with great grief when he heard this request. At first he would on no account agree to it, for he did not want to lose one of his best and most trusty friends; but at length, overcome by his entreaties, he gave his consent.

When the day came which had been fixed for Florus to receive the holy habit, the King went in person to the monastery, attended by all the nobles and Princes of his Court, and when the hour for the beginning of the service arrived, they all went in procession to the church, and sat down not far from the altar.

Florus then appeared, attired in the rich garments of his position. He went up to the King, and asked him to begin to cut off his hair as a sign that he henceforth renounced the world and all its vanities. The King did so with tears streaming from his eyes. Then Florus took off his rich garments, and put on the poor clothes of the monks. The sight he then presented to the nobles, who before used to think him so great, made them all weep. For when they saw one so noble, rich, and powerful, and so much honored by his Prince—one, too, in the prime of life despising all worldly honors to become a poor and despised monk, in order that he might make his salvation still more secure, they felt in their souls that he had chosen the better part. This sight was one that could not fail to have a powerful influence on them all.

When the ceremony was ended, the King dined with the monks, and partook with joy of their humble fare.

Before departing he called Florus, now a monk, to his side, and said to him, while he could scarcely speak for weeping: "My dear Florus, you served me right nobly while you were with me; be as faithful, then, in the service of the great King of Heaven as you were in mine. You defended your country and your sovereign with great valor with your sword; defend it now as valiantly by your prayers, and remember me before God."

The King and his train returned to the palace, but the lesson they had that day received, of the nothingness of the world and the happiness of those who have chosen the better part, was never forgotten.

RIBADENEIRA: *Lives of the Saints.*

You may not have it in your power, my child, to do what Florus did, but there is one great lesson you can learn from his example; you can learn that the things of this world are of no value, because they pass away so soon, and that the only things of any price are those that will last forever.

TANCREDS CHOICE.

In the reign of the Emperor Frederic I., there lived at his Court a pious youth named Tancred, who was a great favorite of the Emperor. This young man, reflecting on the danger to which he was there exposed of losing his soul, earnestly besought the most holy Mother of God to make known to him the state of life he should choose in order to obtain more surely his salvation, being resolved to embrace the one which she would indicate to him. After many days spent in persevering prayer and great fervor the Mother of God herself appeared to him, and said: "Tancred, you have asked me to show you the state of life in which you will most easily gain Heaven and escape the eternal torments of Hell. Go, then, enter my Order." Saying these words she disappeared. Tancred was at a loss to know what Order the Divine Mother referred to. But while he was thinking on this he fell asleep, and in his sleep he imagined he saw two religious of the Order of St. Dominic approaching him, the elder of whom thus addressed him: "You have asked of God through the intercession of His most Blessed Mother, to show you the surest way of saving your soul. Rise, therefore, at once, for you must spend the remainder of your days with us."

In the morning, as he was going to hear Mass, he met on his way the Prior of the Dominican Convent of Bologna, and after looking at him for some time, he recognized in him the person whom he had seen in his dream, and who had spoken to him. Filled with surprise, he went up to him and told him what had happened. Then, no longer doubting what God wanted him to do, he renounced the world and entered the Order of St. Dominic, where he lived and died a Saint.

FLORA AND HER PIOUS FATHER.

When Flora had reached a marriageable age, her father, being anxious to see his daughter honorably married, began to look for a suitable husband for her.

When she heard of this she went to him, and said: "My father, if you really love me as your daughter, do not any longer trouble yourself about me. I have long ago engaged myself to Jesus Christ, and I do not desire any other spouse; and I beg of you to place me in a holy monastery of virgins consecrated to God, that I may be able more freely to serve Him Who calls me to this holy life."

Her father answered her in these beautiful words: "My beloved daughter, since God calls you to Himself, let us prepare to do His will, for it is not lawful for us to keep what the Lord wishes to take for Himself."

But everyone, my child, is not called to these high paths of perfection, and it is in a humbler position that God desires most of His children to serve Him.

BLESSED NICHOLAS OF FLUE.

Blessed Nicholas of Flue was a poor shepherd. He spent the years of his youth in the fields or the meadows, where, at a distance from the noise of the world, everything speaks to the heart about God.

If he had followed his own inclination he would have renounced the world altogether. But such was not the kind of life God had appointed for him. Many were anxious to possess so holy a man for a husband; and Nicholas, seeing that it was the will of God that he should enter the holy state of matrimony, besought Our Lord to send him a wife after His own heart. God answered his prayer, and we read that he married a virtuous young woman who was called Dora.

As this union was begun by God, so did it continue to the end. In course of time a little family grew up at their fireside, who in their turn became Saints like their parents, and transmitted to posterity the amiable virtues they had received as an inheritance from them.

ST. MARGARET OF SCOTLAND.

When King Malcolm III of Scotland saw the virtues of the youthful Margaret, there arose in his heart a desire of making her his wife. As he did not dare of himself to ask her, he went to Agatha, the mother of the Princess, to beg of her to speak to her daughter on his behalf.

When Agatha informed Margaret of the King's request, "a sudden paleness overspread her countenance," says her historian, "and she trembled at her words." She answered that it would be impossible for her to consent to such a union, for she had already given her heart entirely to God.

But when her mother continued to press her to give her consent, she, after a few moments' silence, asked a short delay that she might beg of God to direct her.

Long and fervently did she pray. "O my God," she said, "behold I am in Thy hands; do with me what Thou wilt. I desire only one thing: the accomplishment of Thy holy will. Thou knowest that I have already given my heart to Thee, to love Thee alone; but if Thou callest me to another state, O my God, I am ready."

Her prayer was speedily answered. In a short time she rose from her knees, and went to find her mother. "My mother," she said with calm resignation, "it is the will of God; I consent to accept the King for my husband."

My child, place yourself entirely in the hands of your Heavenly Father, and daily say to Him with so many of His Saints: "O Lord, what dost Thou wish me to do?"

6

FOURTH GIFT OF THE HOLY GHOST —FORTITUDE

The next gift of the Holy Ghost is Fortitude. This gift makes us firm in our Faith, and gives us courage to perform faithfully all our duties.

THE LITTLE BOYS OF OZACA.

At Ozaca there lived two little boys under twelve years of age; they were both pagans. One day they went into a church of the Christians, and, going up to a priest whom they found there, said to him: "Father, we want to be baptized, and to be made Christians."

The priest asked them some questions, and found that they knew well the principal truths of our holy Faith. Yet he did not dare to baptize them, because he knew that their parents were pagans, and he was afraid that they, being so young, might not persevere. So he told them to wait till they grew older.

But the boys would not wait. They threw themselves on their knees before him, and said: "Father, we will not rise up from this place till you have baptized us."

The priest raised up his mind to God by a short prayer to know what he should do. Being sure that the Holy Ghost had specially chosen these children for Himself in this wonderful way, he granted their request, and baptized them.

Not many days after this, it happened that the younger of the boys purchased a little pious picture. He placed it on the wall of the room in which he slept, that he might say his morning and night prayers before it. His father, who hated the Christian religion, seeing this picture on the wall, and knowing it to represent some Christian subject, wondered how it had been placed there.

Sending for his son, he said to him: "Where did you get that picture?"

"Father, it is a picture of Christian devotion."

"What have you to do with these things? You are not a Christian."

"Yes, father, I am!"

"What!" said the father in a passion of anger, "you a Christian! You renounce the worship of our gods! If you do not at once adore them with me I will kill you."

"Father," replied the child calmly, "you can do with me what you like. I am a Christian, and, with God's help, I will be one till I die."

The father, unable to control his anger, seized the child, and, tearing off his clothes, beat him with leathern thongs till the blood flowed from the wounds he had made. From time to time he would stop and ask the boy: "Are you still resolved to adore the God of the Christians?"

"I am a Christian, and I wish to live and die Christian." This was the only answer he gave.

Very soon the child's body was covered with wounds and bruises from head to foot. The father, stopping for a moment, was horrified at what he had done. But, being determined to make the boy yield, he covered him with a thin covering, and brought him before the family, that by their cruel jeers they might make him yield. But this also failed; the boy stood before them calm and patient, and was glad in his heart to suffer something for God.

The Governor of the city, hearing of what had occurred, sent for the boy and his father. Although he was also a pagan, he was melted into tears when he saw the cruel treatment the boy had endured. He turned towards the father, and publicly, with the greatest indignation, reproached him for his barbarous conduct, and declared that from that moment he would place the boy under the Emperor's protection.

NOËL: Catéch. de Rodez.

ST. CONCORDIUS, MARTYR.

Torquatus, the Governor of Tuscia, commanded Concordius to be apprehended and brought before him.

"What is your name?" he asked him.

"I am a Christian," replied Concordius.

"I did not ask you what you were; I asked you to tell me your name."

"I have already told you," answered the Saint, "that I am a Christian, and confess Jesus Christ."

The Governor said: "Sacrifice to the immortal gods, and be my friend. I will be a father to you, and I will go to the Emperor Antoninus, and he will make you a priest of the gods."

Concordius answered: "I beseech and exhort you rather to obey me and offer sacrifice to the Lord Jesus Christ, that you may escape the torments of the world to come, for if you do not obey me you must forever burn along with the gods you worship in the eternal flames of Hell."

Torquatus was enraged at these words, and ordered him to be struck with clubs and to be cast into prison. During the night St. Eutyches came to visit him along with a holy Bishop called Antimus; and as the Bishop was known to the Governor, he obtained permission for the Saint to spend a few days at his house. During that time he ordained him priest.

Not long afterwards, Torquatus sent for him again, and said: "Well, Concordius, have you considered now about preserving your life?"

"Christ is my life and my salvation," answered the martyr, "and to Him daily do I offer up a sacrifice of praise. As for you and your gods, you shall forever burn in hell-fire."

Torquatus became very angry on hearing these words again, and ordered him to be stretched upon the rack. But he, on hearing this, cried out with a joyful voice: "Glory be to Thee, O Lord Jesus Christ."

Being again asked if he would not offer sacrifice to the great Jupiter, he said: "I will never sacrifice to a stone idol which can neither see nor hear, because I adore Jesus Christ Whom alone my soul loves."

The Governor then gave orders that he should be cast into the lowest dungeon, and that his neck and his hands should be bound fast with iron chains. He also forbade anyone to go near him or give him any food, so that he might die of hunger.

These orders of the Governor filled the martyr with great joy. He cried out: "Glory be to God in the highest, and on earth, peace to men of good will." In the middle of the night the prison was filled with bright light, and an angel of the Lord appeared to him, and said: "Be not afraid, Concordius, but act manfully, because I am with thee."

Three days afterwards Torquatus sent two soldiers to the prison, bearing in their hands a little statue of Jupiter. They said to him: "Do you know what the Governor has decreed?"

"No; be pleased to tell me."

"You must either offer sacrifice to Jupiter, or be put to death."

The holy martyr cried out again: "Glory be to Thee, O Lord Jesus Christ." At the same time, as a sign of his hatred for the gods, he spat on the idol they presented to him.

Then one of the soldiers, drawing forth his sword, cut off the head of the martyr, and his spirit flew to Heaven to receive the crown of everlasting glory. The priests, accompanied by many of the faithful, went to the place where his body lay, and, taking it up, they reverently buried it, in the city of Spoleto, near the place where he had suffered martyrdom.

THE LITTLE MARTYR BOY.

The 10th of September, 1622, was a great day in the history of the Catholic Church in Japan, for on that day many of her children received the crown of martyrdom. One of these was the Blessed Ignatius, a little boy only four years old.

His father's name was Dominic; that of his mother, Isabella. Dominic had been put to death when his son was an infant, and Isabella received her crown on the same day as her little boy.

On the very day of his birth this pious mother had offered him up to God, and prayed that He would be pleased to look upon her child as belonging to Himself, watch over him during life, and take him to Heaven when he died.

She called him after St. Ignatius, with the hope that he might one day enter the Order of which that great Saint was the founder, and that the name might always put him in mind of his consecration to God.

But Providence had other designs upon the boy. It is believed that God had made known to him, in some way or other, that he would one day die a martyr. For when he was old enough to know that his father had been put to death for the Faith, he was heard to say: "I am going to be a martyr also."

It was the custom in that country for friends to make little presents to each other, just as it is in our own. When Ignatius made a present to anyone, he used to say: "Be sure and keep this carefully, for the day will come when it will be a relic." And when he was asked what he meant by these words, he would answer: "Because I am going to be a martyr."

On another occasion he happened to see some swords. As soon as he saw them, he cried out: "One of these swords will one day cut off my head, and make a martyr of me."

The prophecy of the little Saint was soon fulfilled. He and his mother, and many other Christians, were cast into prison because they would not give up their holy Faith, and September 10, 1622, was the day fixed for their death.

Isabella, his mother, in token of her joy, put on her richest garments, as for a great festival. In one hand she carried her crucifix, in the other her rosary. Little Ignatius walked by her side, decked out in his best, and looking brimful of happiness. Every eye was fixed on him, and many wept to see so young a child about to die, yet looking so cheerful and so happy.

Father Spinola, of the Society of Jesus, who had baptized Ignatius, was there also to give his life for God.

When Isabella saw him, she bowed to him, and bade him her last farewell.

"Where is my little Ignatius?" cried out the good priest, in the hearing of all the people. A pile of wood, which lay between him and the boy, had prevented the Father from seeing him.

"He is here by my side," she said; and, taking him up in her arms, she said to him: "Look at our dear Father there, who is asking about you; bow your head to him, and ask him for his blessing."

The child did as he was told. Father Spinola, whose hands were tied, could not raise them up to give the blessing, but he looked up to Heaven, and then towards the boy, as a sign that he blessed him, showing that he was touched to his inmost soul.

The mother then, pointing to the child, said to the priest: "Father, this is the most precious offering I can make to God, and I make it with all my heart."

The executioners now came forward with drawn swords, and the heroic mother, taking her last farewell of the Christians near her, and of her child, calmly presented her head to receive the stroke of death.

When his mother's head rolled to the feet of the Blessed Ignatius, the child showed the great courage with which God had filled his soul. He knelt down, crossed his little arms on his breast, and with his eyes fixed on the remains of her who had been his mother and his guardian angel on earth, awaited the blow which was to unite him to her again in Heaven.

The sword was lifted up, and in another instant the soul of the blessed child was safe in the bosom of his Heavenly Father, in those regions of glory where the innocent and the pure follow the Lamb wheresoever He goeth.

7

FIFTH GIFT OF THE HOLY GHOST— KNOWLEDGE

The fifth gift of the Holy Ghost is Knowledge. Knowledge teaches us the will of God, and the way by which the Saints obtained the Kingdom of Heaven.

"HOW MUCH I PITY YOU!"

In one of the great schools of France, to which the sons of gentlemen were sent for their education, there were once two young men who were much attached to each other. They had gone to school together, they were both in the same class, and their parents held a high position in the world.

Before leaving school, they made a promise never to forget each other. For some time they kept this promise, but as years passed by they lost sight of each other altogether.

Now it happened many years afterwards that one of them, who had reached the rank of officer in the Royal Guards, was passing over one of the bridges that cross the River Seine in Paris. He was dressed in all the splendor of his high rank, and walked along as if he thought himself greater than everyone else.

When about the middle of the bridge, he met two monks clad in the rough dress of the Capuchins. He looked at them as they passed with an air of disdain. As he was looking at them, the younger of the two monks chanced to raise his eyes, and they met those of the officer.

The officer suddenly started back. "I have seen that face before," he said to himself, "but where or when I cannot remember."

Going over to the monk, he said to him: "Father, I have met you before somewhere; your face is familiar to me. Kindly tell me your name."

The religious told him who he was, and the officer at once recognized the dear friend of bygone days.

"Oh, how glad I am to see you," he said. "I thought we were never to meet again; but what has induced you to put on that dress and lead so ignoble a life, when it was in your power to occupy a position like mine, and draw upon yourself the esteem and the praise of even the Princes of the State?"

The other answered: "What you say is true; I might have easily obtained honor and glory and fame; but I have thrown all these things at my feet, that I may make more certain of Heaven in the world to come."

While he was saying these words the officer looked more closely at him. He examined him from head to foot. He looked at his coarse garments, and his sandalled feet, and his mortified appearance. "O my old friend," he then said, "what a great sacrifice you must have made to bring yourself to such a deplorable condition. Oh, how I pity you! What if, after all, you should be deceived in what you are trying to procure? What if, after all you have renounced in this world, there should be no Heaven hereafter?"

These words told the religious very plainly that his old companion had forgotten the practice of his duties in the midst of a worldly life. So he answered: "As for me, my dear friend, I do not think I have lost much in throwing away all the brilliant chances in the world that you have spoken of, for I would not have the power of enjoying them always. At most they would last only for a few years, and then what would become of me? In my opinion it is you who are to be pitied, since, as our Faith tells us, there is a Heaven and a Hell hereafter, and you are living as if there was neither the one nor the other."

The officer often thought on these words of the religious, and although we do not know that he followed his example, he was convinced in his heart that his companion was most certainly wiser than he.

It is at the end of your life, my child, that you will see that nothing will be of any use to you then but the good you have done for God. Ask the Holy Ghost to give you this knowledge, that you may lay up for yourself a great store of merits as the Saints have done.

8

SIXTH GIFT OF THE HOLY GHOST— PIETY

The sixth gift of the Holy Ghost is Piety. By this gift we are enabled to live a pious and devout life, and always keep in mind God's holy presence.

ST. WENDELIN THE PIOUS.

Long ago, when Scotland first received the true Faith, there lived in that country a holy young man of the name of Wendelin.

He was the son of one of the Kings who at that time governed the country. His father had embraced the true Faith as soon as it had been preached in his kingdom, and his family as well as himself were fervent Christians.

The more Wendelin thought of God and the life to come, the more earnestly did he wish to go to some place far away from the abodes of men that he might think of nothing else.

The honors of the world, and the dignity which belonged to him by birth, had no attraction for him, because he saw how vain and empty they all were. One day he secretly left his father's house. For many months he wandered about the country, looking for some place where he might live unknown. But when his flight was discovered, search was made for him, and although he often changed his hiding place, he was sometimes nearly found again.

He then crossed over the borders into England, but even there he was in danger of falling into the hands of those who were in search of him. So he finally left Britain altogether, and went over into Germany.

On his arrival there, he met a rich gentleman who possessed immense flocks of sheep. He requested him to take him into his service.

The gentleman asked him what wages he wanted.

"I will serve you for nothing," said Wendelin, "if you will only give me some food to eat, and some little clothing to cover me."

This offer was at once accepted, and Wendelin was sent to tend his master's flocks.

Now he was at the height of his joy. He would have leisure to pray and meditate as long as he wished, and no one would ever dream of looking for him there.

Sometimes when the remembrance of his former greatness would come into his mind, and he began to think of what he might have been had he remained at home, he would call to mind the example of his Divine Master.

"If Jesus Christ calls Himself the Good Shepherd, surely I need not complain in trying to be humble like Him."

He took as much care of his sheep as if Jesus Christ Himself had confided them to him. He brought them to the best pasture-lands and guarded them from every danger, and while his eyes were on his flock his mind was with God. So fervent was he at times that people used to think he was engaged in a familiar conversation with God.

Thus did the holy man live during his long life on earth, and when God took him to see Himself face to face in His glory, people found out who he was, and how he had chosen to serve God in a humble life, rather than to sit on the high throne of a kingdom and they called him Wendelin the Pious.

Life of St. Wendelin.

9

SEVENTH GIFT OF THE HOLY GHOST —THE FEAR OF THE LORD

The Fear of the Lord is the seventh gift of the Holy Ghost. This gift excites in our souls a feeling of great reverence for our Heavenly Father, and a dread of offending Him.

QUEEN BLANCHE AND HER SON ST. LOUIS.

When Queen Blanche became the mother of St. Louis, she received him from God as a treasure to be guarded with the utmost care.

From his earliest years she kept one great thought before his mind—to love above all things his Heavenly Father, and never to offend Him by sin.

Often when the little boy was playing by her side, or sitting on her knee, she would say to him: "My own dear child, God knows how much I love you; no mother could ever love her son more than I love you, yet sooner would I see you lying dead at my feet than know that you had offended God by a mortal sin."

When he grew up, and when the day of temptation came, these words of his good mother came before his mind, and he always remained faithful to God.

From his Life.

My child, the Holy Ghost has chosen your soul as His dwelling-place. Pray to Him frequently to give you these holy gifts, that, like the Saints, you may increase every day in holiness, and persevere to the end in serving and loving Him as they did.

PART VIII
THE CHURCH MILITANT

1

THE CATHOLIC CHURCH FOUNDED

The Ninth Article of the Creed is "The Holy Catholic Church, the Communion of Saints."

There are three parts in the Catholic Church. One part is the *Church Triumphant* in Heaven, where those who were faithful unto death are now in happiness with God; the second part is the *Church Suffering* in Purgatory, where those who have not satisfied God's justice suffer for a time before they are taken into Heaven; and the third part is the *Church Militant* on earth, where God places His children on trial for a time, to see if they will be faithful to Him.

It is of the Church Militant of which you, my child, are a member, that you are now going to read.

My child, Jesus Christ came down from Heaven to show us the way to Heaven; and that we might not go astray and be lost, He, before leaving this world, appointed a sure and faithful guide to lead us there. That guide is His One True and Catholic Church.

JESUS ESTABLISHES HIS CHURCH.

When Jesus began to preach the Gospel to the people, He chose twelve men who were to be always with Him, and to learn from Him the mysteries of the Kingdom of God, that afterwards they might be able to "go forth and teach all nations." These men were the twelve Apostles.

Among these He chose one who was to be their chief and head, and who was to take His place after He went up to Heaven. This one was Simon Peter.

"THOU ART PETER."

When Jesus and His disciples "came into the quarters of Cesarea Philippi, He asked His disciples, saying: 'Whom do men say that the Son of man is?'

"But they said: 'Some John the Baptist, and other some Elias, and others Jeremias or one of the prophets.'

"Jesus saith to them: 'But whom do you say that I am?'

"Simon Peter answered and said: 'Thou art Christ, the Son of the living God.'

"And Jesus answering, said to him: 'Blessed art thou, Simon Barjona; because flesh and blood hath not revealed it to thee, but My Father Who is in Heaven. And I say to thee: that thou art Peter; and upon this rock I will build My Church, and the gates of hell shall not prevail against it. And I will give to thee the keys of the Kingdom of Heaven. And whatsoever thou shalt bind upon earth, it shall be bound also in Heaven: and whatsoever thou shalt loose on earth, it shall be loosed also in Heaven.'"

St. Matthew XVI. 13 *et seq.*

"FEED MY SHEEP."

Another time, after He had risen from the dead, He appeared to His disciples; and when they had dined, "Jesus saith to Simon: 'Simon, son of John, lovest thou Me more than these?'

"He saith to Him: 'Yea, Lord, Thou knowest that I love Thee.'

"He saith to him: 'Feed My lambs.'"

"He saith to him again: 'Simon, son of John, lovest thou Me?'"

"He saith to Him: 'Yea, Lord, Thou knowest that I love Thee.'"

"He saith to him: 'Feed My lambs.'"

"He said to him the third time: 'Simon, son of John, lovest thou Me?'"

"Peter was grieved because He had said to him the third time: 'Lovest thou Me?' And he said to Him: 'Lord, Thou knowest all things: Thou knowest that I love Thee.'"

"He said to him: 'Feed My sheep.'"

St. John XXI. 15 et seq.

It was thus that Jesus, after having established His Church on earth, made St. Peter its visible head, and put under his care His sheep and His lambs —that is, all the faithful.

THE APOSTLES SENT FORTH TO GUIDE AND INSTRUCT US.

On the day of His resurrection, Jesus appeared to His disciples, and said to them: "Peace be unto you. As the Father hath sent Me, I also send you."

When He had said this, He breathed on them, and said: "Receive ye the Holy Ghost; whose sins ye shall forgive they are forgiven them, and whose sins you shall retain, they are retained."

And soon afterwards He appeared to them again and said: "All power is given to Me in Heaven and on earth; go ye into the whole world and preach the Gospel to every creature, teaching them to observe all things whatsoever I have commanded you. He that believeth and is baptized shall be saved; but he that believeth not shall be condemned."

And again Jesus tells us that we are to listen to the Apostles and their successors whom He sends in His Name, just as if He Himself were speaking to us. "He that heareth you heareth Me," He said to them, "and he that despiseth you despiseth Me; and he that despiseth Me, despiseth Him Who sent Me."

2

THE POPE IS INFALLIBLE

St. Peter, as the visible head of the Church, fixed his See at Rome, and from that city he and his successors have governed the world, and will continue to do so until the end of time. The Bishop of Rome is called the Pope, which word signifies "father," because the Pope is the spiritual Father of all Christians.

The Pope is infallible, which means that he cannot fall into any error in teaching the Church, because he is the Shepherd and Teacher of all Christians, and to him as such Jesus Christ promised the guidance of the Holy Spirit, Who would teach all truth in His Church until the end of time.

DECREE OF THE VATICAN COUNCIL.

It was in the following words that the Council of the Vatican defined the dogma of the Papal infallibility:

"Wherefore, adhering faithfully to that tradition which stretches back through all ages, even to the commencement of the Christian Faith, for the glory of God our Savior for the exaltation of the Catholic Religion, and for the salvation of all Christian peoples, We teach and define, with the consent of the Sacred Council, that this is a truth divinely revealed—namely, that when the Roman Pontiff speaks *ex cathedra*—that is to say, when fulfilling the office of Pastor and Doctor of all Christians—he, by virtue of his supreme Apostolic authority, defines as a matter of faith or of morals a certain doctrine to be believed by the universal Church, he, by the Divine assistance promised to blessed Peter himself, possesses that infallibility with which our Divine Redeemer desired His Church to be invested, in defining any doctrine concerning Faith or Morals; and consequently, that these definitions of the Roman Pontiff are of themselves irreformable, without any consent of the Church.

"Hence, if anyone shall presume to contradict this our definition, which may God avert, let him be anathema."

Conc. Vatican.

3

THE FOUR MARKS OF THE CHURCH

My child, Jesus Christ made only one Church, and He said that it was to continue to the end of time. Now, as there are many different sects or Churches in the world, and as only one of them can be the true Church established by Jesus Christ, and since it is necessary to belong to the one true Church if we want to save our souls, there must be certain marks by which the True Church can easily be distinguished from those that are false.

Has the Church of Christ, then, any marks by which we may know her? Yes, the Church of Christ has these four marks: She is One, she is Holy, she is Catholic, she is Apostolic.

The Church is One, because all her members agree in one Faith, have all the same Sacraments and Sacrifice, and are all united under one head.

GONDEBRAND, KING OF BURGUNDY.

Gondebrand, King of the Burgundians, was an Arian, and, though otherwise of an amiable disposition, he refused to believe the teaching of the Catholic Church, and thought that he could get to Heaven in the sect to which he belonged.

Some years after he began to reign he saw that he was wrong, and, as he desired to save his soul, he took the resolution of becoming a Catholic. But he was afraid to do this openly, "being afraid," as he said, "that people might turn against him"; so he went to Avitus, the Bishop, and asked him to receive him privately into the Catholic Church.

But Avitus gave him this answer: "Our Lord has declared that unless we confess Him before men, He will deny us before His Father in Heaven. You must therefore, O King, rise above all worldly consideration, and not lose an eternal kingdom for the sake of an earthly one."

The King did not answer; but his courage failed him, and he lived and died an Arian.

The Church is holy because she teaches a holy doctrine and offers to all the means of becoming holy, and is distinguished by the great holiness of many thousands of her children.

FÉNELON'S PIETY.

Fénelon, the great Bishop of Cambrai, was so illustrious for his piety and great virtues, that those who visited him were obliged to exclaim: "The Church to which that Bishop belongs must indeed be the Church of God, for no other one could produce such a man."

Lord Peterborough, hearing of his eminent merits, was desirous of seeing him. The Bishop received his noble guest with great kindness, and invited him to stay with him. During the few days he spent there he was an eye-witness of the virtuous life of that great prelate; and so great an impression did it make on him that he was heard to say, when about to leave him: "I cannot stay here any longer, because if I did so, I should become a Catholic in spite of myself."

The Church is Catholic, or universal, because she is spread over all nations, and because she has subsisted ever since Christ, and will continue to the end of the world.

THE MAP OF THE WORLD.

In a certain school a teacher had prepared for his pupils a large map of the world, on which were shown all the countries of the universe. He had marked with a red cross upon the map every country and island and place where the Catholic religion was established, and the pupils saw at a glance that God's one true Church was everywhere—not only in civilized countries and in the more thickly inhabited places of the globe, but even in the lands of perpetual snow, and in the midst of pagan kingdoms, so that there was scarcely an islet rising out of the ocean but was marked with a red cross.

"See, my children," he said, "these crosses on the map tell you where you will find the Catholic Church. Go to any of these places you choose, and you will find the same Church as you have at home, the same truths taught, the same Sacrifice offered up, the same Sacraments administered, and all obeying one head—our Holy Father the Pope. Ah! Truly there is no blessing so great as that of being a member of the One True Church."

The Church is Apostolic because she teaches the doctrines and traditions the Apostles taught, and because her pastors are the successors of the Apostles, and because she receives her orders and her mission from them, and teaches what they taught.

THE CURE OF ARS' SERMON.

"My children, there are some who go about saying, 'Priests say just what they please.' No, my children, priests do not say what they please; they say what is in the Gospel. The priests who came before us said what we say, and those who shall come after us will say the same thing. Priests only say what Our Lord has taught.

"Who placed Our Lord Jesus Christ in the tabernacle? It was the priest. Who was it that received your soul on its entrance into life? The priest. Who will prepare it to appear before God by washing it for the last time in the Blood of Jesus Christ? The priest. You cannot recall one single blessing from God without finding side by side with this recollection the image of the priest.

"Who gave the priest all these powers? They came from God. Every priest in the world has been ordained by a Bishop, who has been sent forth for this purpose by the Pope, who is the successor of St. Peter, whom Jesus Christ made Head of His Church."

You see, my child, what a glorious privilege God has bestowed on you in making you a child of His one true Church. Ever esteem this, therefore, as your greatest treasure, and show Him your gratitude by living a dutiful child of His Holy Church as long as you are in this world.

4

THE INFALLIBILITY OF THE CHURCH

My child, the Church of God cannot err in what she teaches, because Jesus Christ said that the gates of Hell would never prevail against her, and that His Holy Spirit would be with her, teaching her all truth to the consummation of the world. It is for this reason that we always say when we make an Act of Faith: "O my God, I believe in Thee, and all Thy Church doth teach, because Thou hast said it, and Thy word is true."

A POOR MAN'S ANSWER.

A poor man who could not read, but who was brought up a good Catholic, was once met by some young men who, although learned in the eyes of the world, were very ignorant of the things of God. They thought that they would be able to put questions to him about his religion which he would not be able to answer. So they asked him to explain to them some things which even learned theologians find difficult to explain.

The poor man did not at first answer them, but when they urged him to do so he said: "Gentlemen, you know that I have no learning and cannot even read, and I am sorry that I cannot give you the explanation you desire. But my heart will answer you better than my lips can. I am happy, and what makes me happy is the knowledge that I belong to that Church which cannot err in what she teaches, and that I put in practice as far as lies in my power the duties it imposes on me. Is there one among you who can say as much as this?"

The young men said no more, but quickly turned away. The poor man without learning showed himself superior to them who thought they knew so much.

It is not ignorance so much as vice that makes people disbelieve the teaching of the Church.

There are many heretics at the present day who are leaving the Church in which they were born and returning to the Catholic Church, because they see that it was the Church Jesus Christ established, and that it must therefore be the true one, since Jesus Christ said He would never allow it to go astray.

THE POET WERNER.

Not very long ago there dwelt in Germany a famous poet called Werner, who in his youth was not a Catholic, but who afterwards became a devout member of "the one fold and the one Shepherd."

It happened that he was in conversation with one of the Protestant Sovereigns who were present at the Congress of Vienna, in the year 1814. The Prince, who knew that he had become a Catholic, said to him; "I do not like those people who change their religion. I think they do what is very wrong."

"O Prince," replied Werner, "I am also of your majesty's opinion. I think that Luther, in changing his religion, did what was indeed very wrong, and it is simply on account of that that I have returned to the religion he had the misfortune to leave."

When a person leaves the religion in which he has been brought up and becomes a Catholic, he only returns to his Father's house after having wandered from it for a time.

5

THE NECESSITY OF BEING A MEMBER OF THE ONE TRUE CHURCH

The greatest blessing that God ever gave you, my child, was that of making you a member of His Holy Church, because if you had not been a member of His Church on earth, you could never hope to be a member of His Church in Heaven.

THE BLESSED CURE OF ARS AND THE PROTESTANT.

The saintly Cure of Ars was one day visited by a Protestant gentleman. The good priest, thinking he was a Catholic, began to speak to him about Our Lord and His Saints, as he was accustomed to do to all those who came to see him.

When he was about to leave, the servant of God gave him a medal as a little remembrance of him.

The gentleman said to him: "Dear sir, you have given a medal to one who is a heretic—at least, I am a heretic from your point of view. But although we are not of the same religion, I hope we shall both one day be in Heaven."

The holy priest took the gentleman's hand in his own, and, giving him a look which seemed to reach his very soul, answered him: "Alas! My friend, we cannot be together in Heaven unless we have begun to live so in this world. Death makes no change in that. As the tree falls, so shall it lie."

"But, dear Father," replied the other, "I put my trust in Jesus Christ, Who said: 'He that believes in Me shall have eternal life.'"

"Ah!" said the priest, "Jesus Christ said many more things than that. He said also: 'He that does not hear the Church, let him be to thee as a heathen and a publican.' And He said again: 'There shall be one fold and one shepherd'; and He made St. Peter the chief shepherd of His flock."

Then, in a voice full of sweetness, he added: "My dear friend, there are not two ways of serving Jesus Christ: there is only one good way, and that is to serve Him as He Himself wishes to be served."

Saying this, the priest left him. But these words sank deeply into the good man's heart, and led him to renounce the errors in which he had been brought up, and he became a fervent Catholic.

Life of the Curé of Ars.

"ONE FOLD AND ONE SHEPHERD."

"I am the Good Shepherd. The Good Shepherd giveth His life for His sheep. But the hireling and he that is not the shepherd, whose own the sheep are not, seeth the wolf coming, and leaveth the sheep and flieth: and the wolf catcheth, and scattereth the sheep: and the hireling flieth, because he is a hireling: and he hath no care for the sheep.

"I am the Good Shepherd; and I know Mine, and Mine know Me. As the Father knoweth Me, and I know the Father; and I lay down My life for My sheep.

"And other sheep I have, that are not of this fold: them also I must bring, and they shall hear My voice, and there shall be one fold and one shepherd."

St. John X. 11 et seq.

VICTORINUS OF ROME.

Many years ago there lived in Rome a great physician, whose name was Victorinus. He professed to be a Catholic, but was never seen to enter the church, not even on Sundays. An old man who knew him well spoke to him of the danger of dying a bad death to which he was thus exposing himself.

Victorinus answered: "Be not afraid; I am a good Catholic, and I hope to die a good death."

"How can you be a good Catholic?" said the old man. "By your conduct you deny your religion, since you do not perform the duties it requires of you. I never see you even within the walls of a church. How, then, can you call yourself a good Catholic?"

"You surely do not mean to say," replied Victorinus, "that the walls of the church make the Christian?"

"No," replied the old man, "but it is by your presence there, and by outwardly attending to your religious duties, that you show men what you are. Do you not remember what Jesus Christ said? 'He that shall deny Me before men I will also deny him before My Father Who is in Heaven.'"

These words had a good result, for Victorinus from that day became a good and fervent Catholic, and died an edifying death.

The grace of being a member of God's true Church is the greatest gift God could bestow on you, my child, because along with it He gives you all other blessings. Oh! Be careful never to lose it, and pray for those whom you love who may not possess it, that He may grant it to them as He has granted it to you.

6

HOW GOD LEADS HIS ELECT INTO THE ONE FOLD

God has His own ways of bringing back His wandering children to His Church, and sometimes those who, like St. Paul, have been most zealous in propagating a false religion are the ones on whom He bestows this great grace.

"I MUST BECOME A CATHOLIC."

St. John Francis Regis one day met a rich lady, who was well known throughout the country for her great zeal in spreading her religion. She was a Calvinist.

"My lady," he said to her, "God has been for a long time calling on you to renounce the errors of the religion in which you have been brought up, and to come into His one true Church. How long are you going to be deaf to His call? Or are you going to lose your soul, which Jesus Christ bought at the price of His precious blood?"

The lady looked at the Saint in surprise; she was astonished at his boldness in thus speaking to her, and she was about to give him an angry answer. But when she saw the heavenly look that was upon his countenance, her anger at once disappeared, and she answered:

"God forbid that I should lose my soul! There is nothing I desire so much as to save it."

"Then," replied the Saint, "you must become a Catholic."

These words caused the lady to start; but the Saint continued:

"The Catholic religion was the religion of your forefathers, and the only one Jesus Christ founded; the one which He promised would endure till the end of time. It is in the Catholic religion alone that you can save your soul."

"You ask me to change my religion! Well," she replied slowly, "I do not know how it is, but there is something within me which seems to tell me that I ought to do so. Many others have already spoken to me as you have done, but I have always refused to listen to them. But when you spoke to me, I heard in my soul, as it were, a voice saying to me: 'You must become a Catholic.'"

"Yes, Father, I must be a Catholic. Do you yourself instruct me, and show me the holy will of God. I cannot explain to you what I feel. I never felt anything like it before; it seems as if it were the voice of God Himself I heard, and I cannot refuse to obey."

"My child, it is indeed the voice of God you have heard. He has given you a great grace in thus calling you into His one true Church. While you live never cease to thank Him and bless Him for it."

After receiving instructions, she was admitted into the Catholic Church by the Bishop of Viviers in France, and for the rest of her life was most zealous in propagating the true Faith which God had so wonderfully given her.

Life of St. John Francis Regis.

7

ZEAL FOR THE CONVERSION OF SOULS

One of the greatest works you can do for God is to bring to the true Faith those who are wandering in the darkness of error. This zeal for the salvation of souls was one of the greatest virtues of the Saints.

ST. GREGORY, APOSTLE OF ENGLAND.

One day St. Gregory, a holy monk, was passing through the forum or marketplace of Rome. Merchants had come from afar with the products of distant countries, and immense multitudes of people flocked to the marketplace to buy them.

Among other things exposed for sale were several boys of fair complexion and with beautiful flaxen hair.

St. Gregory saw them, and, going over to the place where they were standing, asked the merchants who were selling them to what country these beautiful boys belonged.

"They belong to the Island of Britain," they replied; "and all the people of that country are as beautiful as these are."

"Are they Christians," asked the Saint, "or are they still pagans?"

"They are pagans," answered the merchants.

On hearing this, St. Gregory sighed.

"Alas!" he said, "what a pity it is that men whose countenances are so comely should belong to the Prince of Darkness, and that their souls should be devoid of God's grace."

"What do you call the people who inhabit that country?" St. Gregory asked.

"They are called Angles."

"Ah, yes! They have indeed the faces of Angels, and their places should be in Heaven among the Angels of God."

Again he asked: "From what province of Britain do they come?"

"From the province of the Deiri."

"They are well named, because they must be brought from the wrath of God to His grace."

"What is the name of the King who reigns there?"

"He is called Ælle."

"Alleluia! Yes, the praises of God must be sung in that land."

Gregory at once went to the holy Pontiff Benedict, and besought him to send to Britain zealous missionaries who might bring the true faith to that unhappy country.

But as no one seemed to be willing to go, he offered himself for this great work, and having obtained the blessing of the holy Father, set out on his journey accompanied by a few devoted monks.

When the inhabitants of Rome heard of his departure, they besought the Pope to recall him. Messengers were immediately sent after him to bring him back to Rome. The holy man of God obeyed, and returned to Rome with a heavy heart, for he was filled with sorrow to be obliged to leave in the darkness of sin those whom he had hoped to convert to God.

Not long afterwards he himself was made Pope. His first thought was of his beloved Anglia, and very soon might be seen going towards that distant isle a holy band of missionaries with St. Augustine at their head. The banner of the Cross was raised upon our shores, and the Church was established in our land, and Saints and learned men appeared to adorn it, and to go forth to other countries, to bestow on them the grace of the true Faith they had themselves received.

SURIUS: *Vitâ S. Gregorii.*

"THE VOICE OF THE IRISH."

When the great St. Patrick was as yet a boy, God, Who had chosen him to be one of His greatest Apostles, filled him with an overflowing zeal for the propagation of His Holy Church.

One night he had a vision. "There stood before me," he says, "a person of heavenly beauty. He held in his hand a book, which was full of writing. 'I am Victricius,' he said, as he handed me the book to read.

"When I opened the book, I saw written on the first page these words: 'The Voice of the Irish,' and as I continued to glance over the pages of the book, I thought I heard the voices of persons from the forest of Foclut, near the Western Sea, crying out to me with one accord:

"'We entreat thee, O holy youth, to come back to us again, and teach us the way of the Lord.'

"These words moved me to my very soul, and I wept. While I was weeping the vision disappeared, and I awoke.

"The following night I had another vision. I heard the most beautiful music, and the voices of many who sang heavenly hymns; but I saw no one, and I knew not whence the voices came. So I began to pray, and during my prayer I heard someone whispering in my ear, 'I am He Who died to save thee.'

"Next morning I told these visions which I had seen to a dear friend of mine whom I had known from my childhood, and he said to me:

"'Patrick, you shall one day be Bishop of Ireland.'

"These words filled me with great fear, but in God's own time they were fulfilled."

Many years afterwards St. Patrick was in Rome. Pope Celestine then sat in the Chair of St. Peter. As he was speaking to his counselors on the great work of the conversion of Ireland, he asked them whom he should send to convert the people of that country from their idols, and teach them to know God.

With one accord they answered: "There is no one on the face of the earth so fitted for this great work as Patrick is."

Seeing that it was the will of God, St. Patrick at once consented. He asked the blessing of the holy Father, and immediately set out to begin his labors in that far-off country of which he had been chosen the Apostle. He saw the dangers that he must meet, but he feared them not, for an angel of the Lord appeared to him to strengthen and encourage him.

When he arrived in Ireland he began at once to preach the Gospel of Jesus Christ, which he confirmed by many wonderful works that God performed by his hands. Those who listened to him were blessed, but the maledictions of Heaven fell upon those who opposed him.

So great was the success of his labors that he himself was surprised at it.

"How is it," he cried out, "that all these wonderful things have been accomplished? How is it that the children of Erin, who till now had not known the true God, and who had worshiped impure idols, have become a holy people and the generation of the children of God? Never will I leave this land of benediction. I have been asked to go and preach in other lands, but the Spirit of God chains me to this one, and I will never forsake it."

Thus was the good seed of the Gospel sown in Ireland; it grew up, and from that holy island it went forth throughout the world, producing an abundant harvest of souls to God.

Petits Bolland, 17 Mars.

"O MY GOD, GIVE ME THAT SOUL."

There was in the house of a certain Spanish lady called Gratia a poor slave who had been brought up in the religion of Mahomet. She was of a generous and affectionate disposition, and served her mistress with great fidelity.

There sprang up between the lady and her slave a great friendship. Gratia loved her, and the poor girl showed that she loved her mistress in return by attending to her wants with great diligence. One thing alone saddened the affectionate soul of Gratia; she could not look upon the maid without shedding tears, for she beheld in her a soul created to the image of God, a soul for which Jesus died, and yet under the empire of Satan.

"O my God, give me that soul," she prayed; "let not that soul perish for whose salvation Thy Beloved Son died on Calvary."

The pious lady wept and prayed, and performed many works of penance, till at length God granted her what she had so earnestly asked. The slave became a fervent child of God's one true Church, and a faithful imitator of the piety of her mistress.

My child, pray often and fervently for the conversion of those who are not Catholics, that they may become members of His one true Church before they die.

FATHER GASPAR AND THE INDIAN CHIEF.

About the middle of the sixteenth century there lived at Ormuz, a city of India, a holy missionary called Gaspar Berse. He led so holy a life that he used to be called 'the second Francis Xavier.'

Among the multitude whom he converted to the true Faith was one who was the chief of a certain religious tribe of Indians called Yogis. About half a mile from the town, these pagans had a sort of monastery hewn out of the mountain-side. Gaspar was filled with zeal for their conversion. He used to go and speak to them of the truths of the Christian Faith; at first, indeed, without much fruit, but at length, by perseverance and prayer, they began to listen to him.

The sacred truths of our holy Faith found a place in their hearts, and one day they said to Gaspar: "Our Superior is at present absent in Arabia. When he comes home, speak to him the words you have spoken to us, and if he becomes a Christian, we also will all follow his example."

When the chief returned home, Gaspar lost no time in going to see him.

Like the rest of his tribe, he listened to his words, and the teachings of the good Father missionary won his heart; he consented to think seriously over the question of his conversion to the true Faith.

"Give me thirty days," he said, "to consider over this most important question."

Gaspar readily consented, and for thirty days he prayed and did penance for the pagan, and for the same time the pagan lived all alone, thinking over the matter in his mind. It was not an easy thing for him to give up his position, and to forfeit the veneration of his people; but God always helps by His grace those who are anxious to serve Him.

One night the Yogi in his cell heard a voice that said to him: "What are you doing? Why do you hesitate? The religion of the Christians is the only one that leads to heavenly bliss."

The struggle was over; the Yogi resolved to become a Christian. Rising up, he set out at once to find Father Gaspar, and shortly afterwards he had the happiness of being received into the Catholic Church along with all those who had lived under his authority.

The Yogis' temple and their monastery were later on changed into a Church and College of the Society of Jesus.

St. Joseph's Missionary Advocate, 276.

8

IN THIS WORLD WE MUST SUFFER FOR THE FAITH

Those to whom God has given the grace of belonging to His Church on earth must expect to meet with many afflictions. But, my child, you must be willing to lose everything, and even to suffer death itself, as the martyrs did, rather than deny your religion.

ST. JULITTA AND HER LITTLE BOY CYRUS.

Julitta was a noble lady of Lycaonia. By order of the Prefect Alexander, she was arrested because she was a Christian, and brought before his tribunal.

She had a little boy named Cyrus, who at this time was only five or six years old. He was a beautiful child, and the pride of his mother's heart. People who looked upon his angelic countenance thought he was more like one of the blessed spirits of God in Heaven than a child of this world.

When Julitta was led to the tribunal of the Governor, he asked her name and where she came from.

She gave him only one answer to all his questions. She said: "I am a Christian."

Then the Governor became very angry, and ordered her to be scourged.

All this time the child was in his mother's arms. When the Governor had given this order he commanded the child to be brought to him. It was with the greatest difficulty that this could be done, for when the boy saw what they were going to do, he put his little arms around his mother's neck, and clung more closely to her.

When the child was brought to the Governor, he made him sit upon his knees, and tried to stifle his cries by caressing him. But the little boy would not be pacified. He stretched out his arms towards his mother, and made every effort to get back to her again.

In the meantime, the executioners began to scourge Julitta, and while they were scourging her, the only words she said were these: "I am a Christian."

"I am a Christian too," said the child.

The Governor, on hearing this, became filled with great rage. He took the child by the foot, and from the high place on which he sat, threw him down with great violence to the ground. The child's head struck against the corner of the stone steps leading up to the tribunal, and was broken. At the same instant his holy soul ascended to Heaven, to God his Father there, for Whom he had shed his blood.

When the mother saw what had been done she was filled with great joy. "O my God," she said, "I thank Thee with all my heart because Thou hast taken my child to Thyself in Heaven, and hast given him the martyr's crown."

These words increased the fury of the judge, and he gave orders to the executioners to inflict on her still more terrible torments.

While this was being done, a herald cried out to her: "Julitta, have pity on yourself, and sacrifice to the gods."

"I will never sacrifice to devils nor to deaf and dumb idols. I honor Jesus Christ, the only Son of God. My greatest desire now is to see my son again, and it is only in Heaven that I can have that happiness."

The judge, seeing that neither threats nor torments could shake the courage of the heroic woman, commanded her to be beheaded, and her body, as well as that of her son, to be thrown into the place where the bodies of criminals were cast.

On the way to the place of execution, the Saint fell on her knees, and prayed thus to God: "O Lord, I thank Thee for having given my little boy an eternal kingdom in exchange for the sufferings of this life, which end so soon; receive me also, Thy unworthy servant, into the abode of the blessed spirits, where nothing defiled can enter, where my soul shall forever praise Thy Eternal Father, the Creator of all things, and the Holy Ghost. Amen."

When this prayer was ended, the executioner raised his sword, and cut off her head, and the soul of the holy martyr was once more united to that of her beloved boy in Heaven.

Some of her acquaintances secretly took the bodies, and buried them in a field near the city.

Petits Bolland, 16 Juin.

God may not require of you, my child, to die as the martyrs did, but, being a disciple of Jesus Christ, you shall most certainly have to suffer something for His sake, for He says unless we take up our cross we cannot be His disciples.

9

WE MUST NEVER DENY OUR FAITH, NOR BE ASHAMED OF IT

To deny your religion, or even to be ashamed of it, will make Our Lord ashamed of you. Jesus Christ says: "He that shall deny Me before men, I will also deny him before My Father Who is in Heaven" (St. Matt. X. 33).

WHY HE DID NOT OBTAIN THE SITUATION.

It happened not many years ago that there died at the Hague one who had formerly been a Minister of State in Holland.

He was not a Catholic, but he had a great esteem for our religion, and looked down with contempt on those half-hearted Catholics who are ashamed of their Faith.

Whilst holding the above-named office, a young man once came to him to ask him for employment in the service of the Government.

"What religion do you belong to?" said the Minister.

"I am a Catholic," replied the young man, "but I do not care much whether I continue to be one or not."

"Then I have no appointment for you," answered the statesman. "You were born and brought up in the grandest institution in the world, and you do not know how to esteem that privilege. I feel sure that a Catholic who does not esteem and love his Faith as his greatest treasure is not fit for the King's service, because he does not know how to serve his God."

The young man did not expect to receive this rebuke, and hung down his head through shame. He repented of his conduct, but it was too late, for the Minister, after saying these words, abruptly left him, and he was obliged to retire.

"Ave Maria" Notre Dame, Ind., U.S.A.

Ah, my child, if those who are ashamed of their Faith only knew how low they sink in the eyes of people who are not Catholics, they would soon be cured of their slavish fear. For your part, be proud of the honor God has conferred upon you, and esteem the privilege of being a member of His Church as your greatest glory.

THE BRAVE SOLDIER'S ANSWER.

In the city of Orim, in Chaldea, there was a short time ago, a Catholic family which was an example to all the other Catholics in the place, on account of the piety of its members.

The head of this family was a Pole, who, having left his native land, went over to that country, and entered the service of the Shah of Persia. On account of his bravery, he soon reached a high grade in the army, and finally died on the battlefield in defense of his Sovereign's rights.

His children walked faithfully in his footsteps. One of them, called Sukan, became a soldier, and was brave like his father. When he was only seventeen years of age the Shah, who had a great esteem for him, entreated him to renounce the Christian religion and become a Mahometan. "If you do this," he said, "I will raise you to the highest rank, and confer on you my choicest favors."

The young man answered: "O King, my father died for you, and I am ready to do the same. But if you want me to renounce my religion, then take this sword and kill me, for I would die rather than be guilty of such a crime."

The Shah was moved by these generous words. Instead of being angry, he praised the young Christian for his fidelity to his God, and as a mark of his esteem for him, raised him in a short time to the highest honors in the Persian army.

Catéch. en Exemples.

10

THE COMMUNION OF THE SAINTS IN HEAVEN

My child, when brothers and sisters love each other with a real affection, they always help each other in their necessities, and gladly give each other a share of what they possess.

The Holy Catholic Church is our mother, and all the faithful are our brethren. Some are already in Heaven. These are the Saints, with their great Queen, the most holy Mother of God, at their head; some are still on earth, and others are in the prison of Purgatory, but we are all united in the bonds of sincere affection. This union is called the "Communion of Saints."

The Saints who are in Heaven are in communion with us. We ask their prayers, and they help us by praying for us.

OUR HEAVENLY MOTHER MARY.

Mary, the Mother of God, is our mother also, and from her high throne in Heaven she watches over us her beloved ones, prays for us, and showers down on us many graces.

St. Mary Magdalen of Pazzi had a vision, in which she saw a boat sailing on the sea, in which were all the devout servants of Mary. Our Lady herself was at the helm. Although the sea was stormy, and the boat was tossed to and fro by the force of the waves, none of those in the boat seemed to be afraid. Mary at the helm guided it safely to the port to which they were going.

The Saint understood the vision to mean that all those who put themselves under the protection of Our Blessed Lady have nothing to fear on the stormy sea of this world, for she will guide them to the port of salvation in Heaven.

OUR LADY'S REPROACH.

The Blessed Alain was one day assailed by a great temptation, to which he was on the point of yielding, because he forgot to have recourse to the Blessed Mother of God for assistance.

Our Lady appeared to him, and reproached him for this negligence. "If you had only asked me to help you," she said, "I would have done so at once, and you would not have fallen into the danger of losing the grace of God."

ST. FELIX, OUR LADY'S DEAR CHILD.

St. Felix, of the Order of the Capuchins, was dying. He lay on a little straw in one of the cells of his monastery. As he lay there, with the rosary in his hand, praying fervently to the Blessed Mother of God, she appeared to him in the midst of heavenly glory.

"My own dear child Felix," she said, "I have come to bring you good news, you who have served me and loved me so well. The end of your life is now at hand, and you are to come with me to Heaven to receive the reward of your labors."

Saying this, she disappeared, and in a short time afterwards Felix expired, and followed her to Paradise.

O my child, what a happiness it is for us all to know that we have in Heaven a Mother who loves us and helps us so much!

Not only do our angel guardians watch over us in all our ways, but they assist us by their prayers, and obtain many graces for us from God.

BLESSED JANE OF ORVIETO.

Blessed Jane of Orvieto had not only a great respect for her guardian angel, but she placed entire confidence in his protection.

When she was very young she lost both her parents. This was a heavy blow for the affectionate child; but her mother had taught her ever to confide in the care of her guardian angel, and this gave her consolation in her deep sorrow.

A pious lady one day said to her: "My child, how can you support so courageously your terrible loss?"

The child showed her a little picture of a guardian angel her mother had given her, and answered: "Do you not know that my good angel has taken the place of my dear father and mother, and loves me even more than they could do? Why, then, should I give way to sadness?"

Her guardian angel protected her all her lifetime, and at the moment of her death carried her into Heaven.

The Saints who have reached their home in Heaven do not forget their brethren on earth, for it is not possible that one who has loved another on earth should be so ungrateful as to forget him when he has reached his happy home in Heaven.

ST. JEROME'S PRAYER.

St. Jerome had taught St. Paula to love God from her childhood, and watched over her as she grew up. At an early age God took her to Himself.

St. Jerome grieved over her; but knowing how innocently she had lived, he was sure she was already in Paradise. "O dear Saint Paula," he prayed, "help me now by your prayers, and do not forget me, who taught you to live for God and Heaven. Your faith and your piety have already placed you in the bosom of God, and I know He cannot now refuse to hear you. Oh, then, my child, pray, pray for me."

ST. GREGORY AND ST. BASIL.

St. Gregory Nazianzen and St. Basil were united by the bonds of the tenderest friendship. After serving God in holiness for many years, St. Basil died. St. Gregory was filled with grief at his loss; but knowing how piously he had lived, he had the firm hope in his breast that his dear friend was in the bosom of God, and praying for him.

The Saints have many temptations to endure on earth before they can receive the crown of glory in Heaven. St. Gregory also had to endure many of these assaults of Satan. But when they came upon him, he thought of St. Basil, and prayed to him in these words: "O great friend of God, and my dearest friend, O Basil, come and help me. Obtain for me the grace of being freed from these temptations, or at least the strength and courage to overcome them."

11

THE COMMUNION OF THE FAITHFUL ON EARTH

My child, when we speak of the communion of the faithful on earth, we mean that all the members of the true Church throughout the whole world are in communion with each other, by professing the same Faith, obeying the same authority, and assisting each other by their prayers and good works.

A BEAUTIFUL COMPARISON.

The Holy Ghost Himself, in the Sacred Scriptures, has explained this doctrine by a beautiful comparison. In the human body there are many different parts, and each part has its own special work to do. The foot is made for walking, the eye for seeing, the ear for hearing, and so on with each of the other members. Yet each member, although doing its own special duty, is acting for the benefit of the rest of the body. Thus it is for the benefit of the whole body that the eye sees, the ear hears, and the foot walks, because the whole body has a share in what each member does.

So in God's Church all the faithful form but one body, of which Christ Jesus is the Head, and although each person has a certain work given him to do by God, yet whatever he does is for the benefit of all the rest.

Hence it is for the benefit of the whole Church that the priest preaches, says Mass, and administers the Sacraments. It is also for the benefit of the whole Church that the religious pray in their cells, and the faithful people fulfill the duties of their state of life. And although each one receives for himself the merit of the good works he does, these good works benefit all the faithful throughout the world.

The following examples will show how we help each other by our prayers and good works:

ST. PETER IN PRISON.

"And at the same time," says the Scripture, "Herod the King stretched forth his hands to afflict some of the Church, and he killed James, the brother of John, with the sword, and, seeing that it pleased the Jews, he proceeded to take up Peter also. And when he had apprehended him, he cast him into prison, delivering him to four files of soldiers to be kept, intending, after the Pasch, to bring him forth to the people.

"Peter, therefore, was kept in prison, but prayer was made without ceasing by the Church unto God for him. And when Herod would have brought him forth, the same night, Peter was sleeping between two soldiers, bound with two chains. And behold an angel of the Lord stood by him, and a light shined in the room; and he, striking Peter on the side, raised him up, saying: 'Arise quickly!' And the chains fell off from his hands.

"And the angel said to him: 'Gird thyself, and put on thy sandals,' and he did so. And he said to him: 'Cast thy garment about thee and follow me.' And going out, he followed him. And he knew not that it was true which was done by the angel, but thought he saw a vision.

"And passing through the first and the second ward, they came to the iron gate that leadeth to the city, which of itself opened to them. And going out, they passed on, through one street, and immediately the angel departed from him" (Acts XII).

Thus was St. Peter liberated from prison through the prayers of the faithful.

A SISTER'S PRAYERS.

A young man went to Paris to study for the Law. He had been brought up piously by his mother, and many were the good pieces of advice he received from her before he left home, especially to be attentive to his religious duties, and to avoid bad company.

The young man promised most sincerely to his mother to do all she had asked him; but who can tell the terrible temptations to which a young man is exposed in a city like Paris?

It was the time of the Carnival. One of his companions asked him to lay aside for a little his strict way of living, and join with him in the enjoyments of the season.

At first he firmly refused, but at length the seductive words of his companion had their desired effect; he consented to go along with him.

On their way to the place where other evil comrades were waiting, his conscience told him he was about to do wrong, and the nearer he went, the louder that voice seemed to speak.

When he reached the place, and was about to enter, someone seemed to push him back. He looked to see who had done it, but saw no one. Then his conscience began to speak to him more loudly than ever: "Don't go in there."

Immediately he turned around, and without as much as saying a word to his companion, he ran away from the spot as fast as he was able, and did not stop until he had reached the place where he lodged.

It was not until many years after that he knew that he owed his escape to the prayers of his sister, who at that very time had been praying for him. She knew the very great danger to which her dear brother was exposed in Paris, especially at the Carnival-time, so she spent that time in prayer for him.

ST. GENEVIEVE SAVES PARIS.

When news reached Paris that Attila was on his way to destroy it, a panic seized upon the people.

But Genevieve, animated by the Spirit of God, cried out: "O men of Paris, if you do penance for your sins, God will drive back the enemy and save your city."

Many of the people, hearing these words, went along with her to the Church to pray. God heard their prayers, and for the sake of His servant Genevieve He spared the city.

My child, you should be very grateful to your Heavenly Father for making you a member of His family on earth, since it brings you so many blessings.

PART IX
THE CHURCH SUFFERING

1

PURGATORY, AND WHO GO THERE

"Purgatory is a middle state of souls suffering for a time on account of their sins." My child, that is what the Catechism tells us about Purgatory, or the Church Suffering.

Those go to Purgatory who depart this life in venial sin, or have not fully paid the debt of temporal punishment due to those sins, of which the guilt has been forgiven, before the soul left the body.

So great, my child, is the holiness of God, that He cannot permit any one of His children to enter Heaven until entire satisfaction has been made to Him for the sins committed while on earth.

A VOICE FROM BEYOND THE GRAVE.

There lived in one of the Dominican convents a very holy nun called Sister Angela. She had served God with great fervor from her infancy, and had daily made rapid progress towards perfection.

She became ill. The doctors said they had no hopes of her getting better. But she did not wish to die. So she asked her brother, who was already a great Saint, to come and visit her.

"O my brother, pray to God for me, that I may not die yet," she said to him.

But these prayers were not answered, for God had other designs on His servant. Angela daily became worse.

One day, while suffering acute pain, she had a vision. She seemed to be taken to a place where she saw the sufferings of Purgatory. They seemed to her to be terrible beyond all that can be imagined on earth; and she saw, too, the place to which her soul would have to go to suffer for certain faults she had done.

So terrible was this vision that when she came to herself she was trembling from head to foot.

When her brother came again to see her, she said: "My dear brother, if it be God's will that I am to die soon, oh, pray that time may be given me to expiate my faults on earth, so that I may escape the flames of Purgatory."

But this prayer was also without an answer. Angela died.

As they were carrying her body to the grave, her holy brother, by an inspiration from Heaven, commanded his sister, in the Name of Jesus Christ, to rise from the dead.

No sooner had he said the words than his sister rose up on her bier, and appeared once more alive.

God permitted this to happen that we might learn from her lips how terrible are the punishments in the world to come, even for venial sins.

The first thing Angela did was to begin a most penitential life. She was no longer content with ordinary penances, such as fasting and other similar acts of mortification, but she invented the most cruel penances that could be imagined, and performed them with an unceasing earnestness. People who saw her thought she had become insane, and her Superior advised her not to be so hard upon herself.

"Ah!" she answered, "what is all that I am doing in comparison with the sufferings which are reserved in Purgatory for those who have offended God on earth? What is all I am doing, and even if I should suffer a hundred times as much, what would it all be, when compared to the sufferings of Purgatory? Oh, nothing! nothing at all!"

And Angela continued her life of penance till she died, when, let us devoutly hope, her holy soul, purified by her sufferings on earth, went at once to enjoy the vision of God in Heaven.

Fr. Dom. Marchesi, Nov, 9.

WHAT ST. CATHERINE SAW IN PURGATORY.

St. Catherine of Bologna was once permitted by God to see the souls who were suffering in Purgatory. First she saw a raging fire, which burnt even to the inmost soul; it seemed to her as if the flames of hell could not burn more fiercely.

Then she saw a countless number of people, as thick as the leaves in the forest, all burning in these terrible flames. She saw there many who had led holy lives on earth, but who were not yet pure enough to be with God. She also saw there many little children who had never committed great sins, but only venial ones, such as being a little angry, or quarreling with their brothers and sisters, or disobeying their parents in small matters, and the pain she saw them suffering for these sins in those flames was awful to look upon.

God permitted her to see these things that she might warn us to avoid even the smallest sins, since God punishes them with so much severity in the next life.

A VOICE FROM THE TOMB.

Towards the end of the fourth century there lived at Artonne in France, a holy virgin named Vitalina. Besides her virginal purity, she was renowned for many other beautiful virtues, and her life was holy both before God and man.

When she died the people began to honor her as a Saint, and the fame of her holy life and happy death reached the city of Tours, where St. Martin dwelt. This great Saint, being anxious to visit her tomb, went to Artonne, and going to the grave where she lay, saluted it with respect.

At that moment her voice was heard coming out of the grave, humbly asking the Saint for his blessing.

St. Martin gave her his blessing, and asked her to tell him if she was now in Heaven in the presence of God.

"Alas, no!" she replied in a sad tone, "I am still in Purgatory; I will not get to Heaven for some time yet, because on a certain Friday, instead of meditating on the sufferings of my Lord Jesus Christ, as I ought to have done, I allowed my mind to dwell on worldly things."

St. Martin, turning to those who were with him, said: "O my brethren, if this virgin, whose life was so holy and so pure, is for a time kept out of Heaven, and suffers in Purgatory for so small a fault, what shall become of us poor sinners, who have so much to answer for?"

Then, turning towards the tomb, he said to Vitalina: "Be comforted, my child, for in three days you shall be in Paradise, for then the time of your punishment will be ended."

My child, keep away from sin, that you may not have to suffer in the terrible flames of Purgatory, for you cannot enter Heaven so long as there is a single stain upon your soul.

The souls in Purgatory know that one day their sufferings must come to an end; but who can understand how long each moment seems to them in their intense sufferings?

THE SOUL OF ST. MARY MAGDALEN PAZZI SAW.

One evening St. Mary Magdalen of Pazzi was in the chapel saying her prayers. Suddenly she saw before her the soul of one of her deceased Sisters, wrapped in a mantle of fire and suffering great pain. During her lifetime this Sister had been one of the holiest in the convent, and her death had been holy as her life had been.

St. Mary Magdalen was astonished at this terrible vision, and cried out to her: "O my Sister, how is it that you are suffering such awful torments, you who were always so good?"

"My reverend Mother," she replied, "I am suffering because I once neglected one grace which God offered me: I omitted one Communion which I was permitted to make."

With these words, and begging the Saint's prayers, she disappeared.

My dear child, how many graces have you already neglected? And how many sins have you already committed? Ah! Think how much you have already to account for to your Judge, Who is so strict and so just.

SISTER CATHERINE'S VISION.

A certain holy nun received a letter which informed her that her father was dead. He had not only been a good Christian, but was spoken of as a living Saint, so great was his piety. His daughter, knowing how strict are the judgments of God, for a long time offered up fervent prayers and pious works for the repose of his soul.

At last she ceased praying for him, because she thought he must be in Heaven, and that it was useless for her to pray for him any longer. But how great was her astonishment when Our Lord one day showed her in Purgatory the soul of her beloved father, suffering the most excruciating torments, and imploring her help. "O my daughter, pray for me, and do not forget your father who loved you so tenderly."

At the sight of the sad state of his soul she burst into tears, and, casting herself at the feet of Jesus, she besought Him through His most Precious Blood to free her father from his sufferings; or if it was necessary for someone to bear the punishment, she offered herself in his stead.

Our Lord was pleased to accept the offering she made. Her father's soul was immediately set free from Purgatory, but heavy indeed were the crosses and sufferings she had to bear from that day till the end of her life.

My child, you have sometimes heard people say that it does not matter how many little faults you fall into, since it is only mortal sins that can keep you out of Heaven. This is a sad mistake: small sins, it is true, do not keep us out of Heaven, but they are offenses against God, and therefore they must never be committed; and God punishes them in Purgatory with a punishment no one in this world can imagine.

A VOICE IN THE GARDEN.

One evening the venerable Stanislaus of Poland was saying the Rosary in the garden attached to his monastery. Suddenly he heard beside him sounds of grief and wailing. He looked on all sides, but saw nothing. He cried out: "Who is moaning so piteously, and where are you, that I may come to your assistance?" Still there was no answer, and the sad sounds continued as before.

Stanislaus began to think that this must be a temptation of Satan to put distractions in his mind at his prayer; so, making the sign of the Cross, he said: "I command you, in the Name of Jesus Christ, to tell me what you want."

Then he heard these words: "I am a soul from Purgatory, condemned by the justice of God to suffer unutterable sufferings. Oh that I were able to let the living know the awful punishments with which God punishes sin when the soul has left the body. If Christians knew it, even in part only, they would have a horror even for the smallest sin.

"Go and tell everyone what I have just revealed to you," continued the suffering soul, "for God has sent me to ask you to do it. Tell them that the smallest faults are punished in Purgatory with intense sufferings, and that everything they have not blotted out by penance on earth must be satisfied for in these terrible flames."

2

THE INTENSITY OF THE SUFFERINGS OF PURGATORY

The sufferings of Purgatory are more terrible than anything that can be imagined in this world. St. Augustine says: "The smallest pains that these poor souls endure are greater than the most cruel sufferings of this world." And St. Thomas affirms that the fire that burns them is similar to the fire of hell itself.

HIS CHOICE.

Turlot relates the following story:

"There was once a man who suffered great pains for a whole year, without a moment's relief. At the end of that time he prayed to God to take him out of this world, that he might be released from his terrible sufferings.

"God heard his prayer, and sent an angel to offer him his choice—to take three days in Purgatory, or to endure for another year in this world the same pain as he was then suffering.

"The man said within himself, 'I know that the sufferings of Purgatory are most severe, but they cannot be much more so than those I am suffering now; and besides, three days will soon pass by, and then they shall be over. O my God,' he said, 'I choose the three days in Purgatory.'

"His request was granted; he died, and his soul entered Purgatory.

"He had not been many moments there when his angel guardian came to visit him.

"'O angel of God,' cried out that suffering soul, 'why have you deceived me? Why have you left me so many years here, when God said my punishment was to end after three days?'

"'But,' the angel answered, 'you have only just died; your body is still warm on your death-bed, and why do you speak about years?'

"'O holy angel,' said the soul, 'give me my choice again, and I will go back to the world, and suffer gladly for another year all the pains of my former sickness, rather than remain another instant in this awful place.'

"This prayer was also heard, and he returned again to the world. For another year he suffered the same as he had previously done. But to everyone who came to see him he said: 'Oh! accept willingly all the sufferings God sends you in this world, and offer them up in satisfaction for your sins, for the greatest of these sufferings is as nothing when compared with what I suffered during the few moments I was in Purgatory.'"

From the Works of Turlot.

The greatest suffering of the souls in Purgatory is that of not being able to see God. At the moment a person dies he sees God for the first time, and so great is his desire to be with Him, that every moment He is separated from Him is the greatest punishment he can suffer. "O my God, my God, I must be with my God!" he cries. But as long as there is a stain of sin on his soul he is sent away from God into Purgatory till it be blotted out.

BROTHER ANTHONY CORSO.

Soon after Brother Anthony Corso died, he appeared to one of the brothers of his monastery, asking him to pray for him, that he might be freed from his sufferings.

The brother asked him what was the greatest suffering he had to endure.

"It is my not being able to see God; that is the greatest suffering of Purgatory. I do not know how I can bear any longer the pain of being deprived of the sight of my God. As long as I am in this state, I shall be the most unhappy of creatures."

O my child, let this thought continually dwell in your mind; it will enable you to keep from sin, which alone can hinder you from that union with God in heaven which is the supreme happiness of the saints and the reward which surpasses all understanding.

THIRTY YEARS.

A certain religious, when about to leave this world, begged of a priest to say Mass for the repose of his soul immediately after his death.

As soon as the holy man expired, the priest said Mass for him with great fervor and devotion. But scarcely had he finished Mass, when he saw before him the soul of the deceased religious. "O my friend," he said to him, "why did you neglect to fulfill your promise? Why did you leave me in the torments of Purgatory for thirty years?"

"What!" exclaimed the priest; "thirty years? It is not yet an hour since you died!"

"Learn from this," said the holy soul, "how terrible are the pains of Purgatory, since one hour's suffering there appears as long as thirty years."

HOW TIME IS MEASURED IN PURGATORY.

One day a certain religious man appeared to one of his brethren after his death; he had been three days in Purgatory. "O my brother," he said, "the three days I have been in Purgatory seem to me to have been longer than a thousand years, so intense is the pain I suffer."

O my child, keep in mind the terrible justice of God, and when temptation comes, you will be able to resist it.

3

HAPPINESS OF THE SOULS IN PURGATORY

Although the sufferings of Purgatory are so great, the souls there are happy, because they know that God loves them, and that they shall one day most certainly be with Him in Heaven.

THE ANSWER OF A SOUL FROM PURGATORY.

St. Stanislaus of Poland once asked a soul from Purgatory if he would prefer to return to life for a short time to do penance, or remain in that prison of fire till he had satisfied the Divine Justice.

He answered: "Although the sufferings of Purgatory are so great, I should prefer to live in Purgatory, with the certainty of going to Heaven, rather than return to life, and once more be in danger of losing my soul. But the greatest favor you can bestow on me is to pray to God to shorten the time I have yet to spend in Purgatory, so that I may be admitted sooner to the Kingdom of Heaven."

St. Stanislaus promised to pray for him, and the vision ended.

THE NUN'S DEATH.

On July 16, 1636, the Feast of Our Lady of Mount Carmel, about midday, a terrible storm of thunder and lightning broke over the little town of Bassano, in Italy. The hail came down with a loud noise, and the rain fell in torrents. Black and thick clouds hid the sun, and the darkness of night covered the whole country.

In that town there was a convent of holy nuns of the Benedictine Order, among whom was the Blessed Jane Mary Bonomi. There was among the Sisters one for whom this great servant of God had a particular affection; her name was Susanna. During the thunderstorm, as she was passing through one of the corridors, she was struck by the lightning and stretched dead on the ground.

The news of this sudden and terrible death filled the other religious with terror. The Blessed Jane Mary was also filled with grief when she saw dead at her feet the one whom she loved so much. But knowing the power and goodness of her Divine Spouse Jesus, she prostrated herself on the ground, and prayed to Him to restore to life her whom He had so suddenly called to Himself.

When her prayer was ended she made the sign of the Cross on the lips of the dead nun, and commanded her, in the Name of God, to rise to her feet. At the same moment Sister Susanna rose up, and began to speak, to the great joy of the religious who were around her.

When the first moments of surprise were over, they said to her: "Tell us, O Sister, what happened to you, and what you saw during the few moments that you were dead."

She answered: "After receiving the sentence of eternal happiness, I was taken to a very dark place, which I knew to be the prison of my Purgatory. But, O Sister Jane Mary, why did you call me back?" she said in a tone of reproach to that holy Superioress. "Why did you take me out of that dark place, where my salvation was certain, and bring me once more in this weary world, where I may lose my soul?"

Then she continued, after a pause: "Believe me, dear Sisters, it is much better to be in that dark dungeon, where one is sure some day of going into Heaven, than to be in this world, where one cannot be certain of reaching Paradise."

"My Sister," said Blessed Jane Mary, "it is the will of God. You will live here for some time yet, and you will assist at my death."

She lived many years in the convent; but her thoughts were not in this world any longer. After waiting more than thirty years she died in peace.

Lives of the Saints, March 1.

4

WE CAN HELP THE SOULS IN PURGATORY

My child, the Sacred Scriptures tell us that "it is a holy and wholesome thought to pray for the dead that they may be loosed from their sins" (II Macc. XII. 46).

Who can help the souls that are suffering in Purgatory? They cannot do anything for themselves, for their time for meriting is ended. But we can help them. Hence they turn towards those who loved them most dearly when on earth, and they cry to them continually from their prison of fire: "Have pity on us, have pity on us, at least you our friends, for the hand of the Lord hath touched us."

THE CHILDREN'S CRY.

When the Emperor Henry had besieged a certain city for a long time, and the inhabitants still refused to surrender, he gave orders to his soldiers to take it by storm, and to put to death all the inhabitants, young and old, without mercy.

When the people heard this proclamation they were seized with a great fear, for they knew how rigorously these commands would be executed. They held a council to deliberate what they would do to appease his wrath and move him to show them mercy. Then, by the advice of one of their leading citizens, they gathered together all the little children that were in the city, and, forming a long procession, they made them go to the throne of the Emperor, and there throw themselves on the ground, striking their breasts and crying out in accents of grief: "Have pity on us, O Emperor, have pity on us."

When the Emperor saw all the little ones prostrated before him, and heard their sorrowful cries, he burst into tears and pardoned the inhabitants of that city for the sake of the children.

BLESSED CONRAD'S PRAYERS.

In the "Lives of the Saints," on March 14, we read of a wonderful event which happened to Blessed Conrad, whose feast is celebrated on that day.

On one occasion he went to pay a visit to the monastery of Offida. Whilst he was staying there, the religious of that house asked him if he would, in his great charity, try to correct one of the younger brothers, who was leading a very careless life, and was a great trouble, not only to the rest of the brethren, but to everyone who came in his way; and was, moreover, by his bad example, the cause of great scandal.

Conrad promised to speak to him.

Taking the erring brother aside, he spoke to him in words of burning charity, and so full of piety, that the young man, entering into himself, deplored his past irregularities, and became thenceforth a model of virtue to the whole community. He became obedient, kind, pious, full of respect for his Superiors; and, instead of giving them trouble, as he had done in the past, he became for them a subject of consolation, and the object of their affection.

Shortly after his conversion he was struck with a dangerous illness and died, regretted by all the brethren of the monastery.

Some days after his death, Blessed Conrad was saying his prayers before the altar in the chapel. While praying, the soul of the deceased religious appeared to him, and saluted him with great respect, saying to him, "My Father."

"Who are you?" asked Blessed Conrad in surprise.

"I am the soul of that brother who died here a few days ago."

"Well, my brother, tell me how fares it with you in the unseen world? Where are you?"

"Thanks be to God," said the apparition, "I am happy. I have escaped the fire of hell, because I repented when you spoke to me while I yet lived. But I am not in Heaven yet; I am suffering most rigorous chastisement in Purgatory, in expiation of the sins I committed on earth.

"O Father," he continued, "I ask of you in your goodness, and in your charity, that as you came to my assistance when I was living, and took me out of an evil course of life, you will come again to my assistance, and take me out of this awful prison of Purgatory."

"What can I do to help you, my brother?"

"Oh, say an 'Our Father' for me! Pray, pray, my Father, for your prayers are so pleasing to God."

Blessed Conrad, still on his knees, said one "Our Father," and the prayer "Eternal rest give unto him, O Lord, and let perpetual light shine upon him."

"O my Father, what joy, what consolation you have given me by that prayer! Oh, say it again!"

The good Conrad said again the "Our Father" and the prayer "Eternal rest."

"O holy Father," cried out the departed religious, "I conjure you, say it again, and again, and again."

Then Conrad, seeing the consolation he was giving the poor suffering soul, said the prayers one hundred times; and when he had done this, the departed brother said to him: "In God's name, I thank you, holy Conrad, most dear Father, for the charity you have shown me. Your prayers have taken me out of Purgatory, and, behold! I am now going to the Kingdom of Heaven."

At these words the soul of the departed disappeared and went to Heaven, to be in the presence of God forever, and to pray for him who had delivered him from the pains of Purgatory.

Lives of the Saints, March 14.

AN ACT OF THANKSGIVING.

One day a pious young girl, while thinking on the benefits she had received from God, and the loving care He was daily taking of her, cried out to Him: "O my God, what return can I make to Thee Who hast given me so much?"

God answered her in her heart: "My child, there is one thing you can do for Me which will repay Me for what I have done for you. Help the poor suffering souls in Purgatory. Ah! I love them tenderly, because they are My faithful children, and the greatest desire of My heart is to see them in Heaven. But My justice requires that they suffer in Purgatory for the faults for which they have not satisfied Me. But you can, by your prayers, free them from their pains, and send them into Heaven."

The young woman answered: "O my God, I shall then give Thee those souls whom Thou lovest, and I shall go and ask others to pray for them, that they may be the sooner brought to Thee."

5

HOLY MASS OFFERED UP FOR THE SOULS IN PURGATORY

The most powerful means for the release of the souls in Purgatory is the holy sacrifice of the Mass, because in the Mass we offer up to God His well-beloved Son with all the merits of His death and passion in their behalf.

ST. MALACHY OF IRELAND AND HIS SISTER.

St. Malachy, Bishop of Armagh, in Ireland, had a sister whose life was far from being what it ought to have been. The Saint was much grieved at her conduct, and told her that so long as she continued to lead that kind of life he would not visit her nor speak to her.

Some time afterwards word was brought to him that she was dead, and that before her death she had repented of her worldly life.

The Saint was glad to hear of her repentance, and for many days he offered up the holy sacrifice of the Mass for the repose of her soul; then he ceased to pray for her.

One night during his sleep he thought he saw someone come into his room and say to him: "Your sister is standing at the door, and is complaining that for the past thirty days you have not given her any food to refresh her."

The Bishop suddenly awoke, and began to think if what he had seen was a dream or a reality. He counted the days that had elapsed since he last said Mass for his sister, and discovered that it was exactly thirty days.

Next morning he again offered up the holy sacrifice for her, and continued to do so for some days.

One day he thought he saw his sister standing at the door of the church, but on the outside. She tried to go in, but was not able. Her garments, too, were of a dark color.

St. Malachy continued to offer up the holy sacrifice for her as usual. After a few days he saw her again. This time her garments were almost white, and she was able to go into the church, but still could not go near the altar.

On a third occasion he once more saw her. This time she was clad in a robe of dazzling brightness, and seemed to walk in the midst of a company of Saints clad like herself. She stood near the altar of God, and her face wore a look of supreme happiness.

Then the Saint knew that she was with God in Heaven.

Life of St. Malachy.

THE VISION OF ST. THOMAS OF AQUINAS.

One day St. Thomas of Aquinas was saying his prayers. Suddenly there appeared before him the soul of his sister, a very holy nun, who had died a few days previously.

She said to him: "O my brother, pray for me. I am still in Purgatory, suffering acute pains in satisfaction for my sins. Offer up the holy sacrifice of the Mass for me, that I may be delivered from this awful place." She then disappeared.

St. Thomas did as she desired him. Not only did he say Mass for her, but said many other prayers besides, and mortified himself in many ways to obtain her release.

After some days she appeared to him again. This time there was great joy upon her countenance. "My dear brother," she said, "you need not pray for me any longer, for I am going to Heaven now. Many thanks for your prayers and mortifications, and especially for the holy sacrifice of the Mass. I will not forget you before the Throne of God."

When she had said these words, she disappeared, leaving the Saint full of consolation, for he knew that she was now happy with God in Paradise.

Life of St. Thomas of Aquinas.

THE PRIEST'S REQUEST.

In the Life of the Cure of Ars, there is the following story. One day during his instructions, he said to the people, "You remember what I once told you about the holy priest who was praying for his friend who had lately died. God had, it appears, made known to him that he was in Purgatory, and he thought that the best thing he could do for him was to offer up the holy sacrifice for the repose of his soul.

"When he came to the moment of consecration, he took the Sacred Host in his hands and said: 'O holy and eternal Father, let us make an exchange; Thou hast the soul of my friend who is in Purgatory, and I have the body of Thy Son Who is in my hands. Do Thou then deliver my friend, and I offer Thee Thy Son with all the merits of His death and passion.'

"As soon as he had said these words he saw the soul of his friend going up to Heaven all radiant with glory."

O my child, pray fervently for the holy souls in Purgatory, that their sufferings may be the sooner brought to an end, and that they may more speedily enter their home in Heaven.

"MAY THEY REST IN PEACE."

A certain priest was one day saying Mass for the souls of the faithful departed. At the end of Mass, when he said these words, "May they rest in peace," he heard many voices answering joyfully, "Amen."

Whenever you say that little prayer, the holy souls, without doubt, also answer you, although you may not be able to hear them.

"HASTEN! COME QUICKLY! FOR MASS WILL SOON BE ENDED."

Thomas of Cantiprensis relates that a certain holy monk was one day standing at the altar, offering up the holy sacrifice for the souls of the faithful departed.

When he came to that part of the Mass where the priest says, "Lamb of God, Who takest away the sins of the world, give them rest," he heard in the distance, as it were, the voices of a great multitude crying out to each other: "Come quickly, that we may obtain that peace which the priest of God is praying for, for Mass will soon be ended."

When the moment of Holy Communion came, and the monk held in his hands the Sacred Body of Our Lord, he had a vision. A great multitude of souls approached the altar, and, kneeling down reverently before it, seemed to receive some refreshment which filled them with unutterable joy and happiness; and he saw that as those who had been nearest to the altar were retiring, they cried out with a loud voice to others who were in the distance:

"Hasten! Come quickly! For Mass will soon be ended."

The pious monk was rapt in ecstasy for several hours. The brethren who were assisting at Mass could not imagine what was the cause of it. So when he returned to his senses, and finished the holy sacrifice, his Superior commanded him to make known to them what he had seen.

Ever afterwards he endeavored to inspire into the hearts of all he spoke to a deep devotion towards the holy souls in Purgatory; and as often as possible he said Mass devoutly for them, that they might obtain greater relief, and that their deliverance might be hastened.

Thomas Cantrip

A GREAT CONVERSION.

Saint Leonard of Port Maurice relates the following example to show how advantageous it is, even for sinners, to pray for the holy souls in Purgatory.

There lived in Rome a woman who had laid aside all thoughts of God, and lived only to gratify the evil inclinations of her heart. The only good thing she did was to cause the holy sacrifice of the Mass to be offered up for the souls in Purgatory every day of her life.

One day when she was about to yield to temptation, she suddenly felt in her heart a sincere sorrow for her sins, and a great desire to do penance for them. She rose up at once and went to the church, where she made a general confession of her whole life, shedding tears of sorrow at the feet of the priest. From that day till the hour of her death she persevered in the holy life she had begun, and when that hour came she died in peace. She used to say: "Had it not been for my charity to the souls in Purgatory, I would have lived and died in sin, and have been lost forever."

THE MONK'S VISION.

In the days of St. Bernard, a certain monk belonging to the Order of Clairvaux appeared to his brethren after his death to thank them for having delivered his soul from Purgatory.

When they asked him which of all the prayers and good works they had offered up for him had done him the most good, he led them into the church where a priest was offering up the holy sacrifice, and said, as he pointed towards the altar: "Look, my brethren, that is the means by which my deliverance has been effected; that is the great sacrifice that takes away the sins of the world."

You see, my child, the benefit the holy Mass confers on these poor suffering souls. What greater reward could you desire than the happiness of knowing that by causing the holy Mass to be said for them, you have been the means of their deliverance?

ST. PETER DAMIAN.

St. Peter Damian lost his parents when he was only a child. He was left to the care of one of his older brothers, who was very cruel to him. His clothing was only rags scarcely sufficient to cover him, and his food barely enough to sustain his life.

One day the child found on the road a piece of money in silver. This was for him a treasure, and he would now be able to buy some dainty food, or shoes for his feet. As he was thinking of what he would purchase with it, he thought of his parents who were dead, and how kind they had been to him; and he remembered at the same time that perhaps they might be at that moment suffering in Purgatory. So he said to himself: "I shall take this piece of silver to the priest and ask him to offer up the holy Mass for them."

This he did, and from that moment a great change came over his life; for one of his brothers who was living at a distance, hearing of his distress, went and took him to his own house, and treated him with kindness and brotherly affection. Under his care Peter grew up in piety. He afterwards became a priest, and is now a Saint in Heaven.

Thus did God reward him with the greatest spiritual and temporal blessings on account of his devotion to the suffering souls in Purgatory.

6

HOLY COMMUNION HELPS THE SOULS IN PURGATORY

My child, when you go to Holy Communion you can help the suffering souls in Purgatory by offering it up for them. At that happy moment, when Jesus is in your soul, He will most certainly hear your prayers, since there is nothing His Sacred Heart desires so much as to see these holy souls with Himself in Heaven. But, oh! Be sure and pray with fervor.

EFFECTS OF ONE GOOD COMMUNION.

The venerable Louis de Blois tells us that a very great servant of God, whom he knew and loved, was one day visited by a soul from Purgatory suffering intense torments. During his lifetime this soul had been a great friend of this servant of God.

He said to him: "O my friend, I have been condemned to suffer this intense pain, because during life I had received Holy Communion without sufficient preparation and without fervor. I have come to ask you, by that tender friendship we had for each other long ago, to help me now. Go to Holy Communion once for me, and do so with all the fervor and love you can, and I hope that God will accept of it as an act of reparation for my want of fervor and deliver me from these terrible sufferings."

The holy man did so, and the departed soul reappeared to him, all surrounded with a brightness and full of happiness, and said: "At last, thanks to you, my dear friend, I am about to see my adorable Lord and Master, face to face in Heaven."

Catéch. en Exemples.

ST. GERTRUDE'S GREAT CONSOLATION.

St. Gertrude never felt so happy as on the days when she had heard Mass and offered up Holy Communion for the relief of the souls in Purgatory.

One day she asked Our Lord why it was that she felt so happy on these days.

Jesus answered her: "My daughter, it is because it would not be right for Me to refuse to grant you some return for the fervent prayers you offer up to Me for the souls in Purgatory."

O my child, what a consolation it must be for you to remember this—you who so often go to Communion for the souls in Purgatory; and how anxious you should be to hear Mass and receive Holy Communion for them, since it brings so much relief to them, and so many blessings to yourself.

7

PRAYERS AND GOOD WORKS HELP THE SOULS IN PURGATORY

My child, Jesus Christ tells us in the Gospel that if we are merciful to others He will be merciful to us: "Blessed are the merciful, for they shall find mercy." If Our Lord has promised to reward us for every work of mercy we perform for His sake to His children in this world, how great will be our reward, if by our prayers and good works, we send to Heaven the souls in Purgatory who are so dear to Him.

HELP IN THE HOUR OF NEED.

Cardinal Baronius relates that there was once a holy man lying in the agonies of death, whom the devil was tempting with thoughts of despair. During the whole course of his life, this man had done much for the repose of the holy souls in Purgatory.

In the midst of the darkness, he suddenly saw thousands of heavenly spirits clad in shining armor, fighting in his defense against the Evil One.

"Who are you, O blessed beings, who thus defend me?"

"We are those souls," was the answer, "whom by your prayers, penances, and Masses you have released from Purgatory, and we have come to conduct you to Heaven."

"BLESSED ARE THE MERCIFUL."

St. Francis de Sales gives us the following account of an event which took place in the city of Padua while he himself was studying there:

"There was amongst the students of the University a wicked custom which in our day would shock the minds of even the most indifferent. During the night, when it was quite dark, there being no lamps to light up the streets, these students were accustomed to go about armed with swords and guns. If they met anyone, they would ask, 'Who goes there?' and if they got no answer they would instantly kill him.

"Now it happened that one of the students was going home after night had set in. He was met by another student, who asked him the usual question. He neglected to give an answer, and he was at once killed.

"When the young man saw what he had done, he was filled with terror and remorse. He knew that if he should be discovered, he would have to suffer death at the hands of the law. Suddenly he remembered that not far from the place where he stood lived a very pious widow, the mother of one of the students of the University, who was one of his dearest friends. 'I will go to this good woman,' he said to himself, 'tell her what I have done, and I am sure she will conceal me in her house until I can escape from the city.'

"So he went to her, and told her all that had happened, and begged of her to have pity on him, and save him from the hands of the ministers of justice, who would soon be in search of him.

"The good woman, touched with pity, said to him: 'You have nothing now to be afraid of; you are as safe here as in any place in the world; you can stay with me as long as you please.'

"Not many minutes after this someone came in great haste to the door of the widow's house, and cried out: 'Your son has just been killed; his body is lying in the street, and the murderer has escaped.'

"Who can understand the shock this news gave that mother? She was almost beside herself with grief. But who can imagine the horror of the young student when he discovered that the man he had so inhumanly killed was the son of his protectress, and his own dearest friend?

"He began to tear his hair and to cry out as if he had suddenly become insane. He threw himself at her feet, and cried out: 'Oh, wretch that I am! how could I have committed such a crime! I will at once deliver myself up into the hands of justice that I may publicly expiate it with my life.'

"But the pious woman said: 'No, that must not be. As Jesus forgave His murderers, so also will I forgive you; only go at once to Confession, that you may obtain pardon from God for your sin; then go to some place of safety where you may serve God in peace for the rest of your life.'

"When the heroic woman had finished speaking, the soul of her murdered son suddenly stood before her.

"'My mother,' he said, 'your great charity towards that man who killed me has been so pleasing to God that in recompense for it He has been pleased to free me at once from Purgatory and take me into Heaven; whereas, had you not done so, I should have had to remain a very long time in that place of punishment to make satisfaction for my sins.'"

Spirit of St. Francis de Sales.

8

TO HELP THE HOLY SOULS IS BENEFICIAL TO OURSELVES

By offering up your prayers and good works for the relief of the suffering souls in Purgatory, and by applying to them all the indulgences you can gain, you do more to cancel the debt which may be against you than if you kept them all for yourself.

ST. GERTRUDE CONSOLED.

Denis the Carthusian tells us that the holy virgin Gertrude made an offering every morning, in favor of the souls in Purgatory, of all her works of satisfaction and all the indulgences she might gain during the course of the day.

This she continued to do all her lifetime; and frequently did she receive a visit from the holy souls who had been relieved by her prayers. They would appear to her when about to enter Heaven, to thank her for her charity and exhort her to continue to aid their brethren who were still suffering in that prison of fire.

After a long life spent in this manner Gertrude became very ill. As she lay on her sick-bed, Satan came to tempt her, and to fill her soul with thoughts of despair. He represented to her that since she had given up, in favor of the souls in Purgatory, all her good works, she would now justly be sent there to suffer in their stead. He placed before her mind the awful torments she would soon have to endure, to expiate her many faults, since she had reserved nothing for herself of all the good she had done, but had given it all to strangers.

Gertrude was filled with terror at the thought. "Oh, how unfortunate I am!" she said. "In a short time I must die. I shall have to give to God a strict account of every action of my life. Oh! how long I shall have to suffer in Purgatory for the sins of my long life, without hope of obtaining any remission of my punishment, since I have offered up everything in favor of others! I shall have to dwell in that prison till I have paid the last farthing. O my God, will You allow this to happen to me?"

Our Blessed Lord was pleased to come to the assistance of His beloved servant. He appeared to her and said:

"What, O My Gertrude, is the cause of your sorrow?"

She answered: "O my Lord, I am filled with grief because I am about to die, and I have no store of good works laid past to satisfy Your Divine Justice for my sins. I have given them all for the relief of the suffering souls in Purgatory, as You well know."

Jesus smiled on her as He said: "Gertrude, My daughter, that you may know how pleasing to Me has been your great charity to these holy souls, I, from this moment, remit all the punishment due to your faults. More than this, as I promised to reward a hundredfold those who have renounced all for My sake, I will reward you for your charity by increasing the glory due to you in Heaven. By My order all those souls whom you have relieved will come forth to meet you and conduct you amidst hymns of joy to the Heavenly Jerusalem."

Great joy now filled her soul at hearing these glad tidings. She called together the Sisters of the community, and told them what had happened. Then, with a smile upon her lips and her eyes full of heavenly brightness, her happy soul left the body, to enter into the possession of that happiness which her Heavenly Spouse had promised her.

Denis the Carthusian.

When St. Augustine was asked why he prayed so much for the dead, he replied: "I pray for the dead in order that when they reach Heaven they may pray for me." Yes, these holy souls will pray for you, my child, if you pray for them.

"O MY JESUS, HAVE MERCY ON THEM."

Mother Mary of Providence had already as a child a great devotion for the holy souls, so that she would sometimes, even when playing, remind her companions of Purgatory, and exhort them to pray for those poor prisoners. After Communion on All Souls' Day (1853) she felt an inspiration to found a religious institute for the relief of the souls in Purgatory. The saintly Cure d'Ars confirmed her in this design, saying to her: "This idea comes from the Sacred Heart of Our Lord, and He will bless your devotedness." After many great difficulties she succeeded at last in founding in Paris a congregation called the "Helpers of the Holy Souls," the members of which add to the three usual vows a fourth one—namely, to renounce all the satisfactory merit of their prayers, labors and sufferings in favor of the holy souls, and to devote themselves to the service of the sick. Whilst the German troops were besieging Paris (1871), she was prostrated by her last illness. Instead of trembling with nervous alarm at the thunder of the cannon, she reposed quietly, as she had done during her whole life, in the arms of Providence. "I can," she said, "think of nothing but of the souls who are entering into their eternity. O my Jesus, have mercy on them; may each pang of my soul tell Thee of my love, and ask from Thee the deliverance of a soul in Purgatory!" Her last words to her Sisters who surrounded her death-bed were: "May your love for the holy souls increase daily more and more!"

Garside: *The Helpers of the Holy Souls.*

THE VOICES ST. BRIDGET HEARD.

In the revelations of St. Bridget, we read: "One day I heard a great voice, that seemed to come from the prison of Purgatory, which said: 'What return and what recompense shall be given to those who have brought us relief in our affliction?'"

Another voice, louder still, cried out: "O my God and my Savior of Thine infinite goodness, be pleased to reward a hundredfold all those among the living who have come to our assistance, and who by their prayers have raised us up sooner to Thee."

Again she heard the voice of an angel saying: "Blessed are those in the world, who have by their prayers, their alms, and their good works, helped the holy souls of Purgatory."

Revelations of St. Bridget.

9

TO NEGLECT THE HOLY SOULS IS INJURIOUS TO OURSELVES

If you do not pray for the holy souls in Purgatory, my child, you may have to suffer long in Purgatory hereafter for this neglect.

THE VISION OF ST. ANTONINUS.

Antoninus was Bishop of Marseilles in the sixth century. While he occupied that See, it happened that a certain man died, and his pious friends who were left behind caused many masses and prayers to be said for the repose of his soul.

Not very long after his death the deceased man appeared to a holy religious who dwelt in the same city, and said to him:

"My brother, all the masses and all the prayers that have been offered up for me have done me no good. I am in Purgatory, and shall have to remain there till I have satisfied the justice of God, and I have hitherto received no relief from all that has been done for me."

The religious asked him the reason of this.

"It is because, when I was alive, I neglected to pray for the holy souls in Purgatory. All the benefit of the prayers and masses said for me is given to those souls for whom I ought in a special manner to have prayed, and did not do it. They are relieved instead of me, and I have to suffer. O pray for me," he continued, "that God may forgive me my neglect; and go and preach everywhere to people, to pray for the souls of the faithful departed, lest when they themselves die, God may treat them as He has treated me."

After these words the vision disappeared.

Life of St. Antoninus, October 13.

My child, it is sad to see how people neglect to pray for their departed friends, and thus leave those whom they so tenderly loved on earth to suffer so long and so terribly in the prison of Purgatory.

A MOTHER'S USELESS TEARS.

Thomas Cantimprensis tells us the following story about an aunt of his who lost her son, for whom she had a special affection:

"My aunt was inconsolable for the loss of her dear boy. She wept for him day and night.

"One day she had a vision. She thought she saw a company of beautiful boys, all clad in shining garments, and full of joy and happiness. As they passed along, she thought her own son might be amongst them, but he was not there. While she was looking, she saw him coming after them, but at a great distance from them. He seemed to be walking with great difficulty, as if he were carrying a heavy burden.

"'O my son,' said the fond mother, 'why are you not in the company of those beautiful youths, and why do you seem so weary and so fatigued?'

"'Look, mother—look at the burden I am carrying. These are the tears you have shed for me; they have done me no good, but, on the contrary, have kept me from reaching those beautiful young boys you see. O my mother, if you weep for me, weep with resignation to the Holy Will of God. Go and get the holy sacrifice of the Mass offered up for me, and then this weight will be taken from me, and I shall be able to join those companions who are now so happy.'"

There is often a very great mistake made by even good people. It is this: when anyone dies whom they love, and whom they know to have been good, they say: "Such a one is sure to be in Heaven"; and thus they neglect to pray for that one. Now, this is a mistake, my child. You should pray for everyone, no matter how holy they may have been during life.

"O MY FATHER, HAVE PITY ON ME!"

In a monastery belonging to the Friars Minors in Paris, there died a very holy religious. On account of his piety, he had been called "The Angel," for he was as like an Angel as one can be in this world.

In that Order it is the custom for each of the Fathers to say three Masses for every one of their brethren who has passed out of this life.

In that same house one of the Fathers, although he knew of this obligation, did not fulfill it, for, like others, he thought that the good religious must have gone straight to Heaven as soon as he had breathed his last.

After a few days the deceased brother suddenly appeared before him as he was walking in the garden. In a voice that reached the very depths of his soul, he heard the dead man say: "O my Father, have pity on me!"

The Father, full of astonishment, cried out: "What, O holy soul! do you need help from us?"

"Yes, Father, I am in Purgatory, waiting till you have offered up the three Masses you have to say for me. When you shall have said them, God will take me to Heaven."

"My dear brother, I would have said them before this had I thought you stood in need of prayer, but I was certain that after such a holy life as you led you must have gone straight to Heaven."

"Alas! alas!" said the apparition, "no one can tell how severely God judges and punishes. His infinite sanctity finds faults even in our best actions, and we must give an account of everything, even to the last farthing."

That day, and on the two following mornings, the religious offered up the holy sacrifice with great fervor and devotion, and on the third day the deceased again appeared to him to thank him, and to tell him that his time of purgation was ended, and he was about to enter Heaven.

PART X
THE CHURCH TRIUMPHANT

1

WHAT IS HEAVEN LIKE?

God made you, my child, to be happy forever in Heaven. The happiness of Heaven consists in seeing, loving, and enjoying God there. You are now going to read a few examples about the glory of Heaven, that you may often think of it, and so one day possess it.

ST. JOHN IN THE ISLAND OF PATMOS.

In the year 95 a great persecution broke out against the Christians in the East. St. John was the only one of the Apostles then living, for all the others had gone to receive their reward in Heaven.

By order of the Proconsul of Asia, he was arrested and sent to Rome. The Emperor Domitian ordered him to be put to death by being cast into a cauldron of boiling oil; but God preserved him from this death by a miracle.

Then the Emperor, being very angry, banished him into the island of Patmos, that he might die there.

It was whilst in that island that God showed him in a vision the Church Triumphant in Heaven, which will forever be our home if we are faithful to God now.

"I was in the Spirit," he says, "and behold, there was a throne set in Heaven, and upon the throne One sitting; and He that sat was to the sight like the jasper and the sardine stone. And there was a rainbow round about the throne, in sight like unto an emerald. And round about the throne were four-and-twenty seats, and upon the seats four-and-twenty ancients sitting, clothed in white garments, and on their heads were crowns of gold.

"And in the sight of the throne was, as it were, a sea of glass like to crystal, and in the midst of the throne, and round about the throne, were four living creatures; and they rested not day and night, saying: 'Holy, holy, holy, Lord God Almighty, Who was, and Who is, and Who is to come.'

"And when these living creatures gave glory, and honor and benediction to Him that sitteth on the throne, Who liveth forever and ever, the four-and-twenty ancients fell down before Him that sitteth on the throne, and adored Him that liveth forever and ever, and cast their crowns before the throne, saying: 'Thou art worthy, O Lord our God, to receive honor and glory, and power, because Thou hast created all things.'

"After this I saw a great multitude which no man could number, of all nations, and tribes, and peoples, and tongues, standing before the throne, and in sight of the Lamb, clothed with white robes and palms in their hands; and they cried with a loud voice, saying: 'Salvation to our God Who sitteth upon the throne, and to the Lamb.'

"And all the angels stood round about the throne, and the ancients, and the four living creatures; and they fell down before the throne upon their faces and adored God, saying: 'Amen, benediction and glory, and wisdom and thanksgiving, honor and power, and strength to our God forever and ever. Amen.'

"And one of the ancients said to me: 'These that are clothed in white robes, who are they, and whence came they?'

"And I said to him: 'My Lord, Thou knowest.'

"And he said to me: 'These are they who are come out of great tribulation, and have washed their robes, and have made them white in the blood of the Lamb: therefore they are before the throne of God. They shall no more hunger nor thirst, neither shall the sun fall on them, nor any heat; for the Lamb which is in the midst of the throne shall rule them; and God shall wipe away all tears from their eyes.'

"After these things I heard, as it were, the voice of much people in Heaven, saying: 'Alleluia. Salvation and glory and power is to our God, for true and just are His judgments. . . '

"And again they said: 'Alleluia. . . .'

"And the four-and-twenty ancients and the four living creatures fell down and adored God that sitteth upon the throne, saying: 'Amen; Alleluia.'

"And a voice came out from the throne, saying: 'Give praise to our God, all ye His servants; and you that fear Him little and great.'

"And he showed me the holy city Jerusalem coming down out of Heaven from God, having the glory of God; and the light thereof was like to a precious stone. And I saw no temple therein, for the Lord God Almighty is the Temple thereof and the Lamb.

"And the city hath no need of the sun nor of the moon to shine in it, for the glory of God hath enlightened it, and the Lamb is the lamp thereof. And the nations shall walk in the light of it, and the kings of the earth shall bring their glory and honor into it. The Lamb shall be in it, and His servants shall serve Him, and they shall see His face, and His Name shall be on their foreheads; and night shall be no more, and they shall not need the light of the lamp, nor the light of the sun, because the Lord God shall enlighten them, and they shall reign forever and ever.

"He that shall overcome shall possess these things; and I will be his God, and he shall be My son."

Apocalypse of St. John.

THE GLORY OF JESUS CHRIST IN THE CHURCH TRIUMPHANT.

"After these things," continues St. John, "I heard as it were the voice of a great multitude, and as the voice of many waters, and as the voice of great thunders, saying: 'Alleluia; for the Lord our God the Almighty hath reigned. Let us be glad and rejoice and give glory to Him; for the marriage of the Lamb is come, and His wife hath prepared herself. And it is granted to her that she should clothe herself with fine linen, glittering and white; for the fine linen are the justifications of saints.'

"And he said to me: 'Write: Blessed are they that are called to the marriage supper of the Lamb.'

"And he said to me: These words of God are true...

"And I saw Heaven opened, and behold a white horse; and He that sat upon him was called 'Faithful and True,' and with justice doth He judge and fight. And His eyes were as a flame of fire, and on His head were many diadems, and He had a name written which no man knoweth but Himself. And He was clothed with a garment sprinkled with blood; and His Name is called 'The Word of God.' And the armies that are in Heaven followed Him on white horses clothed in fine linen, white and clean. And He hath on His garment and on His thigh written, 'King of kings and Lord of lords.'"

THE GLORY OF THE SAINTS AND ANGELS.

The Holy Scriptures describe to us, as far as it is possible for man to understand it, the incomprehensible glory of the Saints and Angels in Heaven.

Reigning supreme in the Church Triumphant is our most glorious Lady, Mary, Mother of God.

"O Virgin, prudent above all!" exclaims the Church on the day of her glorious Assumption, when she was placed on that magnificent throne of glory prepared by the Omnipotent Father for the Mother of His only-begotten Son—"O Virgin most prudent, whither art thou going, radiant as the aurora in its splendor? O Daughter of Sion, thou art all beautiful and full of sweetness, fair as the moon, shining as the sun in the splendor of its noonday brightness! Thou art all fair, O Mary, and the original stain is not in thee. Thy raiment is white as the driven snow, and thy countenance is like the sun. Thou art the glory of Jerusalem, thou art the joy of Israel, thou art the honor of our people. Blessed art thou, O Mary ever Virgin in the Lord, the most high God, above all women of the entire universe."

The most holy Mother of God is exalted above all the choirs of Angels in the Kingdom of Heaven. "And a great sign appeared in the Heaven," adds St. John; "a woman clothed with the sun, and the moon under her feet, and on her head a crown of twelve stars."

"From the beginning, and before the world, was I created, and into the world to come I shall not cease to be, and in the holy dwelling-place I have ministered before Him. And so I was established in Sion, and in the holy city likewise I rested, and my power was in Jerusalem. And I took root in an honorable people, and in the portion of my God His inheritance, and my abode is in the full assembly of the Saints. Because He has regarded the humility of His handmaid, behold, from henceforth, all generations shall call me blessed; because He that is mighty hath done great things to me; and holy is His name.

"Hail Mary, full of grace, the Lord is with thee; blessed art thou amongst women!"

But what human lips could ever proclaim her sublime glory?

Then the Angels of God are there in their uncountable multitudes: "thousands of thousands minister to Him, and ten hundred times a hundred thousand stand before Him; and they rest not, day and night, saying: 'Holy, holy, holy, Lord God Almighty, Who was, and Who is, and Who is to come.'"

And the Saints are there, standing before the throne in the sight of the Lamb, clothed with white robes and palms in their hands, shining like the sun in the Kingdom of their Father, like the Angels of God, even brighter still like to God Himself; for St. John says: "We know that when He shall appear, we shall be like to Him, because we shall see Him as He is."

The martyrs are there in inconceivable numbers; they have come out of great tribulation, and washed their robes and made them white in the blood of the Lamb, and serve Him day and night in His temple.

The confessors and all the elect are along with them, who, having overcome, are clothed in white and walk with Him, because they are worthy.

Then, following the Lamb wherever He goeth, are the holy virgins, who have not defiled their souls, in whose mouth there was found no lie, but are without spot before the throne of God.

The glory and happiness of the Saints can never be understood by anyone while in this world, for no eye hath ever seen, nor ear heard, nor has it entered into the heart of man, what God has prepared for those that love Him. But the Holy Scriptures have given us some little idea of what it is, in these words: "... The city of the living God, the Heavenly Jerusalem; in it is the throne of God and of the Lamb; and His servants shall serve Him; and they shall see His face, and His name shall be on their foreheads; and night shall be no more, and they shall not need the light of the lamp nor the light of the sun, for the Lord God shall enlighten them, and they shall reign forever and ever.

"They shall no more hunger nor thirst, neither shall the sun fall upon them, nor any heat, for the Lamb which is in the midst of the throne shall lead them to the living fountains of water, and God shall wipe away all tears from their eyes. They are His people, and God Himself with them shall be their God; and death shall be no more, nor mourning, nor crying, nor sorrow shall be any more, for the former things are passed away.

"He that shall overcome shall possess these things; and I will be his God, and he shall be My son. To him that shall overcome, I will give to sit with Me in My throne, as I also have overcome, and am set down with my Father in His throne."

Then the just reply to Him in the fullness of the happiness they possess: "Oh! how hast thou multiplied Thy mercy, O God! We are inebriated with the plenty of Thy house: with Thee is the fountain of life, and in Thy light we shall see light. Thou hast made known to us the ways of life! Oh! how great is the multitude of Thy sweetness, O Lord, which Thou hast hidden for them that fear Thee!"

Oh, my child, love God and serve God as the Saints did, and the glory of Heaven will one day be yours also. Say to Him with the holy prophet David: "As the hart panteth after the fountains of water, so my soul panteth after Thee, my God; my soul hath thirsted after the strong, the living God. When shall I come and appear before the face of God?" (Ps xlii).

2

A GLIMPSE OF THE GLORY OF HEAVEN

God sometimes gives to His faithful servants even in this world a glimpse of the glory of Heaven. He does this either as a reward for their holy lives, or to encourage us to love and serve Him, that we also may one day obtain that glory.

EMMANUEL, THE PIOUS DOCTOR.

In the town of Ranran, in Cochin China, there was, not many years ago, a great doctor, who was at the same time a most fervent Christian. His greatest joy was to convert his heathen countrymen to the Faith, and while most zealous in healing their bodily maladies, he was still more so in attending to their spiritual wants.

One of the missionary fathers gives us an account of a vision this good man had of the great happiness God was to bestow upon him as the reward of his holy life. He writes:

"Not long after I arrived in that province he was attacked by a dangerous illness. Everyone thought that he was about to die, and those who were waiting upon him expected every moment to see him breathe his last.

"The people of the town, who loved him as a father, flocked round his death-bed to pray for him.

"One day as they were saying the prayers for a departing soul, he suddenly ceased to breathe. They thought he was dead; and for some time they remained kneeling at his bedside praying for him.

"Suddenly, to their great surprise, he began to speak. 'Oh! I have seen such beautiful things! I have seen Heaven!'

"The people said: 'Tell us what God has shown you.'

"'That is impossible,' he said; 'no tongue could describe nor mind conceive the beautiful things I have seen.' After a few moments he continued: 'I saw in Heaven many whom I knew on earth, who during life gave good example by their piety.' But he did not mention who they were.

"To show that it was not a mere dream, but a real vision from God, he rose at once from his bed, free from all sickness, without the least trace of his recent illness.

"From that time he became disgusted with the things of this world: the most beautiful things that were shown to him had no attraction for him; he could think of one thing only, the beauty of Heaven. When he was with his family and friends, he could speak of nothing else; and his eyes were generally fixed on Heaven, where his heart already was. Time seemed to him unsupportable. 'When shall that happy day come, when God will place me in that glory which He showed me?'

"At length it did come, and he died in a transport of heavenly joy. He had no regret in leaving this world; his only sorrow was that he had been kept so long on earth. So true is it that when one knows the real value of heavenly things, everything on earth appears vain and worthless."

Voyages du P. Alex de Rhodes.

"HEAVEN AT LAST."

The blessed Isemberg had left the world and gone into a monastery, that he might prepare himself for a happy death.

He spent thirty long years there; and as these years passed slowly by, he used to wonder how long it would be before the happy day would come when he would be called from this world to see God in Heaven.

He knew that if he persevered day by day in serving God, that time would certainly come; for he always kept in mind the solemn promise that Jesus Christ had made, of giving everlasting life to everyone who had left all things to follow Him.

After these lonely years of patient waiting, the time at length drew near. The holy man lay on his bed dying. A lay brother was watching by his side. One night this brother was surprised to hear him utter beautiful words about God and Heaven. He seemed also to be gazing in rapture at something, for his eyes were turned towards Heaven and a sweet smile was on his lips.

The brother went at once for the Father Abbot, who came immediately to the room.

As soon as the dying man saw him, he said: "O my Father, what a happy night I have spent! I was in Paradise among the Saints, singing the praises of God. Oh, how beautiful it was! Those who sing on earth become weary, but in Heaven it is quite different. There the blessed praise God without pain or weariness. The more they praise Him, the greater is their desire to sing His praises still, and their only rest is in praising Him without end.

"I also saw some of those whom I knew on earth: they were clad in white raiment—so white that my eyes could not endure the glorious brightness. I asked them if it should be given to me to be clothed in garments as white as these.

"They answered me: 'He who desires to be clothed as we are must live a holy life, and be without spot before God.'

"O my Father," he continued, "how beautiful, how lovely are the good things that God has prepared in Heaven for those who love Him and serve Him on earth! They far, far exceed all that man can imagine. Oh, how happy are those blessed ones who shall enjoy them in Heaven forever and ever!"

Now, it happened that at this time there were living in the monastery two men who were much attached to the world and the pleasures of this life. The Abbot sent for them, that, hearing the dying man's words, they might be converted.

At first they refused to come, but after some persuasion they consented.

"O my brother," they said to the dying man on their arrival, "how happy you are to have always lived for God alone! We also have often wished to leave the world and do as you have done, but we had not the courage to do it."

"Ah!" he answered, "if God had shown you what I have seen, you would utterly despise the world and all its empty glory."

These simple words led to their conversion.

That same day the holy man died, and his soul went to drink of that torrent of pleasure in Heaven, of which he had received a foretaste here below.

This was about the year 1180.

Lives of the Cist. Fathers.

Your Heavenly Father has not shown you, my child, the joys of Heaven as He showed them to the blessed Isemberg; but if you serve Him to the end of your life as he did, you may be quite sure that He will give them to you, for He has promised them to you as well as to him.

3
―――

OF THOSE TO WHOM GOD HAS PROMISED HEAVEN

Jesus Christ has promised us everlasting glory in His Church Triumphant if we, in this world, take up our cross and persevere in His holy service to the end. "To him that shall overcome, I will give to sit with Me in My throne: as I also have overcome and am set down with My Father in His throne" (Apoc. III. 21). What a beautiful promise! And it is to you, dear child, that God has made it!

ST. CYRIL, THE BOY-MARTYR.

During the persecution of the Emperor Valerian, in the third century, there lived in Cesarea a little boy whose name was Cyril.

His parents were both pagans, and in his infancy he was a pagan too. But when he was able to go to school, he had the good fortune to become acquainted with some children who were Christians, and from them he learned to know and love God. He used to go with them to the church, where he would kneel at their side, and listen with the greatest attention to the Holy Word of God.

But he never told his parents that he went there, because he knew how much they hated the very name of Christian, and that if they found out where he went, they would never allow him to go back again.

Years went on in this way, and Cyril was no longer a child, but had grown up to be a big boy. The love of God had also grown in his heart, so that when he heard of how the martyrs died to show how much they loved God, he often wished that he also might one day be a martyr. He had not long to wait for the martyr's crown.

One day his father told him that now he was old enough to accompany him to the temples of the gods to worship them. "You will make yourself ready and go with me tomorrow," he said.

"No, father," said the boy, "I will not go. The gods you wish me to adore are only blocks of wood or stone; there is only one true God, and He is the God whom the Christians adore."

His father looked at him in amazement; his lips became white with rage, and his eyes flashed with anger. "What!" he cried out as soon as he could speak–"what is this I hear? Has a son of mine gone over to that infamous sect? No, boy, we will soon put an end to this."

So saying, he rudely seized the child, and inflicted upon him a most severe chastisement. Cyril bore it patiently, and rejoiced in his soul that he was already able to suffer something for the love of God.

When his father saw that this had no effect upon him, but, on the contrary, made him only more determined, he subjected him to still harsher treatment.

"Begone from my house," he said to him, "and never enter it again till you have made up your mind to obey me."

But even this did not shake his constancy.

Then his father, seeing that he himself could not move him, resolved to frighten him into obedience. So he went to the Governor of the city, and asked him to summon the boy before him, and threaten to put him to death if he would not yield.

The Judge ordered Cyril to be brought before him.

"Cyril, my dear child," said he, in the kindest tone, "what is this I hear about you? Why do you refuse to obey your father, and to worship the gods of the Empire?"

"I am a Christian," answered the brave child, "and I glory in the

Name of Jesus Christ, my Lord and my God, Whom I love above all things."

The tyrant was very angry when he heard these words spoken by so young a boy, but, pretending to be kind and gentle, he said: "O my boy, how foolish you are! Do you not know that you have made yourself liable to suffer a great punishment for having spoken in that manner to me? I could even put you to death for having said these words. But I will not do so. If you now renounce Jesus Christ, and promise me that you will have nothing to do with the Christian sect for the time to come, I will forgive you; and, more than that, I will go to your father, and will obtain for you his pardon also, and I will give you great honors and make you very rich. But if you refuse, I will inflict upon you most severe punishments, and if you still remain obstinate and disobedient, I will put you to a cruel death."

But Cyril answered: "I am glad to stand here and confess my Faith. I am happy because I am able to suffer something for it. My father has cast me out, but I have a Father in Heaven Who will not forsake me. I would like to be poor in this world that I may be rich in Heaven; and as for death, I do not fear it, because it will open Heaven to me."

"O foolish boy!" cried the Judge, "you shall die a cruel death. Here, executioners, take this boy and bind him, and cast him into that great fire, that he may suffer for his obstinacy."

In the meantime he secretly gave orders to the men not to throw him into the fire, but only to pretend to do it. So when they brought him to the place where the fire was burning, they in the first place showed him the instruments of torture, and told him that these were made to punish those who, like him, were disobedient. Then, seeing that this made no impression on him, they bound him with ropes and lifted him up, as if to throw him into the flames. Cyril made no resistance.

When they had gone thus far they took him back to the Judge, as they had secretly been told to do; and he, with a smile on his countenance, said: "Now, my boy, you have seen the swords and the fire; I am going to give you still one more opportunity of escaping them. Obey me, and you will yet obtain what I promised you; disobey, and you shall certainly be cast, without mercy, into that terrible fire which I showed you."

The boy answered: "You have done me a great wrong by calling me back. I do not fear your threats nor all your instruments of torture, nor the great fire you showed me: for I burn with a great desire to see my God in Heaven, Whom I love with my whole heart. Be quick, then, and put me to death, that I may see Him the sooner."

When the people, who stood around heard these words, they began to weep. Cyril said to them: "Why do you weep? You ought rather to be very glad. But you do not know the happy Kingdom I am going to, nor the beautiful things my God is about to give me because I love Him. Oh no, you do not know this; otherwise you would not weep for me."

When he had said this the angry Judge ordered him to be cast into the flames. The fierce fire soon consumed his body, but his innocent soul flew to Paradise, there to rest in the bosom of his God forever and ever.

The short sufferings of this world are soon over, and if they are endured patiently for the love of God, they will procure an eternity of glory and happiness in Heaven.

Lives of the Saints.

"ONE DAY I SHALL REIGN!"

There was, long ago, a very holy man named John, who renounced the world and became a monk, that he might more surely save his soul.

It happened that he was sent by his Superior into Egypt, on some affair of importance. There he met another solitary, called Leo, of whose virtues and great piety he had often heard, and whom he had much desired to see.

During the time they were conversing together, Brother Leo often said these words: "One day I shall reign."

John did not understand the meaning of them, and asked him to tell him what he meant.

The holy man, raising his hands and his eyes towards Heaven, said: "Is it not true, my brother, that God has promised His own Kingdom to us if we be faithful? In it we are to be placed along with Him on His throne. Therefore I am only saying what is true when I say that one day I shall reign."

Lives of the Fathers of the Desert,

THE VISION OF THEODOSIUS.

God has promised to give us "the crown of life" in Heaven if we serve Him faithfully while we are on earth.

The Abbot Theodosius tells us the following story of what happened to himself when he was a young man.

"One day, when I was at my prayers, I thought I saw by my side a person who was surrounded with a bright light, brighter even than the sun. He took me by the hand and said to me: 'Theodosius, come along with me, for you have to fight to gain a crown.'

"Then it seemed to me that he led me into a large hall full of people, who had come to see the fight. Some of them were clad in white, like the one who had brought me, and others wore dark garments and were dreadful to look at.

"When I was placed in the middle of the hall, I saw standing there a negro of great size and strength. The man who had brought me to this place said to me: 'This is the one with whom you have to fight.'

"I was filled with great fear at these words, and I answered: 'O sir, it will be impossible for me to overcome this monster, for he is so much stronger than I am; no man on earth could conquer him!'

"But he replied: 'You must fight with him: I brought you hither for that very purpose. Go, then; attack him courageously. I will stand beside you and help you; be not afraid.'

"When I heard these words I advanced towards my enemy. He was indeed very strong, and certainly would easily have gained the victory over me; but my guide came to my assistance, and the negro was soon overcome.

"As soon as he fell, the people in the hall who were clothed in black began to cry out in dismay, and fled in haste, but those who were clad in white sang a beautiful hymn of joy in honor of him who had helped me in the fight. Then they came forward to the place where I stood, and congratulated me on my success. 'Come with us,' they said to me, 'and dwell forever in our beautiful home, where you will be filled with happiness which will never end.'

"As soon as I entered their dwelling, which was beautiful above all I had ever seen, or had been able to imagine, he who had led me to the fight, and who had helped me to gain the victory, put upon my head a beautiful crown, and said to me that this was the reward he had promised, and that it was now mine forever, because I had overcome my adversary.

"When I returned to my senses, I began to think what was the meaning of the vision. God seemed to answer me in my heart, saying: 'The negro is Satan, who tries to destroy the souls of men; the hall in which you had to fight represents the world; the people whom you saw in the hall were the good and evil spirits, who are witnesses of your contest; He who assisted you to gain the victory is Myself, and the crown given to you is the glory of Heaven, which I will give to everyone who is victorious over Satan and sin'"

We also are engaged in this war. If we want to gain the crown of victory in Heaven, we must fight bravely during our short life in this world. God's grace will help us to gain it.

Lives of the Fathers of the Desert.

4

HAPPY THOSE WHO DIE IN BAPTISMAL INNOCENCE

When God takes away from us those whom we love, and who have never lost their innocence, we ought to be full of joy, because they will begin at once to enjoy the happiness of Heaven, and will pray for us who are left behind.

"I WANT THAT CHILD."

Anna of Seville was a poor woman who had none of those things which this world calls "the comforts of life," but was rich in good works for the world to come.

She was married to a man poor as herself, and by him had several children: these she loved with all the tender affection of a mother. She watched over them with the greatest care, and was ever mindful that they belonged to God rather than to herself.

God wished to send her a great trial. One of her children became very ill. The paleness of death was upon its countenance, and it was evident to everyone that she was soon to lose it.

When she saw that there was no hope, she fell on her knees and wept. She prayed to God to spare her little one, whom she so tenderly loved. And as she prayed Our Lord was pleased to console her. He said to her: "My daughter, what are you afraid of? and why do you weep? I want that child."

Anna replied: "O my God, take it, then, for everything I possess belongs to You."

Thus did God console her in her grief.

But He was not satisfied with that trial; He had another and a greater one in store for her.

She had a little daughter, five years old, who was her very image and bore her own name. After her first child's death she bestowed on this one a double share of affection, and was never happy when the little girl was for a moment out of her sight.

One day the child complained of being ill. A sudden fear came upon the mother that she, too, was to be taken from her. The little Anna daily grew worse, and in a short time went to bless and praise God in Heaven.

The poor mother was pierced with grief at her double loss. She knew, indeed, that both her little ones were happy with God; but what would she not give to see them and speak to them again? God again consoled her, as He does all those who love Him.

One day she was thinking of the beauty and glory of Heaven. Suddenly she seemed to be rapt up, as St. Paul was, into Paradise, where she saw its beauty and glory and happiness, which St. John describes in the Scriptures. She saw the glorious choirs of angels and white-robed army of Saints, each one enjoying the glory he had merited by his good life on earth. She heard also most ravishing music sung by that multitude of holy ones who stand before the throne of God.

Then she beheld the Lamb of God Himself, surrounded and followed wherever He went with a countless band of virgins, clothed in garments of the purest white, and singing a hymn which none could sing but themselves. And oh! delight! there were her own two little ones amongst them, so beautiful and so happy, plunged as it were in an ocean of joy.

When the vision was over, Anna no longer grieved for the loss of her darling children; she would not now for a moment think of calling them back from their supreme happiness. But the view of Heaven which had been granted her filled her soul with a dislike for everything on earth, and inflamed her with the desire of becoming more and more perfect, that she herself might gain more and more glory hereafter.

Life of St. Anna of Seville.

EVANGELIST AND AGNES.

St. Frances of Rome had many children, two of whom died young. One of these, a little boy called Evangelist, died when he was only nine years old. The other one was named Agnes.

When the plague broke out in Rome in the year 1411, Evangelist was struck by it. Just before dying he said to his mother: "Don't you remember, mother, how often I said to you that there was nothing in this world that gave me any pleasure, and that I wanted and prayed to be with the angels in Heaven? God has heard my prayer, and I am going to leave you; but don't weep, mother, because I shall be very happy in Heaven, and I will pray for you when I get there. See! Here are my dear patron Saints come to take me to Heaven; and oh! Such a multitude of beautiful angels! O mother, give me your blessing that I may go with them!"

When his weeping mother did so, the holy child composed himself on his bed and gently died. At that same moment, a little girl who stayed in the next house, and who was also dying, suddenly cried out: "Look! Look! There is Evangelist going up to Heaven between two angels!"

One night, about a year afterwards, as his mother was watching at the bedside of her little daughter Agnes, she saw a snow-white dove fly into the room, and after hovering over the child for a few moments, disappear. She thought for a long time over this, but could not discover the meaning of it.

As she was pondering over it, the room was suddenly filled with a bright light, and in the midst of it she saw her little boy who had died the previous year. He had the same appearance as he had when living, only he was incomparably more beautiful. He was accompanied by a young man still more beautiful than himself.

Frances was full of joy at seeing her dear boy again, especially as he drew near to her and saluted her most affectionately. She stretched out her arms to embrace him, just as if he had been alive. "O my own dear boy," she cried out, "what are you doing now? Where are you? Do you ever think of me now that you are in Heaven?"

Evangelist raised his eyes towards Heaven and answered: "My dearest mother, our occupation in Heaven is to look upon the eternal beauty of God, and to praise and bless His Majesty in transports of joy and love. There is no sorrow in Heaven, mother; there could not be any, and we are enjoying a peace which will never end.

"And since you wish to know where I am, I will tell you that God has placed me in the second choir of Heaven. This young man who is with me is there also; he is more beautiful than I, because he is higher up than I am. God sent him to you to give you consolation in your pilgrimage in this world; but I am come today to tell you that I am going to take little Agnes with me. She shall die in a few days, and then she shall have a share along with me in the joys of Paradise."

Then Frances understood the vision of the white dove flying round her little child. After a whole hour's conversation with her son, he asked her permission to leave her, and then disappeared. So great was the splendor of the apparition, that she could not have been able to look upon her holy child had not God assisted her to endure it.

Since she now knew that her darling Agnes was soon to leave her, she bestowed on her all the care and affection in her power. She looked on her with a kind of reverence, as one so soon to be with the holy angels in Heaven, before the throne of God.

Agnes fell sick and left this weary world in the fifth year of her age. Angels carried her innocent soul to Heaven, where she will be forever happy in the bosom of her Heavenly Father.

Life of St. Frances of Rome.

5

HAPPY THOSE WHO DO PENANCE HERE

I f God has not taken you to Himself in your baptismal innocence, you can reach Heaven by another way—the path of Penance.

THE REWARD OF PENANCE.

St. Peter of Alcantara died on October 18, 1562. He had spent upwards of fifty years in the practice of good works, and in doing penance. Many, many were the trials he had to meet and the crosses he had to bear, and often had he to drink of the bitter chalice of suffering during his long life.

But it came to an end at last. He had patiently persevered, and now the day of the promised reward had come.

Immediately after his death he appeared to St. Teresa, who was then living. She saw him all at once enter her cell, brilliant as the sun, and so surrounded with glory, that she could not find words to describe it.

"What is this, my Father?" she said.

The Saint replied: "I am going to eternal repose. I am filled with unutterable joy; and the glory to which God has now raised me, on account of the humble life I led, far exceeds all comprehension."

He spoke then of the great reward God bestows on His Saints for each little act of penance done for His sake, and said: "O thrice happy penances that have merited for me so great a reward!"

After this he exhorted the Saint to serve God as she was doing to the very end of her life, and then left her. She saw his soul pierce the clouds, and, surrounded with brightness far surpassing that of the sun, enter the presence of God. He was clothed in a very rich robe, with a mantle of snowy whiteness, covered with pearls of great value. He was then placed on a throne of glory, around which stood a multitude of holy angels.

This revelation filled St. Teresa with a holy joy, and encouraged her to bear her trials with resignation, since they would bring to her so much happiness in Heaven.

Life of St. Peter of Alcant., II. 215.

6

JOY OF THE SAINTS ENTERING HEAVEN

What a joy filled the Saints, my child, when they heard God call them to Paradise, and tell them that He was now to give them an eternal reward because they had served Him so well! Oh! serve Him and love Him now, and one day you will experience the same joy.

THE GOOD AND FAITHFUL SERVANT.

St. Erasmus, who lived towards the end of the third century, gained many souls to God not only by his eloquent sermons, but even more by his virtuous life.

The time at length came when he was to receive his reward. While he was at prayer one day with his whole soul fixed on God, he suddenly heard a voice from Heaven:

"Erasmus, good and faithful servant, since you have so bravely fought the good fight, come now and receive the crown of justice which I have prepared for you."

Looking up to Heaven, he saw a most beautiful crown, which a company of angels were bringing to him. Then, bowing down his head, he said: "O Lord, receive my soul."

When he had said these words his soul left his body, and went up towards Heaven, under the appearance of a snow-white dove. An escort of angels accompanied it, and brought it before the throne of God. He is there now, and will be there for all eternity, because he fulfilled here below the Will of his Heavenly Father.

Lives of the Saints, June 2.

THE HUNDREDFOLD REWARD.

St. Catherine of Sienna was once praying in a church dedicated to St. Dominic in her native city. A poor man, seeing her there, went up to her and asked her for the love of God to give him an alms.

The Saint answered: "My good man, I have nothing to give you. If I had anything, most certainly I would give it to you."

"Have you nothing at all? I will be content even with the smallest offering," said the poor man.

St. Catherine searched again, but found nothing to give him. The beggar was going sadly away, when, seeing the little cross hanging at the end of her beads, she took it off and gave it to him.

The next night Our Lord appeared to her with the same cross in His hands, but covered with jewels and diamonds. He said to her: "Catherine, do you recognize this cross?"

"Oh yes," she answered with surprise; "it is the cross I gave the poor man yesterday, but it is far more beautiful now."

Jesus answered: "At the day of judgment I will return it to you in the presence of all My angels and of all men as shining and beautiful as it is now; and this will be your reward in Heaven for this work of charity."

Another day she gave some clothing to a poor person. Jesus again appeared to her as if covered with a most magnificent garment, and said: "You must wear this garment as a pledge of the eternal glory which I will one day bestow on you in Heaven."

Life of St. Catherine.

ST. TERESA'S EXCLAMATION.

When St. Teresa was quite a child her greatest desire was to be alone, that she might think of God and speak to Him. The thought of eternity was always before her mind, and the words "forever, forever, forever," always on her lips.

This world had no attractions for her, because she knew that it would end so soon; hence her constant prayer was that God would be pleased to let her die soon, in order that she might at once get to Heaven, to see Him there and to live forever with Him.

THE SHIPWRECKED FAMILY.

A little family, consisting of the father and mother with their two infant boys, left their native land in a noble ship bound for the East Indies.

During the voyage, a hurricane drove the vessel out of its course, and it was wrecked. The only ones known to be saved were the members of this family who, by clinging to some pieces of wreck, were driven upon the shores of an uninhabited island.

For many years they lived there unknown to the rest of the world, subsisting on herbs and the wild fruit which grew on the island, and living in a cave they found in the rock. At best their life was a desolate one, for they seemed to be alone in the great world God had made.

Time wore on; the two children, who were only infants when they were cast upon the island, had now grown up to be stout and healthy boys. Their desert home was the only one they had ever known, for they did not remember anything about the continent on which they had been born.

Their parents often spoke of it to them, and of the stately trees and magnificent houses which were upon it, and of the immense number of people who lived far away. The two boys tried sometimes to picture to themselves what it could be like, but the idea was very imperfect, for they had never seen a house nor a high tree, and the only people they had ever seen were their father and mother.

One day, after many years' sojourn in this place they saw a little boat approaching their island, and in the boat four negroes. Hope and fear filled the parents' hearts; on the one hand they hoped that they would now be taken away from their dreary home, and once more dwell amongst men; but, on the other hand, knowing the barbarity of some of the savage tribes who inhabit the islands of those seas, they were afraid lest they might be killed. The negroes were surprised when they found the strangers on the island, but showed signs of kindness to them.

The father also made signs that he wanted them to take him and his family along with them to the place where they dwelt.

But they showed him that their boat was too small to carry them all at once. What was to be done? The father, after a little reflection, said: "My dear wife and children, I will go first, and when I have reached the mainland, they will come back for you, and while they are away I will prepare a home for you."

The children and their mother objected to this, because they did not like to be separated from him. But he showed them that it was expedient for him to go before them; that in a short time the boat would come back and take them also; and that soon they would all meet again in a far more beautiful country, where they would be so happy, and never be separated during their lifetime again.

So the father entered the boat, and very soon it disappeared on the horizon from the eyes of dear ones left behind. "Our father is gone now, and we will never see him again," sobbed the children. But the mother, though full of fear and sadness, encouraged them to wait patiently for a little time, and they would see him again.

For the next two days they kept their eyes fixed on the wide ocean, watching for the return of the boat. At length a black speck was seen in the distance, and they were again full of joy.

But their joy was not of long duration. It was the same little boat and the same negroes that returned, and they saw it could not carry them all. Who would now remain, the mother or the boys? The mother wished her children to go first, but they said: "No, mother, you must go, and we will remain till the boat returns."

The mother was at last persuaded to go into the boat, after embracing the dear ones whom she left on the shore weeping. "Do not weep, my children," she said; "these good men will come back again, and we will soon meet in a better and happier country."

Two days afterwards the little boat returned, and the two children entered it. A strong wind was blowing, and the sea was very rough, so that the boat was tossed about by the rolling waves. The boys were frightened, and clung to the sides of the skiff; they thought that it might sink, and that they would never reach the beautiful country where their parents were.

But the good negroes knew how to manage the boat, and soon they came near to the place to which they were going.

When the boat neared the shore, the boys looked, and, oh, joy! there were their dear parents standing to welcome them. They leaped out of the canoe and threw themselves into their parents' arms.

For some time none of them could speak, their hearts were so full of joy, for they knew that they were now freed from the miseries they had so long endured on their desolate island, and would enjoy the plenty which their new home afforded.

The parents then gave them food to eat they had never tasted before, so different from the poor fare to which they had been accustomed, and showed them the many beauties which abounded in their new country, which far surpassed anything they had been able to imagine. Moreover, the prince who ruled over that country caused a comfortable dwelling to be erected for them, and from that time forward they lived as happily together as it is possible to do in this world.

This story contains a beautiful moral. Like that poor family, we are in the desert island of this world; it is not our home—our home is far away from this. We may have to live a long time in this world before we reach our home in Heaven. Sometimes our parents, and many others whom we love, are taken away before us, and we are left behind; but if we have only a little patience, and keep our eye fixed on Heaven above, the messenger will come and take us also over the rough sea of death, and bring us into our own true country, Heaven, where we will see again all those dearly loved ones who have gone before us, and where the Great King, our good God Himself, will fill us with every happiness, and crown us with the crown of everlasting glory.

Rep. du Catéchiste.

7

ALWAYS THINK OF HEAVEN'S JOYS

Let the thought of the beauty of Heaven be always before your mind; and take a firm resolution to live piously in this world, that it may one day be yours.

"THAT CITY MUST BE MINE."

Philip of Macedon was a King whose name was famous over the whole world. One day there came to his palace a man called Demades; he was one of the chief magistrates of the city of Athens.

When Philip knew that he came from Athens, he ordered him to be treated with every kindness, and even invited him to dine with him at his own table.

"I have often heard of your good city," said the King, "and I have been told that it is exceedingly beautiful."

"My lord," answered Demades, "you have been told the truth; but no one can describe the greatness and beauty of our city, except one who has seen it, and even his words could never convey to your mind what it really is."

Philip urged him to give him a description of it, "for," said he, "I am anxious to hear about it from one who dwells there."

Demades did not require to be asked a second time. He gave an account of its rise and progress, and of the greatness it had reached. He spoke of the wealth of its inhabitants, and the beauty of its buildings, and the renown it had obtained for learning, and how people from all parts of the world went thither to visit it.

The King listened in silence to the account of Demades. When he had finished, he said: "That city must be mine, cost what it may. I will risk everything I have to make that city mine."

There is a city far more beautiful than Athens. That city is Heaven. It is to be given to us forever, if we love and serve God faithfully. My child, say to yourself what Philip of Macedon said: "That city shall be mine, cost what it may; I will spare no pains that I may gain it."

ST. ADRIAN, MARTYR.

St. Adrian was a young pagan soldier of eighteen years. Seeing the invincible constancy displayed by the martyrs in the midst of the most terrible torments to which they were subjected, he asked them what they hoped to gain in exchange for them.

They answered him: "We confidently hope to receive imperishable glory greater than the mind of man can imagine. It is this that encourages us to support them so joyously and so manfully; it is this also that makes these tortures so sweet and so easy to bear. If we had each a thousand lives, we would with the same joy sacrifice them all; for the direst tortures are but short, and will soon be over, and the happiness that will be bestowed on us in return will endure forever and ever."

The youthful soldier was so touched by this answer that he asked to receive baptism, and in a short time he also gave his life for Jesus Christ, that he might partake of the endless joys of Heaven.

Acts of the Martyrs.

THE PROPHET DANIEL IN BABYLON.

The King of Babylon, having obtained a victory over the Jews in Jerusalem, took all the people whom he found there captives into his own country. Daniel the prophet was one of them. Now, nothing was so dear to the hearts of the Jews as the city of Jerusalem, the capital of their kingdom. Every day Daniel used to open the window of his house which looked towards the Holy City, and falling down on his knees, would pray to God that the day might soon come when he would see it again.

This also ought to be your only desire and prayer, my child. Heaven is your home; this world is the land of your exile. Oh! then every day of your life think of Heaven, and pray to God that the day may come when you may be found worthy to enter your eternal Home above.

PART XI

SIN AND ITS FORGIVENESS

1

OUR OBLIGATION TO OBSERVE THE COMMANDMENTS OF GOD

God has given us a law which we are bound to keep if we desire to obtain everlasting life. He gave it to Moses in the Old Law, and Jesus Christ our Lord confirmed it in the New Law. To willfully break any of the Commandments is to disobey God and to commit sin.

GOD GAVE THE COMMANDMENTS IN THE OLD LAW.

"In the third month of the departure of Israel out of the land of Egypt, on this day, they came into the wilderness of Sinai.

"And Moses went up to God, and the Lord called unto him from the mountain, and said: 'Thus shalt thou say to the house of Jacob, and tell the children of Israel: You have seen what I have done to the Egyptians, how I have carried you upon the wings of eagles, and have taken you to Myself. If, therefore, you will hear My voice and keep My covenant, you shall be My peculiar possession above all people: for all the earth is Mine: and you shall be to Me a priestly kingdom and a holy nation. These are the words thou shalt speak to the children of Israel.'

"Moses came, and calling together the elders of the people, he declared all the words which the Lord had commanded. And all the people answered together: 'All that the Lord hath spoken, we will do.' And when Moses had related the people's words to the Lord, the Lord said to him: 'Lo, now I will come to thee in the darkness of a cloud, that the people may hear Me speaking to thee, and may believe thee forever.' And Moses told the words of the people to the Lord.

"And He said to him: 'Go to the people, and sanctify them today, and tomorrow, let them wash their garments, and let them be ready against the third day: for on the third day the Lord will come down in the sight of all the people upon Mount Sinai.'

"And now the third day was come, and the morning appeared: and behold, thunders began to be heard, and lightning to flash, and a very thick cloud to cover the mount, and the noise of the trumpet sounded exceeding loud, and the people that was in the camp feared. And when Moses had brought them forth to meet God from the place of the camp, they stood at the bottom of the mount. And all Mount Sinai was in a smoke; because the Lord was come down upon it in fire, and the smoke arose from it as out of a furnace: and all the mount was terrible. And the sound of the trumpet grew by degrees louder and louder, and was drawn out to a greater length; Moses spoke, and God answered him. And the Lord came down upon Mount Sinai, in the very top of the mount, and He called Moses unto the top thereof. And when he was gone up thither... the Lord spoke all these words: 'I am the Lord thy God, Who brought thee out of the land of Egypt, and out of the house of bondage.

"'Thou shalt not have strange gods before me.

"'Thou shalt not take the name of the Lord thy God in vain.

"'Remember that thou keep holy the Sabbath Day.

"'Honor thy father and thy mother.

"'Thou shalt not kill.

"'Thou shalt not commit adultery.

"'Thou shalt not steal.

"'Thou shalt not bear false witness against thy neighbor.

"'Thou shalt not covet thy neighbor's wife.

"'Thou shalt not covet thy neighbor's goods.'

"And all the people saw the voices and the flames, and the sound of the trumpet, and the mount smoking; and being terrified and struck with fear, they stood afar off, saying to Moses: 'Speak thou to us, and we will hear: let not the Lord speak to us, lest we die.'

"And Moses said to the people: 'Fear not; for God has come to prove you, and that the dread of Him might be in you, and you should not sin' (Exod XIX., XX.)."

CHRIST CONFIRMED THE COMMANDMENTS IN THE NEW LAW.

Although the Ten Commandments were given in the Old Law to the people of God, they are also binding on all Christians in the New Law. Jesus Christ tells us that if we desire to enter life we must keep the Commandments.

"I am come," says Jesus Christ, "not to destroy the law, but to fulfill the law"—that is, by His words and actions to teach us how to observe it.

Jesus Christ also tells us that the observance of the law is the mark by which we show Him that we love Him. "If you love Me," He says, "keep My Commandments." And again: "He that hath My Commandments and keepeth them, he it is that loveth Me. If any one love Me, he will keep My word, and every one that heareth these My words and doth them shall be likened to a wise man that built his house upon a rock."

He also announces the terrible fate that will befall those who neglect to do the Will of God—that is, to keep His Commandments—in these words: "Not every one that saith to Me, 'Lord, Lord,' shall enter into the Kingdom of Heaven: but he that doth the Will of My Father, Who is in Heaven, he shall enter into the Kingdom of Heaven."

From the Holy Gospels.

2

WHAT SIN IS

When we disobey our Heavenly Father by breaking His Commandments, we commit sin. Sin is the greatest evil that can happen in this world, because it is an offense against God, Who is infinitely good in Himself, and infinitely good to us. It was sin, also, that nailed our Savior Jesus to the cross.

WHAT SIN DOES.

When St. Bridget was ten years old, she heard a sermon on the sufferings of our Lord. The following night she had a vision, in which she saw Jesus hanging on the cross.

Jesus said to her: "Bridget, look at Me nailed to the cross."

"O my Jesus," she cried out, "who was it that nailed You to that cross?"

Jesus answered: "My own children did it, because they would not love Me, but despised Me, and committed sin."

When St. Bridget awoke, she was so touched by what she had seen, that for the rest of her life she could never think of the sufferings of our Lord without weeping.

SURIUS: *in Vit, S. Birgittae.*

THE SAINT WHO WAS FOUND WEEPING.

St. Isidore, a holy priest and hermit of Scete, was once found weeping very bitterly. Someone asked him why he wept so much.

"I am weeping because I have offended God by my sins," he replied.

"But, my Father," the other one said, "we all know how earnestly you have loved and served God, and how carefully you have avoided every sin."

"It is true, my brother," he answered, "I am not conscious of having committed any grievous sin against God, but I have been guilty of many faults; and if I had offended God but once, and although that offense were only a venial sin, all the tears I could shed during my lifetime would not be enough to blot it out."

This is what the Saints thought about the greatness of the evil of sin.

Life of St. Isidore.

THE IMITATORS OF HEROD.

The venerable Sister Jane, of the Order of St. Francis, was one day meditating on the cruel persecution which Herod raised against the Divine child Jesus. Suddenly she heard a great noise as if a multitude of armed men were running after someone.

At the same instant there appeared a beautiful little boy coming towards her in great haste, crying out to her: "O Jane, save me, help me! I am Jesus of Nazareth, and I am trying to escape from sinners, who are continually seeking to take away My life as Herod did."

By these words, my child, Jesus wished her to understand that everyone who yields to sin treats our Lord in the same way as Herod did. Oh, then, keep away from sin, since it offends our Divine Lord so much.

ST. PHILIP AND THE NOISY BOYS.

St. Philip Neri loved God so much that he could think of nothing else all day long but God; and he spent his long life in trying to make other people love God also.

He used to say: "Oh! if I could only keep people from offending God, how happy would I be!"

He was especially anxious about children and young people, for he knew that they were in more danger of falling into sin, on account of the Devil's temptations; and his greatest study was to find out ways and means of keeping them from sin.

So he would often gather together all the boys of the neighborhood and make them join in games near his house, and he himself often took part in them. People were surprised to see him—a man already advanced in years, and one who was considered so holy—spend so much of his time playing with children.

One day a multitude of boys were thus amusing themselves in front of the room where St. Philip was reading. They were making so great a noise that some of the people in the house went to the Saint and complained to him about it.

St. Philip answered: "Let the good boys alone: let them play and amuse themselves as much as they like. There is only one thing I desire, and that is, that they keep away from sin."

Another day, a gentleman of distinction came to see him. It happened that the boys were playing near the house where he dwelt, and as usual were making a great noise.

The gentleman said to St. Philip: "I am astonished, dear reverend Father, that you can allow these boys to play and make such a noise there, under your very window. How can you permit such conduct?"

The Saint answered: "I can bear with anything if it will only keep them out of sin. Oh! if they would only keep from offending God they are welcome even to chop wood on my back!"

Life of St. Philip Neri,

3

GOD'S LOVE FOR THOSE WHO ARE INNOCENT

One who has never committed sin is like a child who has never disobeyed his father.

There is nothing God loves so much as a good child. The soul of an innocent child—that is, of one who does not commit sin—is the place in which God loves to dwell.

WHY JESUS LOVED ST. NICHOLAS SO MUCH.

One day, when St. Nicholas of Tolentino was only seven years old, he was hearing Mass with great devotion. At the elevation of the Sacred Host, Jesus showed Himself to the boy under the appearance of a little child of great beauty. Nicholas was filled with love and admiration at what he saw, and gazed on the Divine Child with motionless earnestness.

Jesus spoke to him: "Nicholas, My child," He said, "do you know why I love you so much, and why I have appeared to you today under this beautiful form? It is because you are so like Me by the innocence and beauty of your soul. Those who are clean of heart are My most dear children. I love them with a special affection, I shower down on them My richest blessings, and I bestow on them My most precious and sweetest graces.

"You are indeed clean of heart," continued Our Blessed Lord, "and I would like to see every child resemble you. Oh, keep always free from sin, and we shall dwell together in mutual love."

These words made so great an impression on the soul of the young Nicholas that to the end of his life he preserved that innocence which made him so pleasing to God. Happy will you be, my child, if, like him, you keep from sin, because you shall one day see God in Heaven. "Blessed are the clean of heart, for they shall see God." Keep in mind that there is no evil so great as that of sin.

4

THE TERRIBLE STATE OF A SOUL IN SIN

My child, a soul in the state of mortal sin is such a frightful thing that nothing we can imagine in this world can bear any comparison to it.

THE ANGEL AND THE MONK.

One day a holy monk was favored by the vision of his angel guardian walking at his side.

As they were going along, they came upon the carcass of a dead animal lying by the wayside. The stench which came from it was so great that the air for some distance around was polluted by it.

When they came near, the good man could not endure the awful smell. He put his hand upon his nostrils, and hurried past the place as fast as he could. But the angel did not seem to feel it at all.

After a little while they saw a young man coming towards them. He was dressed in the highest style of fashion, and was of a beautiful and pleasing appearance. As soon as the angel saw this man his countenance became very sad. He showed signs of the greatest abhorrence, and tried to get past him as fast as he could, keeping his eyes turned in an opposite direction, that he might not see him.

The monk asked the angel why he showed no signs of disgust when he passed the place where the dead animal was lying, and seemed to feel so much horror when he met the well-dressed young man.

The angel answered: "The smell and the sight of the dead animal were indeed bad; but if you only saw, as we angels see, the frightful state of that young man's soul, for he has been guilty of mortal sin, you would have died of fright.

Catéch. en Hist.

O my child, keep away from sin, since it would make your soul so hideous in the sight of God and of His holy angels.

5

THE INGRATITUDE OF ONE WHO COMMITS SIN

To commit a sin is to be guilty of an act of cruel ingratitude to God, Who has always been so good to us. The Saints preferred to die rather than be ungrateful to God.

ST. POLYCARP BEFORE THE JUDGE.

When St. Polycarp was standing before the judge who was about to condemn him to death, the judge said to him: "Polycarp, if you renounce the Christian Faith, and no longer serve Jesus Christ, I will spare your life."

The Saint answered: "How could I ever do that? For eighty-six years have I served Jesus Christ, and He has never done me any harm; on the contrary, He has always given me every good thing I could desire. You ask me to deny Him, my Lord and my Master, Who has been so good to me! Never! How could I be guilty of such ingratitude!"

The judge then condemned St. Polycarp to a most cruel death, which he endured with the greatest joy, for he was glad to be able to show his Father in Heaven that he would die rather than offend Him.

Life of St. Polycarp.

"NEVER! NEVER!"

St. James, surnamed the "Mutilated," was ordered by the judge to deny Jesus Christ, to burn incense to the false gods, and to trample under his feet the image of Jesus crucified.

But to each command his only answer was "Never!"

The judge said: "If you refuse to do what I command you, I will cut your body to pieces."

"You may do with my body what you like. Do you think that I could be so ungrateful to my God as to deny Him? Never! You may pull out my tongue, you may cut off my hands and feet, but I will never deny my Savior and my God."

Then commenced his martyrdom, which lasted for nine hours. They cut off each member of his body one by one. In the midst of these cruel tortures he was calm, and never ceased praising and blessing God.

When they were cutting off his hands and his feet, he said: "Go, my hand; go, my foot; we will meet again when the Day of Judgment comes. You have been faithful to your Maker here, and you will have an eternal reward hereafter."

Saying these words, he died.

THE PICTURE OF JESUS CRUCIFIED.

One day St. Teresa went into her cell, where there was a picture of Jesus hanging on the cross. As she looked on the picture, there came into her mind so great a sorrow for the sins she had committed that she thought she would have died of grief.

She threw herself on her knees before it and besought Our Divine Lord, with many tears, never to allow her to offend Him again, and never to permit her to commit even one sin. "Since that time," she said afterwards, "I became better and received from God more abundant grace to make me more holy and pleasing to Him."

ST. CATHERINE'S WORDS TO JESUS.

St. Catherine of Genoa was once thinking of the infinite love of Jesus in dying for us on the cross. At the same moment, Jesus appeared to her carrying His cross and covered with blood.

"O my Jesus!" she exclaimed. "O my Love! Oh, never again will I commit a sin, since it has cost You so much!"

ST. ALPHONSUS AT TWELVE YEARS OF AGE.

When St. Alphonsus was about twelve years of age, he was placed by his parents under the care of the Fathers of St. Jerome for his education.

It was the custom in their college for the young students to go into the country once every week for amusements. On one occasion Alphonsus was asked to join them in a certain game; but he tried to excuse himself, saying that he did not know how to play it. His companions, however, urged him so much that at length he consented, and so great was his success that he gained thirty times.

This made his comrades jealous, and one of them, older than himself, exclaimed in great anger: "So it was you who pretended not to know the game, was it?" adding at the same time a very improper word. When Alphonsus heard it, he cast on him a look of great severity, and said: "How is this? Shall God be offended all for a few miserable pence? Take back your money."

Saying this, he threw down at his feet the money he had gained, and, turning away from his companions with a holy indignation, he went by himself to another part of the woods.

But this was not all; for when evening came and it was time to return home, Alphonsus could nowhere be found. They called on him, but received no answer; and as darkness was beginning to set in, everyone went to seek for him. What was their surprise when they discovered him on his knees before a picture of the Blessed Virgin which he had with him, and which he had placed on a branch of a tree. He was so absorbed in God that it was some time before he came to himself, notwithstanding the noise his companions made.

O my child, what a beautiful example for your imitation. Look on sin as the greatest evil that is in the world, since it displeases God, and, like St. Alphonsus, you will flee from the very appearance of it. For it is an act of the greatest ingratitude to offend God, Who has done us so much good.

WHY ST. VINCENT DE PAUL HATED SIN SO MUCH.

What grieved St. Vincent more than anything else was to see his Beloved Lord so much offended by sin. His constant thought was how to diminish sin. He saw he could not destroy it altogether, and even, that he could do but little to diminish it, yet he tried to do what he could, with all the powers of his soul.

One day he said to some people who came to see him: "If Our Divine Master is going to receive fifty strokes of the lash, let us try to make that number less, by hindering some of these strokes from reaching Him, and try to condole with Him for those we cannot keep back."

He meant to say that, since we cannot hinder all mortal sins from being committed, we should try to hinder as many as we can, and to offer Him our heartfelt sympathy for those that are committed against Him.

6

ORIGINAL SIN

Original sin is the sin in which we were born. We were born in sin because our first parents disobeyed God in eating of the fruit which He had forbidden them.

CHRISTINA'S PRESENT.

Christina was a child nine years old, and was at school under the charge of a nun called Sister Josephine.

One day when she returned home, she seemed more thoughtful than usual. Her mother wondered what had happened to make her so serious, because she was usually so noisy. So she asked her what was the matter with her.

"O mother," she answered, "Sister Josephine told us today about Adam and Eve, and how they disobeyed God by eating the forbidden fruit; and I was thinking how wrong it was in them to have done this, and how easy it would have been for them to have left that tree alone, since they had permission to eat of the fruit of all the other trees. I am sure I would not have done it."

Her mother answered: "I am very glad, dearest, to see how attentive you have been to what the good Sister told you. But are you quite sure you would not have touched that apple if you had been in their place?"

"Oh yes, mother, quite sure!"

"What makes you so sure?"

"Because if God told me not to do a thing, I would not do it, because I would displease Him if I did it."

"But are you not sometimes disobedient to me? and do you not know that when a child disobeys her parents she disobeys God?"

Christina did not answer; she knew she was guilty: so she hung down her head and began to weep. Her mother kissed her, and the child promised never to be disobedient again.

Now, not many days after this, it happened that Christina went to see a companion called Dorothy. This girl had just received a canary-bird as a present, and it sang so beautifully as it sat in its cage at the open window. Christina ran home and told her mother about it, and ended by asking her to buy one for her.

"Yes, I will give you a bird like the one Dorothy has, if you promise to be always obedient."

"Oh yes, mamma, I will never disobey you; I will always do what you want me."

So the mother promised to buy her a bird.

Next day when Christina came home from school her mother put a little box into her hand, saying "Take care of this box; don't open it till I come back, and you will be very glad when you know what it contains. I will not tell you what is in it just now, but when I return you will then see what it is." When she had said this she went away.

Now, when the child was left alone, she began to examine the box. "It is not heavy," she said; "I wonder what is in it? The lid, too, is full of little holes: I wonder what these holes are made for. I think I'll open the box to see. But no! I mustn't do that; mother forbade me, and it would be wrong to disobey her. Yet there is no one here to see me do it. Yes, I will open it, and just peep into it: then I will shut it with great care. No, I will not; I must not disobey mamma." And she laid down the box and went away.

A few minutes afterwards her eyes again fell upon the little box in the place where she had laid it. She went over to it, took it into her hands again, examined it on every side, then began to work with the catch that kept it shut. Again she said, "No! I will not do it; but I am *so* anxious to know what it contains."

For a few moments she hesitated, but at last, with a heart beating loudly within her—for she knew she was going to yield to the temptation—she quickly opened the lid. Immediately a beautiful canary flew out of the box up to the ceiling of the room, singing joyfully at being released from its prison.

Christina threw down the box and tried to catch the bird, but in vain, for it flew all over the room far above her head; and sometimes just as she thought she was about to catch it, it flew to another place.

In the midst of this scene the door opened, and her mother entered. "Ah! my little Miss Curiosity! what has become of your promise? Did you not say that you would never disobey me again, and that you would do all I wanted you? And you *have* disobeyed me! The little bird in the box was to be given to you as a present; but before giving it, I wished to see if you deserved it. But as you have been disobedient, you shall not get the bird. I will take it back at once to the merchant from whom I bought it."

The child began to weep, and now repented of her sin. But it was too late. Her mother took back the bird; and Christina, by her own fault, lost what would have given her great joy and pleasure.

Choix d'Histoires Morales.

Our first parents offended God by their disobedience. Had you, my child, been in their place, you might have done what they did. Thank God that He has blotted out that sin from your soul by Baptism, and during your whole lifetime show that you are grateful to Him by keeping His commandments.

THE LOST INHERITANCE.

Not long ago there was a poor man who from morning to night labored to procure food for himself and his little ones.

But it happened that a distant relative died, and left him sole heir of all his property; so that from being poor he suddenly became rich, and his children, instead of being obliged to lead a laborious life, would inherit a great fortune, which would provide for all their wants, and raise them to a high position in the world.

Great was the joy of these children at their present good fortune and their future prospects. But it did not last long; for their father, seeing so much money in his possession, and wishing to gain still more, rashly engaged in a foolish undertaking, at the request of one who pretended to be his friend, but who was his enemy. In a short time he lost all his fortune, and was reduced to a more pitiable condition than before. His children also, who expected to inherit so much wealth, saw themselves reduced to beggary by their father's fault; and after his death they were obliged to wander over the world, without a home to shelter them, and to earn their bread by the sweat of their brow.

My child, our first parents by their sin lost the inheritance of Heaven, which God gave them, and we, their children, were involved in their ruin. But God, in His infinite goodness, promised to send a Savior Who would restore to us that inheritance which was lost. That Savior was Jesus Christ.

By His death upon the Cross, Jesus made reparation to God for the sins of mankind, and He instituted the Sacrament of Baptism to apply to our souls the merits of His death, so that Original Sin might be blotted out, and that we might become His children again.

THE PEARL IN THE MIRE.

There was once a rich man who possessed a pearl of great beauty, which he valued above all his other possessions. One day, as he was showing it to a friend, it fell from his hands into a pool of mud at his feet. No sooner had it fallen than he put forth his hand and took it up. But oh! how changed it now was. Its beauty had disappeared under the thick mud which covered it.

He carried it into the house, and, putting some water into a dish, began to wash it. In a few minutes all the mud was washed away, and the pearl shone with the same brightness as before.

My child, when you were born your soul was soiled by Original Sin. But when you were brought to the church, and the waters of Baptism were poured upon your forehead, the mire of Original Sin was washed away, and your soul became beautiful in the eyes of God. Oh, how good has God been to you in making you His child again by that holy Sacrament.

7

MORTAL SIN

You know, my child, what mortal sin is. The Catechism tells us that it is a grievous offense against God; that it kills the soul, because it destroys the life of the soul, which is the grace of God; and that those who die in mortal sin will be punished in hell for all eternity.

There is only one real evil in the world, and that evil is mortal sin. All the evils and misfortunes that could possibly happen can bear no comparison to one mortal sin.

ST. LOUIS HATRED OF SIN.

St. Louis, King of France, asked one of his nobles named Joinville what he would do if he were asked to choose between committing a mortal sin and being struck with leprosy.

Joinville, without any hesitation, answered the King: "I would sooner commit ten mortal sins than be infected even once with that terrible plague."

The King looked sadly on his friend and said "Ah! my dear sir, it is evident you do not know what an evil it is to commit a mortal sin. There is no evil so terrible as sin is: for no matter how much we detest our sins, we can never be sure so long as we live whether or not God has forgiven us, or that we have sufficiently repented of them."

Life of St. Louis.

DON PEDRO'S CONVERSION.

St. Dominic received from God the gift of converting the most obstinate sinners into great saints. One of these was Don Pedro, a nobleman of Aragon.

When the Saint was preaching in that part of the country, this gentleman, hearing of the wonders he wrought, had a great desire to see him.

So he set out one day, accompanied by a crowd of servants, and entered the church where St. Dominic was going to preach. It was not with the intention of changing his life that he went there—there was nothing further from his mind—but only to gratify his curiosity. The people, who knew of the bad life he was leading, were astonished to see him; but as he was great and powerful, they all made way for him, and bowed their heads before him as he passed.

St. Dominic was kneeling before the altar as Don Pedro entered. God was pleased to make known to him the dreadful state of this man's soul. He seemed to behold entering the church a hideous negro, with eyes starting from his head, and his hands like eagle's claws. He seemed also to be enveloped in flames, in the midst of which there was a multitude of evil spirits, who held him by a chain attached to his neck.

At this sight the holy man of God was filled with terror. "O my God, I beseech Thee," he cried out, "change the heart of this great sinner, and make him truly penitent."

He then went into the pulpit, and preached a sermon upon the awful effects of mortal sin. But all the eloquence of the Saint was lost on this poor sinner; he remained as hardened as ever.

Not many days afterwards the same nobleman returned to the church, dressed with splendor as before, and with the same multitude of attendants. St. Dominic was preaching as he came in. He suddenly ceased his sermon, and, turning towards the crucifix, said: "O Jesus, full of mercy, O Jesus, all-powerful, let Thy people here see with their bodily eyes the sad state of the soul of him who has just entered Thy holy house."

This prayer was heard. In an instant the proud Don Pedro appeared before them as a hideous monster, surrounded by a multitude of evil spirits, who held him by a chain. Terror and fear came upon all the people. Some began to scream, others fled in dismay, others covered their eyes with their hands, and a great tumult arose in the house of God.

Don Pedro was astonished at seeing the dismay his appearance had caused, nor could he understand whence it arose. Going up to one of his servants, who was trembling from head to foot with fear, he asked him what it all meant.

"My lord," answered the servant, "is it possible that you alone do not see the terrible change that has come over you? You no longer look like man: you seem to be changed into some frightful specter surrounded by evil spirits that hold you by a great chain. It is this that has filled us all with fear."

The unfortunate man at once remembered the state of sin in which he had so long lived, and saw that God had manifested the state of his soul to those who were present, and that it was this that had frightened them so much.

St. Dominic exhorted the people to cease their cries, and rather to pray. He himself knelt down before the altar, and again asked God to have mercy on this poor sinner. He felt in his inmost soul that his prayer was heard, and that it would soon be answered.

Calling one of his disciples to his side, he gave him his rosary-beads, and told him to give them to Don Pedro. "Tell him," he said, "to repent of his past misdeeds, and ask mercy and pardon from God, and to say at the same time on these beads the sweet words of the 'Hail, Mary!'"

No sooner had Don Pedro taken the beads into his hands than he assumed his usual appearance. He kissed the beads devoutly, and went at once to the altar of Our Blessed Lady to ask her intercession. He felt so great a compunction in his heart that the tears fell in torrents from his eyes.

In a few moments he was seen kneeling at the feet of St. Dominic. There he confessed the sins of his life, and obtained pardon. Not content with this, he publicly asked pardon of all the people for the scandal he had hitherto given them.

His life ever afterwards was one of penance and piety; and we read that, when he was near his last hour, the Blessed Virgin herself appeared to him, to strengthen and console him, and that when he died a smile of joy was upon his countenance, as if he had at once entered the Kingdom of Heaven, the home of holy penitents as well as of those who have never sinned.

Ecclesiastical History, A.D. 1220.

THE BOY AND THE ROSE-BUSH.

There was once a little boy who was very fond of roses. One day he asked his mother to let him choose one of the rose-bushes in the garden which he might attend to himself. His mother willingly consented, and he chose one which was the prettiest of them all.

Every day he went to see it and to count the flowers that were growing on it, and when the bush was covered with them, he seemed to be the happiest boy in the world.

But one morning, when he went as usual to see his rose-bush, he immediately perceived that something was wrong. The leaves were hanging loosely, and the flowers, which the day before were so beautiful, seemed to have now lost their brightness, and gave out a sickly odor instead of the fragrant perfume he so much enjoyed; it was evident the bush was dead. He looked everywhere to see what had killed his beloved plant, but could see nothing; it was as firmly rooted to the ground as ever.

With tears in his eyes, he went to his uncle, and told him what had happened. "My child," replied his uncle, "I think I can tell you what has killed the bush; come with me, and I will show you."

When they reached the place, his uncle pulled it out of the ground and examined the roots. "Ah, here it is," he said. "Do you see that worm which has eaten its way into the very center of the stem? It is that worm that has killed your tree."

"My dear uncle," said the boy, "who could have imagined that one worm should have destroyed all the beautiful roses and leaves that made my bush so lovely, for it was the prettiest one in the whole garden?"

"Ah, my child!" said the old man, "one worm is sufficient to destroy the finest plant that ever grew. Just in the same way one mortal sin kills the soul and destroys its beauty and all the merits of the good works of a lifetime. Learn, then, from what has happened to your rose-bush to hate sin, which can do so much harm to your soul."

Those who live in the state of mortal sin can never be happy so long as they remain in that state, because they know that if they die they shall be lost forever.

THE SUSPENDED SWORD.

A certain Prince called Damocles, who was very ambitious, thought that there was no one so happy as a King. "Oh, I wish I were a King!" he was often heard to say. "I would then be rich, and have no cares nor sorrows, and I would live in perfect happiness."

Dionysius the King heard this, and to teach him a lesson, he one day said to him: "Since you think my dignity to be so full of happiness, I will permit you for a time to rule in my place."

So Damocles was placed on a throne of gold, and clad in robes of the finest texture. Servants attended to all his wants, and everything that his heart desired was given to him.

Fortune now seemed to smile on him, and he thought his happiness complete. But one day as he was at the table he happened to raise his eyes, and saw suspended over his head a sharp sword. It hung by a single thread, and he saw that if that thread broke he would most certainly be hurt, and perhaps even killed.

As soon as he perceived it, he became pale; he was afraid to move lest he might in doing so break the slender thread, and he sat on his rich throne as immovable as a statue, crying out to someone to come and take away the sword. By the King's order this was not immediately done, and Damocles was almost dead from fear.

Those who are in mortal sin are in even greater danger: they are hanging over the abyss of hell; all that keeps them from falling into it is the slender thread of life. O my child, keep out of mortal sin.

To avoid mortal sin, keep away from those who do evil: if you go with them, you also shall certainly become as bad as they are, and fall into sin.

EMELIA AND THE PIECE OF COAL

There was once a young girl of sixteen who was as innocent as she was beautiful: her name was Emelia. She had a father who loved her with true father's love by watching over her continually, that she might never do anything to spoil the beauty of her soul.

Emelia met another young girl who was giddy and vain, but whose pleasing conversation made her love her company. Her father soon saw this, and at once said to her: "Emelia, my dearest child, you must not go with that girl any more."

But Emelia answered: "My dear father, I know that she is not so good as she ought to be; but, then, I am not a child now, and there is not any danger for me, because I know how to take care of myself."

Her father said nothing, but taking up a piece of coal which was lying near the fire, he gave it to her. "Take it," he said; "it will not hurt you, because it is not burning."

She took it from him, and in a moment her pure white hand became stained by the piece of coal, although she held it as carefully as she could, and her dress on which it happened to fall was also soiled by it.

She said: "See, the coal has made my hand and my dress quite soiled. But why did you give it to me?"

"To show you that if you go near anyone whose conduct is bad, you also will lose the purity of your soul."

Emelia understood the lesson, and ever afterwards avoided the young woman's company.

8

MORTAL SIN DESTROYS THE MERIT OF ALL OUR GOOD WORKS

Mortal sin not only kills the soul, but it also destroys all the merit we have gained by the good works done in a state of grace. O my child, what a terrible evil is mortal sin!

THE WORK OF ART DESTROYED.

Albert the Great spent thirty years in making a wonderful piece of work. It was a human figure, which, by means of certain contrivances, was made to move and act, as if it were alive. The pious Albert had spent all his leisure time at this work during these thirty years, and as it was all done in secret, no one knew about it.

At length it was finished. It happened that at that very time one of his friends from a distance, whom he had not seen for a long time, came to visit him. He thought he would give him an agreeable surprise by showing him this wonderful figure which he had just completed.

So he told him to go to a certain part of the house. "You will see something there," he said, "which I am sure will astonish you."

In the meantime he went to the place where the figure was and set it in motion, then hid himself, that he might enjoy unseen the surprise of his friend.

When the man went into the room, and saw the figure moving so naturally, and uttering sounds so like the human voice, he began to think that there must be some evil spirit about it.

So he suddenly seized a great piece of wood which was lying near, and dealt a blow at the figure, which in an instant broke it into a thousand pieces.

"Stop! stop!" cried out Albert, rushing from his hiding-place. But it was too late; the beautiful work was destroyed. The man now saw what he had done, and was filled with regret at his hasty act. Albert said to him, with a sadness in his voice, "My friend, for thirty years I have labored to bring that work to perfection, and in one instant you have utterly destroyed it. The loss can never be repaired." And the two friends separated.

From his Life.

My child, your soul is beautiful so long as it remains in a state of grace; but the moment you commit a mortal sin all is changed. The good works of many years, perhaps, are utterly destroyed in an instant. Oh, be careful to avoid mortal sin!

9

VENIAL SIN

My child, venial sin is a lesser evil than mortal sin, because it does not kill the soul. Yet it is a very great evil, and must never be committed, because it displeases God. It is sad to see so many people who pretend to be very pious, and yet think so little about venial sins. It is not in this way that the Saints of God thought about them.

"ONLY A VENIAL SIN."

Maria Theresa, wife of Louis XIV, had a great horror of sin. One day someone asked her to do something which was wrong.

She answered: "No, I will never wilfully consent to offend God."

"But," said the other, "after all, it is a very small offense; at most it is only a venial sin."

The pious Queen answered: "Only a venial sin! And do you think it is nothing to commit a venial sin? A venial sin is an offense against God, and whatever offends Him is grievous enough, no matter how small it may appear."

Life of Maria Theresa.

ST. MACARIUS AND THE STOLEN FIG.

When St. Macarius was a little boy, he was playing along with some other children in a garden. At a little distance stood a fig-tree, laden with ripe fruit.

The boys said: "What beautiful figs! Let us take some." So they plucked a few, and began to eat them.

While Macarius was eating, his conscience seemed to be always saying to him, "You have done wrong! You have done wrong!" And he found no pleasure in eating the fig he had taken.

Afterwards, when he grew up to manhood, his disciples would often see him weeping. "I am weeping," he said, "for the sin I committed when I was a child, by stealing a fig."

"But, dear Father, that was only a venial sin."

"Ah! My brethren, it was an offense against God, and that is enough."

Fathers of the Desert.

A HOLY CHILD'S GRIEF.

When St. Aloysius was about five years old, his father took him to live in the camp for about three months, because he wanted him to be a soldier. His mother tried to keep him at home, for she was afraid lest he might see and hear things that would stain the innocence of his soul. But his father's resolution was not to be changed; so he went to the camp, with no one but his tutor to take care of him.

During the time he was there it happened, as his mother had foreseen, that he heard one of the soldiers say some unbecoming words of which he did not know the meaning. He repeated these words in the hearing of his tutor.

"O my child," said the tutor, "do not say these words again, because they are bad, and those who say them offend God."

Aloysius burst into tears, and promised never to say them again.

Ever afterwards, when he thought of what he had done, tears of sorrow would run down his cheeks.

If even the appearance of sin caused the Saint so much sorrow, how much more ought you to grieve, my child, who have so often wilfully offended God?

VENIAL SIN IN THE EYES OF GOD.

Father Alphonsus Rodriguez relates that there was a very holy man who desired to know himself as he really was in the eyes of God. "O my God," he prayed, "be pleased to show me my soul just as it is in Thy holy sight."

God heard his prayer and showed him his soul, which, though free from grievous sin, was nevertheless stained with venial faults. The sight of it filled his heart with so much disgust that he could not bear to look at it, but immediately cried out: "O my God, do not show me my soul again, when there are venial sins upon it, otherwise I shall faint from fear."

So, my child, keep away from even venial sin, since it is so terrible in the eyes of God.

If you, my child, had been on Mount Calvary during the Passion of Jesus Christ, and if you had been a witness of His cruel sufferings, you would now be better able to understand what a terrible evil sin is, even those sins that are venial, because they caused Him to suffer so much.

ST. MARGARET MARY'S LITTLE FAULTS.

When St. Margaret Mary was a little girl, she was very pious, and loved God above all things. But as she grew up she allowed vain thoughts to come into her mind. She became fond of dress, and of the praise people gave her, and soon began to give more time to the world than to God. Yet, in all this, she never committed a mortal sin; she would have died sooner than have yielded to such an evil. The faults she committed were only venial sins.

One evening, when she came home from a place where she had received much flattery on account of her dress and elegant manners, she lay down to rest, her mind at the same time being full of these vain thoughts.

Jesus in His mercy appeared to her just as He had been when the soldiers were scourging Him—covered with wounds and blood.

"O my Jesus," she exclaimed in horror at the sight, "oh, how cruel were those wretches who caused Thee to suffer so much!"

"My child," said Our Lord to her, "it was you yourself who helped to make Me suffer so much; your pride and vanity were the cause of some of these sufferings."

From that moment Margaret Mary renounced all the vanity of the world, and by her love tried to make reparation to her beloved Master for these faults of her childhood.

You must also be careful never to commit venial sin, because those who commit venial sins very easily fall into mortal ones.

DRAWN BY A HAIR.

There was once a girl who worked in a factory. The day's work was nearly done, and it was time to go home. She saw on her dress some white lint, and she stooped down to brush it off.

As she bent forward the quickly revolving machinery caught her loose hair and drew her by it. She could not get away, and in a moment her head and body were drawn in among the wheels, and she was crushed to pieces.

It was by a few hairs only that she was at first caught. You would have thought it would have been easy to have broken them and so escape. But no; while each hair is so very small of itself, they all together are stronger than a rope. So it is with venial sins. O my child, keep away from venial sin.

10

HOW SIN IS PARDONED

God wishes everyone to be saved, and gives to everyone, even the greatest sinners, pardon for the sins they have committed, if they are sorry for them. He has given power to the Apostles and their successors, the Bishops and priests of His Church, to forgive sins in His Name, and has appointed the Sacraments of Baptism and Penance as the means of obtaining that forgiveness.

THE LITTLE CHILD IN THE FIRE.

Not long ago a mother went out of her house for a few moments, leaving her little girl alone in the room. She told her not to go near the fire until she returned. The child promised to obey.

But scarcely had her mother gone out when the girl, forgetting her promise, went near the fire.

Whilst standing there, she stumbled and fell upon the burning coals. In an instant her clothes were on fire, and the flames rising up around her, caused her to suffer intense pain.

She began to scream and to cry out, "O mother! mother!" These were the only words she could utter.

Fortunately, her mother, who was not far distant, heard her

screams, and, knowing that something terrible must have happened to her, she rushed back to the room.

When she saw her child enveloped in flames, and heard her calling on her for help, she flew towards her. In an instant she lifted her in her arms and extinguished the flames. The poor child was badly burned; many people said she could not live, but, by her mother's care, she recovered. She was sorry for her disobedience, and it was a lesson for her never to be guilty of that sin again.

In this example you see how speedily this mother came to her child's assistance, and rescued her from the evil she had brought upon herself by her disobedience. God, Who loves us with a greater love than even that of a mother, will snatch us from the state of sin when we call upon Him, more speedily than this mother snatched her child from the fire.

ST. FRANCIS DE SALES AND THE GREAT SINNER.

St. Francis de Sales was hearing confessions in his church at Annecy. Among other penitents who went to him was a woman who had led a very bad life, but who, touched by God's grace, made a good and sincere confession of all the evil she had done.

St. Francis blessed God for her conversion, and felt his soul full of happiness when giving her absolution.

When she had received it she said to him: "My Father, what do you think of me now, since you have heard all the crimes I have been guilty of?"

"My dear child," he answered, "I now look upon you as a Saint."

"Ah, how can you say such a thing? Have I not just told you of my great crimes? You are not saying what you think."

"I am saying the truth: you may have one time been a sinner, but now you are a Saint."

"But how can the past be forgotten? I have sinned, and I cannot recall my evil deeds."

"My child," answered the Saint, "let people say and think what they like; they may judge you as the Pharisee judged Mary Magdalen after her conversion, but you know what Jesus Christ thought of her, and how He judged her."

"But, my Father," she replied, "what do you think now of my past life?"

"Nothing, I assure you," he answered. "How can I think of a thing that has now no longer any existence. I think of nothing but of praising God and celebrating the feast of your conversion. Ah! I wish I could join myself now to the angels in Heaven, who at this moment are singing a canticle of joy because of your return to God." Saying these words, tears came running down his cheeks.

The penitent saw these tears. "Ah, dear Father," she said, "you are weeping. I am sure you are weeping because of the abominations of my past life."

"No, no, my child," he answered again; "I am weeping tears of joy, because of your resurrection from the grave of sin to a life of grace."

The penitent was not only consoled by these words of St. Francis, but when the devil came to try to make her fall into despair by thinking of her past iniquities, they enabled her to drive the temptation away.

A SPARK THAT FELL INTO THE SEA.

A man once let a spark fall into the sea. Immediately it was extinguished in the great ocean, and forever disappeared.

The sins which we commit, when compared to the infinite mercy and goodness of God, are even less than a spark when compared to the ocean; for the ocean, although so great, has limits, but the mercy of God and His goodness are infinite.

This, then, should give hope to the greatest sinner. And has not God Himself said to those who return to Him with their whole hearts: "If your sins be as scarlet, they shall be made as white as snow; and if they be red as crimson, they shall be white as wool"? (Is. I. 18).

HOPE OF PARDON.

There was a young Spanish gentleman who had in his youth led a very wicked life. Touched by the grace of God, he left off his evil ways, and began to lead a life of fervor in the practice of every Christian virtue.

Satan was full of wrath when he saw that God had snatched from him a soul he had thought would most certainly be his forever. He tried to fill him with thoughts of despair, by bringing before his mind the grievous sins of the past.

One day he appeared to him under the form of a hideous monster, dragging after him a heavy chain. "I am come," he said, "to bind you with this chain and take you along with me to hell, to punish you for all the crimes you have been guilty of against God."

The young man said: "Satan, you need not think to frighten me in this way. God is much stronger than you are, and Jesus Christ, by His death, has merited my pardon, and protects me. I do indeed fear God, but at the same time I love Him, and I know that He does not wish me to perish, but to live forever. As for yourself," he added, "I am not afraid of you, and I hate you. You shall never be able to make me offend God by tempting me to despair of my salvation, for I love God too much to fall into such a temptation."

This firm confidence in God put the devil to flight, and the young man was never again troubled with these thoughts.

O my child, how grateful you should be to God for His infinite goodness in being so ready to pardon you, and promise Him that you will be faithful to Him by never again committing sin.

PART XII

THE RESURRECTION OF THE BODY AND LIFE EVERLASTING

1

THE RESURRECTION OF THE BODY

My child, when you look on the face of one who is dead, and behold the eyes that can no longer see you, the mouth that can no longer speak to you, and the ears that can no longer hear you, you are filled with sadness, and tears flow from your eyes.

But to the good Christian death has also its joys, because he knows that it is the only gate through which he can pass into the joys of eternity. And he knows also that the body, now so cold and lifeless, shall one day rise again from the grave.

St. John says: "The hour cometh, wherein all that are in the graves shall hear the voice of the Son of God. And they that have done good things shall come forth unto the resurrection of life: and they that have done evil unto the resurrection of judgment" (John V. 28, 29).

ST. EULALIA'S LAST WORDS.

St. Eulalia was only twelve years old when she was seized as a Christian and condemned to die. It was towards the beginning of the fourth century.

Calpurnian, an officer of the Emperor, commanded her to be cruelly beaten with rods; but the holy virgin remained firm. When her body was all one wound, she turned towards the officer, and with a firmness with which the Holy Ghost inspired the martyrs, she cried out: "O Calpurnian, open your eyes and look at me. Take care to observe well my countenance, that you may know me again on the terrible day of judgment. You and I shall on that day have to appear before Jesus Christ, I to receive the reward of my sufferings, you to receive the chastisement due for your cruelty."

After these words the faithful martyr was put to death. Her pure soul went to Paradise, and her body was laid in the grave to await the day of its glorious resurrection.

THE MACHABEES.

When Antiochus the King was tormenting the Machabees because they would not deny their faith, one of them said to him: "Thou, indeed, O most wicked man, destroyest us out of this present life; but the King of the world will raise us up, who die for His laws, in the resurrection of eternal life."

And when the tyrant ordered one of the others to put forth his tongue that it might be cut out, he quickly did so, and courageously stretching out his hands, said with confidence: "These I have from Heaven; but, for the laws of God, I now despise them, because I hope to receive them again from him" (2 Macc. VII. 9-11).

The bodies of the just shall rise again at the last day in splendor clothed with the brightness of Heaven. Jesus Christ says in the Scripture: "The just shall shine as the sun in the kingdom of their Father."

BLESSED WILLIAM OF CLAIRVAUX.

On the night when Blessed William of Clairvaux died, he appeared to a certain pious religious sister surrounded with the brightness of a most glorious light, so dazzling that the eye could not look on him. His garments appeared to be of the most precious material, adorned with the richest gems, and on his head he wore a crown of gold sparkling with many jewels.

Now when the religious saw him in this magnificent attire she was filled with amazement, for she had not heard of his death. As soon as she could speak she said to him: "Reverend Father, how is it that I see you so gloriously arrayed? You were not accustomed to be so."

Blessed William replied: "I have left the world, and have received my never-fading crown of glory in Heaven."

"What mean those precious stones, and that glorious crown you wear?"

He answered: "The precious stones are my reward for the tribulations and trials I suffered for God's sake while on earth, and the rich crown is the recompense for my labors in His holy service."

Saying these words, he disappeared.

My child, you also must one day rise from the tomb; may you on that day be numbered with the Saints.

A LITTLE CHILD'S QUESTIONS.

When the venerable Sister Magdalen Dubois was only four years old, she was standing at the door of her father's house as a funeral procession was passing by. She asked her nurse, who was with her, what they were doing.

"They are carrying the body of a young woman to the grave, because she is dead."

"And must I also die?" asked the little Magdalen.

"Yes, my child, we must all die, and our souls must go to Heaven or to Hell for all eternity."

"And how long is eternity? Is it longer than one day?"

"Ah! my child, eternity has no end; eternity means for ever and ever."

Magdalen said no more, but from that moment the thought of eternity never left her mind. Sometimes she was heard to say to herself: "An eternity in Heaven, or an eternity in Hell. We must all one day die, and when this life is over there begins one that will never end."

Magdalen lived a holy life, and her death was that of the Saints.

You are made to the likeness of God, my child; your soul is like to God, because it can never die; and although your body must be laid in the grave, it shall rise again at the last day, and, soul and body united, you must live as long as God is God, either with Him in happiness, or separated from Him in Hell. This thought should make you careful to avoid every sin, and to love God in this life, that you may be with Him for ever in Heaven.

2

WHAT LIFE EVERLASTING MEANS

My child, there is a verse of a beautiful hymn you often sing, which explains to you what 'life everlasting' means; it is as follows:

"The good with God in Heaven above
Shall ever happy be
The wicked in the flames of Hell
Shall burn eternally."

The happiness of Heaven, then, is to see, love, and enjoy God forevermore.

APPARITION OF THE CHILD JESUS.

St. Boniface, Bishop of Lausanne, was once suffering from a long and tedious illness. One night, as he lay on his bed, he complained to Our Blessed Lady, whom he loved with all the affection of his heart, that he felt so sad and weary.

The Blessed Virgin immediately appeared to him, bearing in her arms the Divine Child Jesus, wrapped in swaddling-clothes, as He was long ago in the stable of Bethlehem. The face of the Holy Child was also covered.

The good Bishop was full of joy at the beautiful vision; but he desired most ardently to look upon the sweet face of his Redeemer.

Jesus, knowing the thoughts that were passing in his mind, lifted up His hand, and raised the veil which concealed His holy countenance, and Boniface was able to behold it.

The holy man was ravished at its celestial beauty, and cried out in ecstasy: "Oh! if in Paradise there were nothing else but that Blessed Face, it were worth while to suffer all tribulations here on earth, that we might be able to gaze upon a countenance so glorious."

Whilst he continued in prayer, he was rapt in the Spirit, and was led into Paradise, and saw the cherubim, how they burn with love of God. Afterwards he was led into each choir of angels, and into that of the prophets, and saw their various dignities. Then the glory of the Apostles was unfolded before him. Then he came to the choirs of the martyrs, and saw their glory.

After that he came to the choirs of the confessors who edified the Church of God by word and by example, and he contemplated their glory. Then he came to the choirs of virgins who follow the Lamb wheresoever He goeth; he beheld their dignity, and was filled with rapture at their splendor and their beauty.

Then above them all he beheld the Immaculate Mother of God herself, enthroned in unspeakable glory, and he beheld also with what love she is honored by her Son, and with what reverence she is venerated by all the blessed.

At last he came before the Majesty of God, where he saw the Son in the Father and the Father in the Son, and the Holy Ghost proceeding from both, and how God is glorified in His Saints.

When he returned to his senses after this ecstasy, and tried to describe what he saw, "I cannot do it," he said; "no mortal tongue can describe it, no mortal mind conceive it. The glory of Heaven cannot be imagined on earth."

Lives of the Cistercian Fathers.

And yet, my child, such is your home, the home for which God made you. You are to be forever, not only a spectator of all that beauty, but also to share in it, and to be one of that thrice blessed company. Oh! What a glorious future is in store for you, my child, if you are good now, and it will be forever and ever. You see now what "life everlasting" means.

ST. THOMAS MORE'S FIDELITY.

Thomas More was Lord High Chancellor of England in the reign of King Henry VIII. He was a fervent Catholic, and although zealous in the service of his King, was still more so in the service of God.

When Henry rebelled against the Church, he put into prison, and sometimes even condemned to death, those who would not acknowledge him to be head of the Church in England.

When he informed Sir Thomas More of this law which he had made, requiring his subjects to submit to his authority in spiritual things, Sir Thomas at once replied that he for one would never obey it, "because," he said, "it is against the law of God."

The King was very much grieved at Thomas's refusal, not only because he himself had a great esteem for him, but also because he knew the great influence his example would have over others. So he tried, first by promises, and then by threats, to make him submit.

But it was all in vain, for the faithful servant of the King of Heaven firmly declared that he would sooner die than neglect his duty to God.

This answer put the King into a great passion, and he ordered him to be immediately put into prison. "You shall see," he said, "that I am your master, and that you must do what I wish."

"You have, indeed, power over my life, and over everything I have that passes away with life," replied the intrepid Thomas, "but more than that you have no power over."

The King condemned him to death. But wishing to give him yet an opportunity of saving his life, he went to Margaret, his wife, and persuaded her to go to her husband and to try and influence him by those endearing motives which have most effect upon the human heart.

"O my husband," she said to him, "*do* obey the command of the King as others have done, and your life will be spared."

"And how long, my dear wife," he answered— "how long do you think I shall live if I do what you ask me?"

"For at least twenty years," she said.

"Well, if you had said twenty thousand years, that would have been something; but it would, indeed, be a very poor thing to live even that number of years, and run the risk of losing my God in eternity! Oh no, dear wife, I thought you would have spoken more wisely to me than that. I will never consent to disobey my God in that way; I promised Him over and over again that I would serve Him faithfully all my days, and love Him with my whole heart, and by His grace I will do it."

Sir Thomas More died on the scaffold on the sixth day of July, 1535.

From his Life.

My child, Heaven is your home. In Heaven your Father dwells, and your beloved Mother Mary, and all the angels and the Saints. For Heaven you were made, and Heaven is to be your dwelling-place forever if you are good now. What is more profitable, then, for you than often to think of Heaven now, that you may the more surely reach it when you die?

ST. IGNATIUS ALWAYS THINKS OF HEAVEN.

St. Ignatius of Loyola sometimes spent the whole night thinking of his home in Heaven. When he was in Rome, he used to go to the highest part of the house where he dwelt, and keep his eyes fixed on Heaven. Then he would think of the happy home God had prepared for His servants, and the infinite rewards those who loved Him would receive; and he was often heard to exclaim: "Oh, how vile and worthless does this world appear to me when I think of the joys of Heaven!"

3

THE JOY OF THE GOOD CHRISTIAN AT DEATH

Our home is in Heaven. How very foolish, then, is it for us to live as if our home were on this earth! How happy are those, when death comes, who in this world have lived for Heaven only! And how many are the regrets, at that hour, of those who have lived only for the world and forgot Heaven, or did but little for it!

THE DYING MAN'S SMILE.

A poor old man was lying on his deathbed. For many years he had been confined to his bed, and had suffered much from his great infirmities. But no one ever heard him complain; he was always resigned to the holy will of God, and always happy. Everyone who had heard of him was edified by his holy life, and already they gave him the name of "The Saint."

One day he became worse than usual. The report was soon spread that "The Saint" was dying, and the people of the neighborhood came to see him, and speak to him once more before he left them. As they stood around his bed, tears were upon their cheeks, and sobs choked their speech. He alone was calm and serene, and a smile of joy was upon his countenance.

One of his friends said to him: "Tell us how you, who are suffering so much, and are so near your end, can smile and be without fear, since it is a terrible thing to die."

"Ah! my friend," he replied, "I am glad because I am going home. It is the remembrance of my past life that makes me so happy. I never loved the world nor its follies. I always lived for Heaven, and had always fixed my thoughts there. I have accepted from God's hands all the afflictions He has thought fit to send me, to satisfy for my sins, and because I knew that would please Him and I united them all and all my sorrows to those of Jesus on the cross. I always kept away from those who were wicked, and I tried to do all the good I could to my neighbor. I tried also to attend to my religious duties, and to serve my God as faithfully as I could, in the humble condition in life in which He placed me. And now, when I see that I am dying, I lovingly, and with great confidence in my Heavenly Father, resign my soul into His hands. It is this that makes me so happy now."

The people were filled with admiration at these words. Soon after this he breathed his last. One of the bystanders said: "Oh, how beautiful it is to die as this man has died!"

"Yes," said another, "it is indeed beautiful. But to die as he did, we must live as he lived."

Choix d'*Histoires Morales.*

VANITY, OR THE DYING GIRL.

There was once a young lady who was very beautiful and clever. People used to flatter her and praise her, and, like many others of her age, she believed every word they said. This made her proud and haughty, and she spent most of her time in seeking after things which would make her still more beautiful in the eyes of those who admired her, that she might gain more praise from them.

In the midst of all this vanity, she forgot her duties to God, and lived in this world as if there was no God at all.

But in the midst of these enjoyments she suddenly became very ill. The sickness at first was slight, and everyone said that it would soon pass away.

But in this they were mistaken; the doctor soon saw that it had become very dangerous, and he told her parents that they might prepare for the worst.

This information filled them with great dismay, but they did not tell her of the danger she was in, lest this might make her worse.

So time went on, and as she felt herself becoming daily weaker, and saw the sad countenances of her parents, she began to feel alarmed. The thought that perhaps she was really going to die filled her mind with fear, for she knew well that she had not lived as she ought to have done.

God is good to His children, even when He sends them afflictions. For it is often in this way that He brings back again those whom the world has led away from Him.

So, when she began to think on her past life and her present illness, tears came into her eyes. "O my God," she said, "what a miserable girl I have been! Instead of loving You and pleasing You, I have forgotten You altogether, and sought for the empty flattery of the world instead. But it shall be so no longer. I will begin now to be good; and if I do become well again, how different will be my whole conduct!"

That very moment she asked her mother to send for the priest. When he came he confirmed what the doctor had already said—that there was great danger, and that it was time to think of receiving the Sacraments of the dying.

This at first made her tremble more and more, but the words of the priest encouraged her, and before he left her bedside he had reconciled her to God, and tears of happiness and contrition bedewed her cheeks.

"O my God," she said, "if I cannot live for You, let me die for You. I offer up my death to make some little reparation for my past sinful, vain life."

After this she sent for her friends to come and see her, those especially who had encouraged her in her vanity. When they came to her bedside they began to weep.

"You may weep," she said, "and weep bitterly, too, as I have done, for the folly of your past lives. I sent for you to say goodbye to you before I die, and that you may see the vanity of the things of this world. A few days ago I was the object of your admiration, and the world smiled upon me. Tomorrow, perhaps, or at least in a few days, I will be in the cold, cold grave, forsaken by you all, and forgotten.

"Oh, my friends, if you could only see the things of the world as I see them now, how clearly you would see how vain and empty they all are! Ah yes! you would see then that there is nothing in this world of any real value except to love God and serve Him alone. My hour has now come; yours will soon come also. Oh, then, remember my dying words—the dying words of one whom you used to call your friend: do not delay a moment longer; begin at once a new life, and live for God alone. These are the last words you will ever hear from me. Pray for me; and if God in His mercy, as I now hope, will admit me into Heaven, I will not forget to pray for you."

She did not live long after this, but her death was not without its fruits. Those who had lived with her in following the vanities of life became after her death pious and attentive to their religious duties. The words she had uttered on her deathbed were never forgotten.

Philothea, 9 *Année,* p. 167.

JOY AT DEATH.

A pious and faithful missionary had consecrated his life to the service of God and the salvation of souls. Many were the trials and sufferings he had met with in the discharge of his duty, and at length, wasted and worn out, he lay on his deathbed.

Those who came to visit him were in admiration at his patience and the calm serenity of his countenance, and some of them asked him how he could be so calm and happy. He answered:

"Long, long ago I read of a poor pagan who desired very much to die; and when people asked him the reason of this strange wish, he replied that he wished to die because he was anxious to see certain famous heroes of whom he had heard. Now, with how much greater reason ought I to rejoice when I see the hour of death coming, since I am going to see my Divine Savior and His holy mother Mary, and all the angels and Saints in Paradise." Then, looking up to Heaven, he prayed thus: "O my God, what a beautiful thought—when I enter Heaven I will see Jesus Christ and all His Saints, and be forever happy in their company."

If even the thought of being in the company of the blessed in Heaven could bring so much joy, how much greater must it be to be actually in their company forever?

THE GOOD NEWS.

When St. Aloysius had been for a long time ill of the malady which caused his death, the physicians, seeing that he was drawing near his end, told him that he could not depend on more than eight days to live.

When they retired, one of his companions came into the room where he lay.

"Oh!" he cried out, with an expression of great joy on his countenance, as soon as he saw him, "do you know the news? Do you know the news, the good news, I have received? The doctors have just told me I cannot live longer than eight days. Oh! come, let us sing a hymn of joy to thank God for this great happiness: the danger of losing my soul will soon be past."

After this he wrote a letter to his mother, in which he said: "My dearest mother, I have good news to give you today, and I am sure you will rejoice with me when you hear it. I am now near the end of my life—near that time when there shall be no longer any danger of me losing my soul. As for myself, I look upon death as the greatest blessing God could bestow on me, and I ask you to join with me in thanking Him."

After this a scruple came into his mind that perhaps it was wrong to give expression in this way to the joy he felt at the approach of death. So, sending for his confessor, he asked him if it were sin.

"No, my child," he replied, "the joy which you feel is caused by the great desire you have of seeing God, Who is the Sovereign Good, and of seeing your soul safe from all danger. Rejoice, then, as much as you wish, and say with the holy King David, 'I am filled with joy at the things which have been said to me: we shall go into the house of the Lord.'"

Life of St. Aloysius.

My child, what a joyful moment that will be for you, if you, at the last day of your life, when the moment of your judgment comes, hear these words from the mouth of the Great Judge of the living and the dead: "Come, thou blessed of My Father, possess the kingdom which was prepared for thee from the foundation of the world." Yet those who persevere till the end of their lives in the service of God shall one day most certainly hear these blessed words.

QUEEN ESTHER.

We read in the Scriptures that there was a monarch in the East whose name was Assuerus, who chose for his spouse one of the young women of the Children of Israel who were then in captivity, and took her into his palace, where she might receive the honors that were due to her exalted rank. Her name was Esther.

When she entered the palace, and saw the great magnificence of the King, and the greatness of the courtiers who surrounded him, and all the glory of his attendants, Esther was filled with a terrible fear, and would have fainted at the feet of the King had not the monarch held out to her his hand in which was his golden scepter and said to her in a tone of the greatest sweetness: "Fear not, Esther, for I am thy brother; thou shalt not die."

This is a picture of what happens to the souls of those who have served God during life. God has chosen you, my child, from among those who are living in the captivity of sin, and has made you His child, and has sent you to live in His palace, that is His Church in this life, and has prepared a home for you in the Kingdom of Heaven in the next. At the moment when you enter the abode of the Blessed above, and see the magnificence of God's house, and the glory of His kingdom, like Esther, you will be so filled with fear and wonder that you will almost faint away.

How glorious it shall then be to hear the voice of the Eternal King saying to you: "Be not afraid, my child, for I am thy Brother; thou shalt not die."

Yet this is the truth, and not a mere fancy. Oh, then, love the good God now when you are on earth, that one day you may enjoy that happy reality.

THE WORDS A SAINT HEARD IN HEAVEN.

Jesus Christ one day gave St. Mechtildes a view of the glory of Heaven. And as she was gazing on it in rapture and wishing that the happy day were come when she also would enjoy the happiness of the Saints, she heard a voice that seemed to come from the immense multitude of the blessed, saying: "O thrice happy are you who still live in the world, because it is in your power to increase your glory and your merit forever."

"Oh!" cried out the Saint, "if men did but know how much they might increase their merit every day, they would never awake in the morning without their hearts being filled with gratitude to God for His goodness in giving them another day in which they might increase their glory for Heaven, their eternal home. This thought alone ought to be sufficient to strengthen them in all their difficulties and trials, and to give them courage to lead a mortified life, since each one of these things is of so much avail for them in eternity."

THE BRIGHT CROWN.

We read in the Lives of the ancient Fathers that there was one of them who labored without ceasing to become more and more perfect. Day by day he increased his austerities and good works without allowing himself any repose or rest from his labors.

The brethren, thinking that he would become wearied, and might shorten his life by his excessive labors, one day begged of him to take a little rest.

"No, my brethren," he answered; "let me labor and suffer as long as I am upon the earth, that I may receive a brighter crown in Heaven. It is the thought of that crown of glory that consoles me and sustains me in my weariness. Believe me, my children, I am of opinion that Abraham himself, when he saw the greatness of the eternal rewards of Heaven, was sorry he had not labored more while he was here on earth."

4

THE ETERNAL REWARD FOR BEARING PATIENTLY OUR CROSS IN THIS WORLD

God requires of us in this world to go against our own natural inclinations, and to deny ourselves. If we only knew the eternal reward He will give us in Heaven for doing this, we would daily try to suffer more, that our reward there might be greater.

COUNT OTHO'S DAUGHTER.

There was one time a rich Count called Otho, who had a daughter whom he loved with great affection, and whom he brought up in the fear of God.

One day the child was amusing herself with some beads of various colors made of glass, with which she seemed to be much pleased. Her father was sitting by the fire watching her.

"My child," he said, "these are pretty beads you are playing with."

"Yes, papa, they are very beautiful."

"You are pleased with them, then, and feel quite happy while amusing yourself with them."

"Yes, dear papa, I am," said the child.

"Well, then," said the father, "take them up and throw them all into the fire."

The child looked up into her father's face to see if he was in earnest. One glance told her he was. Tears at once came into her eyes, and for a moment she hesitated to obey.

"Well, dear child, you may do as you choose, but you know that when I ask you to do something, it is always because I, who love you so tenderly, see that it will be the best for you."

The girl at these words gathered together all the beautiful beads she had esteemed so much, and threw them into the fire, where in a few moments they became destroyed by the flames.

Her father said nothing till she had done what he had asked of her. But when the beads began to crackle in the flames, he took her into his arms, and, kissing away the tears that trickled down her cheeks, said to her: "Now, my child, you will soon see how your father can reward you for that heroic sacrifice you made to please him."

He then drew forth from a drawer a little casket, and when he had opened it, the child saw a beautiful necklace, made of glittering diamonds and rare and costly stones set in gold.

"This, my child, is for you. I wanted to see if you loved me more than yourself. You have proved to me that you do so because, rather than displease me, you have sacrificed for my sake what gave you great pleasure.

"Take this, then, my dearest little one, and when you wear it, it will remind you that your Father in Heaven will reward you with a reward surpassing all understanding in the world to come if you obey Him in this life, and sacrifice everything rather than displease Him by breaking His commandments."

Choix d'Hist. Morales.

THE BEAUTIFUL CROWN.

A holy monk called William dwelt in a monastery in Denmark. He had lived for the long period of ninety-one years, and during all that time he had to endure afflictions and trials without number. But by the grace of God, he had borne them all patiently.

One day he had a vision. He seemed to see one of God's holy angels making a beautiful crown; it was formed of precious stones and glittering diamonds.

The old man said to the angel, "For whom are you making that crown?"

And the angel answered him, "I am making it for you."

"And when will it be finished?" he asked.

"When you have suffered patiently all that God has designed to send you."

This answer consoled the holy monk, and encouraged him to suffer with patience till the end of his life, that he might receive it from the hand of God as the reward of his long life on earth.

HAUTRIEVE : *Catech de Pers.,* II. 470.

My child, when a person is anxious to obtain a prize, or something he desires to possess, he says to himself, "I am determined to get it"; then he thinks of it alone, and how he is to obtain it. That determination is called a firm resolution.

Now, as there is nothing so important for you as to obtain Heaven, and as you cannot obtain Heaven without perseverance in the service of God, you must first of all take a firm resolution to serve God as long as you are on earth.

ST. PLATO COMFORTED.

St. Plato was condemned to suffer terrible tortures because he would not renounce his Faith. The soldiers scourged him so cruelly that his body seemed to be one wound from head to feet. Yet in the midst of all these sufferings he was never heard to utter one word of complaint. When they had scourged him in this inhuman manner, they put him into prison.

Many of the faithful who had been witnesses of his sufferings and of his heroic patience went to the prison to visit and console him.

He said to them: "Do you think, my dearest brethren, that it is for a trifling reward that I am suffering in this manner? No, no! Oh, how terrible are these tortures! No mind can conceive the intense pain I suffer. Yet I do not complain, because I have always before my eyes the eternal reward, the glorious immortality that awaits me in Heaven. At every instant I say to myself: 'Courage, my soul; you have resolved to serve God to the end. It is coming; it will soon be here, and then you shall enjoy eternal rest.'

"O my brethren," he continued, "you have also taken a firm resolution to serve God till the end of your lives. Continue, I beseech you, to do so, and in order that you may not be overcome by the temptations that arise before you, keep your eyes fixed on Jesus, your Master in Heaven, Who is holding in His hands the crown of life, which He will place upon your heads if you are faithful to the end."

My child, that beautiful lesson is for you also. You shall have many trials in your journey to Heaven, but keep to the end the firm resolution you have taken of serving God, and you also shall receive the reward God has promised.

"CONSIDER THY LAST END."

An ancient Father who had for many years led a holy, mortified life in the desert was asked by some of his brethren how he had been able to persevere in enduring so many trials and the great sufferings he had to undergo in that frightful solitude.

"O brethren," he said, "all the labors and sufferings of the many years I have been here are not to be compared to one hour of the torments of Hell. Wherefore, in order to escape them and to obtain the eternal rewards of Heaven, we must cheerfully undergo the hardships and labors of the short time of our mortal life. Then look up to Heaven, think of its eternal glory, its never-ending joys. Ah! let us, then, mortify ourselves here, that we may find that everlasting rest hereafter in our happy home in Heaven."

5

OUR ETERNAL REWARD WILL BE MEASURED BY THE GOOD WE HAVE DONE ON EARTH

In Heaven, God will give to each one the reward he has merited by his good life on earth. Blessed are those, then, who are poor now and in suffering, for if they bear all this for love of God, He will grant them a beautiful reward.

THE DUKE OF CARINTHIA'S FEAST.

The Duke of Carinthia was very rich, and his palace was filled with many wealthy nobles. The good Duke himself was a Christian, but the nobles were all pagans, and although he used every means to bring about their conversion, they always turned a deaf ear to his words.

One day he prepared a great feast in his palace, to which he invited all these wealthy nobles. He also sent an invitation to all the Christians in the neighborhood, asking them to come and share in the banquet. Now, most of these Christians were poor, and when the Faith had been preached to them they had readily embraced it.

In the meantime, great preparations were being made. The banquet-hall was decorated with great splendor. The tables were covered with gold and silver vessels. Wines of great price filled the goblets; most delicious food was served up; and everything was prepared with a magnificence never before seen in that country.

In the lower apartments of the palace, the Duke caused other arrangements to be made. Tables of rough wood and benches of the same material filled the hall. On these tables were placed vessels of clay and food of the plainest kind. Instead of rich and costly wines, water was the only kind of drink; even the poorest amongst the poor had seldom seen such bad and common fare.

When all was ready and the hour had come, the guests were seen approaching. The nobles, clad in garments of the richest material, glittering with jewels of great price, came in great numbers, looking forward with pleasure to the joys of the feast. As each arrived at the palace he was met by an attendant, and at once, to his great amazement, ushered into the room below, and ordered to sit down on the rough chairs, and to eat of the hard and dry bread on the rough tables.

The poor people also came, and as they entered the Duke himself met them at the door, spoke kind words of welcome, and led them into the grand banquet-hall, there to regale themselves with the dainty food set before them. They also were astonished at this act, the reason of which they could not understand.

Then some of the nobles, filled with great wrath, went to the Duke as he stood amongst the poor, and asked him the meaning of this.

"You have treated us," they said, "with the greatest indignity. You have invited us to a feast, and when we have come, you place before us food which the poorest of your subjects would scarcely touch, and you have put these ignorant savages in the place which by rank and dignity is ours."

The Duke answered: "I know well what I have done; I have treated each of my guests according to his dignity."

"Impossible!" they answered. "Do you mean to say that these poor ragged tillers of the soil are greater than we are?"

"Yes," said the Duke. "You are indeed rich according to the world, but before God you are poor. But these men, who are Christians, are the children of God, and for them an eternal kingdom is prepared hereafter. Judge, then, for yourselves. They are heirs of Heaven, and shall forever reign with God in unspeakable glory. You who know not God can never reach Heaven; eternal misery in Hell will be your portion, for God has said: 'Blessed are the poor, for theirs is the kingdom of Heaven. Woe to you that are rich.'"

The Duke's guests, both rich and poor, then understood the meaning of the lesson they had that day received. Many of the nobles, touched by the grace of God, became Christians, that they might have a share with the poor in the eternal kingdom of God; and the poor themselves were consoled in their poverty with the thought of what would one day be given them in exchange for the miseries they had to bear here on earth.

BRUNNER: *Annales.*

"O PARADISE! O PARADISE!"

Father Picolomini was dying. The other Fathers were kneeling around his bed praying. He also from time to time joined his voice to theirs in fervent aspirations. But they, thinking that speaking so much would hasten the moment of his death, asked him to remain quiet, and not utter so many ejaculations, lest he might die sooner.

"O my brethren," he said, "what does it matter if I die a few hours sooner when there is a question of gaining merit for eternity? Every moment is most precious to me, and I do not wish to lose even one. Let me, therefore, pray as long as I am able to speak."

The pain which this good Father suffered was intense. To encourage himself to bear it patiently, he ordered the window of his room to be opened, that he might look up to Heaven. "Oh, how easy it is to suffer these terrible pains when I keep my eyes fixed on Heaven! O Paradise! O Paradise! Soon—yes, very soon, I hope to be there—to be there forever!"

O my child, you will receive from God an eternal life in Heaven if you serve Him during this short life on earth. Ask your Father in Heaven, then, through the intercession of Our Blessed Lady, to protect you now in the day of trial, that you may forever enjoy that eternal happiness.

6

THE SOULS OF THE JUST SHALL FIND ETERNAL REST IN GOD

St. Augustine used to say, "Our souls are made for God in eternity, and they can find no rest but in God."

AN OFFICER CONVERTED.

An officer once gave a grand ball to certain ladies of the town in which his regiment was quartered.

Towards midnight, when they were at the height of their enjoyment, and everyone seemed to be perfectly happy, the officer felt a weariness and disgust which he could not overcome. This melancholy soon became so great that, seeing it impossible to remain longer in the room, he asked one of his friends to be so kind as to do the honors of the feast for him during the rest of the evening, and then retired.

He went out to the seashore and walked upon the sands. Over his head was a beautiful starlight sky; before him a calm sea, the waves of which rippled with a gentle murmur at his feet. Everything around him was still and silent, and all nature seemed to speak to his heart.

"What am I doing?" he asked himself; "and where am I looking for a happiness which I can never find? Why do I take up so much of my time with created things, in which I can find no real enjoyment, while I run away from Him Who alone can give me everything that my heart can desire?

"O my God," he continued, "how true it is that our hearts are made for Thee alone, and can find no rest but in Thee. My mind is now quite made up. I will be Thine alone from this time forth and forever."

When he had taken this resolution, he felt in his soul a calm and holy joy he had never felt before. He went home, put all his temporal affairs in order, and began to lead a very holy life. As soon as he could get his discharge from the army, he left the world altogether and became a religious. By his holy life he was a model to everyone who knew or heard of him, and by his zeal converted many sinners to God.

RAINERI: *Instructions.*

WHY HE WISHED TO DIE.

St. Francis de Sales was one day told that a poor man who was dying wanted to see him. The Saint went immediately, and found the man very ill. On seeing the Bishop he was filled with joy, and asked him to hear his confession and give him his blessing. When this was done he said: "My lord, do you think I will get better?"

"My child," replied the Saint, "God is the Master of our lives, and I have sometimes seen people get better who were worse than you are."

"But, my lord," said again the poor man, "do you think I am going to die?"

St. Francis, supposing from these words that he was exceedingly afraid of death, tried to give him confidence by telling him to resign himself without fear into the hands of God his Father in Heaven.

"O my lord," he exclaimed, "I asked you that question, not because I am afraid to die—oh no, it is quite the contrary: I was afraid

I might get better, for I wish with all my heart to leave this wretched world."

The Saint now imagined that this great desire to die might arise from some imperfect motive, and he said to him: "Why, my child, are you so disgusted with this world? Have you had much to grieve you since you came into it? Or are you afraid of any new misfortunes about to befall you?"

"No, my lord," he answered; "I am perfectly contented and happy in the state of life in which God has placed me, for He has been good to me all my days. But what makes me so anxious to die is that I may get to Heaven to see my God, Whom alone I love. You have so often spoken in your sermons of the love of God, and of the happiness of Heaven, that this world seems to me to be a prison, out of which I wish to be delivered."

"Thanks be to Thee, O God," ejaculated St. Francis, "Who hast hidden the secrets of Thy wisdom from the wise ones of the world, and hast revealed them to those who are humble."

The dying man received the last Sacraments from the hands of the Bishop with great fervor and on the following day calmly yielded up his soul to God, Whom he had loved and served so faithfully.

Abbé Migne.

"MY FRIENDS, TO PARADISE! TO PARADISE!"

When St. Nicholas of Lombardy was a little child, he was told that God made him for Heaven, and from that moment he took the resolution that all his life should be spent in keeping the Commandments, that at the day of his death God might take him to that happy place.

He had to suffer many things during the course of his life, but the thought of the joys of Heaven made him bear them all patiently. At length, after a long life, the hour of his death came, and when all around him were weeping, he was full of joy. "My friends," he exclaimed, "to Paradise! to Paradise!" Saying these words, he sweetly expired, and his holy soul went to receive from Jesus the crown of life he had gained, because he had kept to the end of his life the resolution he had made in his childhood of serving God faithfully.

A SAINT WHO WAS ALWAYS TREMBLING.

St. Isidore was always a holy man. He had begun to serve God in his childhood, and had served Him faithfully during the whole of his life; yet he was never seen to smile, and was always trembling.

One of his disciples once said to him: "Father Isidore, why are you always so sad, and what makes you tremble so much? You always seem to be full of fear, as if some terrible evil was about to fall upon you."

"My child," he answered, "I am afraid that I may not persevere to the end, and that I may lose my soul."

"But you have always tried to serve God," said his disciple; "why, then, should you be so much afraid, since God has promised Heaven to those who serve Him faithfully?"

The Saint answered: "When a poor man is expecting to receive a rich legacy or a great fortune, and is afraid that something may arise to deprive him of it, how can he have an easy mind? It is only when the money is given to him that he can be free from anxiety. So it is with me. I have not yet received the crown of glory, and as long as I am in this world I am in danger of losing it: have I not cause, therefore, to tremble?"

"WE DESIRE GOD ALONE AND HEAVEN."

St. Augustine, who often spoke to the faithful under his charge of the joys of Heaven, one day said to them: "My brethren, if God came down here amongst us, and told us that He would grant each of us a hundred years more to live, or even a thousand, and that during these years we should have whatever our hearts could desire, but on condition that we should never see Him or be with Him in Heaven, would any of you accept that offer?"

But the whole multitude with one voice cried out: "Never! May all earthly things perish; we desire God alone and Heaven."

O my child, let that also be your answer when Satan asks you to offend God. Think of Heaven, and you shall be able to persevere.

7

AN ETERNITY OF PUNISHMENT FOR THE WICKED

My child, the end of those who do not serve God is terrible. They see that they have not served and loved God, and they know that those who have not done so can never be happy with Him in Heaven: so they fall into despair, die at enmity with God, and are lost forever.

"MAXIMUS, MY SON!"

St. Gregory the Great relates that there was once a rich man who had, during his whole lifetime, lived for the world and its pleasures, and had neglected to labor for the salvation of his soul. He had a large family, whom he brought up like himself—to please the world instead of serving God.

At length he became ill, and his body was racked by terrible sufferings. But the sufferings of his soul were infinitely greater. He saw before his eyes the long list of his sins, and he knew that in a short time he must die and be lost forever.

Already he seemed to see the evil spirits around his bed. They appeared to be waiting till he drew his last breath, that they might carry his soul to Hell. He turned from side to side on his bed of agony, but wherever he looked he thought he saw the same terrible specters. He began now to tremble, and the cold sweat covered his face. He cried out in terrible accents: "Maximus, my son! Maximus, come here."

The young man ran to his father's side.

"O my dear son!" he cried out again, when he saw him; "oh! think of all that I have done for you, and help me now. Save me from those terrible demons whom I see all around me!"

But Maximus could not understand him. He called together in haste all his relatives, and told them that his father's mind must be wandering, since he imagined he saw such terrible things.

"No," exclaimed the dying man, "my mind is not wandering. See! they are overwhelming me;" and he tried to raise himself up on his bed, as if to escape from them, but he was so weak that he could not move. At last he cried out, as if speaking to the demons: "Oh, leave me, leave me till tomorrow!" With these words, and in a terrible agony of despair, he died.

He died a bad death, because he had not served God.

VICTORINE'S RESOLUTION.

There was in the South of France a little girl whose father was a blacksmith. In her father's forge there always burned a great fire, which sometimes gave forth so much heat that she could not go near it.

One day her father had some work to do that required a greater and more intense fire than ever she saw before. The whole forge seemed to be one mass of fire. Victorine stood at a great distance and gazed on it with terror. "O my God," she exclaimed, "if this fire which my father has kindled is so terrible to look at, how terrible must be the fire of Hell which God in His anger has kindled for the punishment of sin!

"Oh, what an awful thing it must be to be condemned to Hell forever! To be forever burning along with the wicked angels, never to see God, our dear Father in Heaven—never! Never!

"O my God, from this moment I take the resolution never to commit sin. The thought of Hell will always check me when I am tempted to do evil, and make me accept with resignation every evil that can befall me in this world, rather than break Thy Commandments."

Victorine is still living, and she has till now faithfully kept her resolution. My child, imitate her good example.

TWO SOLDIERS AT A SERMON.

Two soldiers were one day passing through a place where a mission was being given. They had but little religion, and were living wicked lives. One of the soldiers said to his comrade: "Let us go in and hear the sermon." So they went into the church. The missionary was preaching on Hell.

When the sermon was ended they rose up and left the church together. "Do you believe all the priest said?" asked the least wicked of the two when they reached the street.

"Oh no!" replied the other; "I believe it is all nonsense invented to frighten people."

"Well, for my part," said the first one who spoke, "I believe it; and to prove to you that I believe it, I shall give up being a soldier and go into a monastery."

"Go where you please," said the other soldier "I will continue my journey."

But while he was on his journey he fell ill and died. His companion, who had just entered the monastery, heard of his death, and a terrible fear came upon him. "O my God," he prayed, "show me in what state is my comrade who has just died."

God was pleased to grant his request. One day, as he was praying, his companion appeared to him. He at once recognized him, and said to him: "Tell me, where are you now?"

"I am in Hell," he answered. "I am lost."

"O wretched man, do you now believe what the missionary said about Hell?"

"Yes, I believe it. The missionary was wrong in one thing: he did not tell us a hundredth part of what is suffered here."

With these words he disappeared, leaving the penitent soldier thanking God for the grace he had received.

Life of the Curé of Ars.

SATAN COMPELLED TO GIVE AN ANSWER.

A holy priest was once casting the devil out of a man who was possessed, and while he was doing so he said to him: "In the Name of God, tell me what are the punishments the wicked suffer in Hell."

Satan answered: "The punishments the lost suffer in Hell are a continual burning in an abyss of fire, remorse, and despair; but the greatest of all is not to be able to see God, Who made them, and Whom by their own fault they have lost."

"What would you now do to be able to obtain the opportunity of re-entering God's grace?"

"I would willingly suffer all the torments of Hell for ten thousand years if I could only see God for one moment; and if I had a body like you, I would be always at His feet, begging for mercy. Oh, if men only knew what it is to lose the grace of God!"

"I CANNOT BEAR THIS MUCH LONGER!"

One day St. Bernard went to see a man who was very ill. He had all his lifetime been negligent in his religious duties, and now, when he was so near the end of his life, he would not hear of returning to God by a sincere repentance.

St. Bernard asked God very earnestly to show mercy to this poor sinner. So when he went to see him he sat down at his bedside and began to speak to him about his sickness.

"Yes, sir," said the man, as he tossed about in his bed from the greatness of the pain, "I am indeed suffering awful torments. Oh, I cannot bear this any longer—I cannot bear this any longer! It *must* come to an end soon!"

St. Bernard looked with eyes full of pity on the poor sufferer as he lay there in anguish, and very soon the tears began to fall from his eyes.

The sick man saw him weeping. "Ah! dear sir," he said, "I see you feel for me! I see you are moved at the sight of what I am suffering. Is not my condition one to be pitied?"

"Yes, my poor man, your condition is indeed one to be pitied, and I weep when I think of it. But those tears flow from my eyes, not so much on account of the state of your body, but because of the state of your soul at this moment. I am thinking that in a very short time, perhaps in a few hours after this, your poor soul must leave the body, and then be cast into Hell forever and ever, because you have not served God on earth. And I imagine that I hear it saying there the same words you said a little time ago, 'I cannot bear this much longer!' and yet it shall have to bear forever and ever and ever torments infinitely greater than those you are now suffering.

"Oh, how terrible are the punishments of God, punishments which can never end, and yet it is in your power to escape them, and you refuse to do so! Poor unfortunate man!"

The Saint could say no more, his emotion was so great. He hid his head in his hands, and prayed and wept for the poor sinner's conversion.

When he looked up he saw moisture on the poor man's cheeks; he too was weeping.

"Father," he said, "help me to be reconciled to God before I die, and pray for me that I may escape those endless torments."

St. Bernard returned thanks to God for His mercy to this poor sinner, and had the happiness of seeing him a true penitent.

At the end of three days he died the death of the just, and is now, let us hope, happy with God in Heaven.

Flor. Exempl.

8

AMEN

THE AMEN OF THE STONES

The following legend is related of a venerable missionary by a German poet: Though blind with age, the holy priest continued with unceasing zeal to carry the Gospel tidings from town to town and village to village.

Led by the hand of a boy, he went from place to place, and preached the Word of God with almost the fire and fervor of his youth.

One day his guide led him into a valley strewn all over with huge stones. The old man sat down to rest on one of them, when the boy, more from love of mischief than anything else, suddenly said: "Venerable Father, many people are assembled to hear thy Word."

Then the old man rose, chose a text, and discoursed on it with so much eloquence and loving fervor that the tears fell down his white beard.

He repeated the Lord's Prayer, and when he came to the closing petition, many thousand voices responded, "Amen! Amen! Amen!"

The boy was struck with fear. Penitently he kneeled at the feet of the holy man, and confessed his sin. "My son," said the missionary, "hast thou not read that if men are silent, the stones will cry out and praise the Lord? Do not jest with God's Word; it is quick and powerful, and sharper than a two-edged sword. And if all men's hearts should turn into hardness of stone, to the stones might be given human hearts. In other words, Christ our Lord 'is able of the very stones to raise up children unto Abraham.'"